T0302036

# The Globality of Governmentality

This book reinvigorates the governmentality debate in International Relations (IR) by stressing the interconnectedness between governmentality and globality.

It addresses a widening gap in the social sciences and humanities by reconciling Michel Foucault's concept of "governmentality" with global politics. The volume assembles leading scholars who draw attention to the importance of approaching governmentality in IR from the perspective of globality, and thereby suggests to consider governmentality and globality as fundamentally entangled. Accordingly, the contributors engage in a multifaceted debate about the relationship of governmentality and globality, relating their views to the proposition that globality cannot be equated with the international level and should rather be considered as a genuine context of its own requiring distinct consideration. The book builds on the increasing importance and popularity of governmentality studies, not only by updating Foucault's concepts at a theoretical level, but also by introducing novel empirical problems and practices of global governmentality that have not hitherto been explored in IR.

With a wide theoretical and empirical range, it is relevant not only to IR in general and International Political Sociology in particular, but to any student or practitioner in political science, political theory, geography, sociology, or the humanities.

**Jan Busse** is Senior Research Fellow and Lecturer at the Institute of Political Science at the Bundeswehr University Munich, Germany.

# The New International Relations

The field of international relations has changed dramatically in recent years. This new series will cover the major issues that have emerged and reflect the latest academic thinking in this particular dynamic area.

Edited by Richard Little, *University of Bristol*, Iver B. Neumann, *Norwegian Institute of International Affairs (NUPI), Norway* and Jutta Weldes, *University of Bristol*.

**Small States and Shelter Theory**
Iceland's External Affairs
*Baldur Thorhallsson*

**The Use of Force under International Law**
Lawyerized States in a Legalized World
*Fernando G. Nuñez-Mietz*

**Discourse and Affect in Foreign Policy**
Germany and the Iraq War
*Jakub Eberle*

**Tactical Constructivism, Method, and International Relations**
*Edited by Brent J. Steele, Harry D. Gould and Oliver Kessler*

**International Relations Narratives**
*Riikka Kuusisto*

**The Globality of Governmentality**
Governing an Entangled World
*Edited by Jan Busse*

For more information about this series, please visit:
www.routledge.com/New-International-Relations/book-series/NEWIR
New International Relations

# The Globality of Governmentality

Governing an Entangled World

**Edited by
Jan Busse**

Routledge
Taylor & Francis Group

LONDON AND NEW YORK

First published 2021
by Routledge
2 Park Square, Milton Park, Abingdon, Oxon OX14 4RN

and by Routledge
52 Vanderbilt Avenue, New York, NY 10017

*Routledge is an imprint of the Taylor & Francis Group, an informa business*

*British Library Cataloguing-in-Publication Data*
A catalogue record for this book is available from the British Library

*Library of Congress Cataloging-in-Publication Data*
Names: Busse, Jan, editor.
Title: The globality of governmentality : governing
an entangled world / edited by Jan Busse.
Description: Abingdon, Oxon ; New York, NY : Routledge, 2021. |
Series: New international relations |
Includes bibliographical references and index.
Identifiers: LCCN 2020053605 (print) | LCCN 2020053606 (ebook) |
ISBN 9780367491321 (hardback) | ISBN 9781003044727 (ebook)
Subjects: LCSH: Foucault, Michel, 1926–1984. |
Globalization. | International relations.
Classification: LCC JZ1318 .G57854 2021 (print) |
LCC JZ1318 (ebook) | DDC 327.101–dc23
LC record available at https://lccn.loc.gov/2020053605
LC ebook record available at https://lccn.loc.gov/2020053606

ISBN: 978-0-367-49132-1 (hbk)
ISBN: 978-1-032-00289-7 (pbk)
ISBN: 978-1-003-04472-7 (ebk)

Typeset in Times New Roman
by Newgen Publishing UK

# Contents

# Contributors

## The editor

**Jan Busse** is Senior Research Fellow and Lecturer at the Institute of Political Science at the Bundeswehr University Munich, Germany. In 2016 he obtained his PhD degree, and he holds a master's degree in Global Politics from the London School of Economics and Political Science (LSE) and a bachelor's degree in Political Science from Bielefeld University. He is a member of the Arab-German Young Academy of Sciences and Humanities and Co-Coordinator of the Israeli-Palestinian Policy Network (IEPN). His research focuses on global historical sociologies of political order, the Israeli-Arab conflict, political dynamics in the Middle East and North Africa, and EU-Mediterranean Relations. He has published in peer-reviewed journals such as *International Political Sociology*, *Middle East Critique*, and *Global Affairs*. He is author of the book *De-Constructing the Dynamics of World-Societal Order: The Power of Governmentality in Palestine* (Routledge, 2018).

## The contributors

**Mathias Albert** is Professor of Political Science at Bielefeld University, Germany. He has published widely on the history and sociology of world politics, IR Theory, youth studies, and polar studies. His latest book publications include: *A Theory of World Politics* (Cambridge University Press 2016); *The Politics of International Political Theory* (ed. with A. Lang, Palgrave 2019); *Jugend 2019* (with K. Hurrelmann et al., Beltz 2019); *What in the World? Understanding Global Social Change* (ed. with T. Werron, Bristol University Press 2021); *Envisioning the World: Mapping and Making the Global* (ed. with S. Holtgreve and K. Preuß, Transcript, forthcoming 2021).

**Mitchell Dean** is Professor and Head of Department, Department of Management, Politics and Philosophy, Copenhagen Business School, Denmark. He is well-known for his book *Governmentality: power and rule* *in modern society* (Sage, 1999/2010). He has been cited in the first edition of Foucault's governmentality lectures (in French and English) and quoted in the Oxford English Dictionary entry on government. He has completed a new book on the historical and political context of Foucault's work in the 1970s, *The Last Man Takes LSD: Foucault, Neoliberalism and the End of Revolution*, with Daniel Zamora of the University of Brussels, which will be published by Verso in 2021. Today he works on political and economic theology, focusing on practices such as oath-taking, political acclamation and political liturgies.

**Scott Hamilton** is currently the Research Coordinator at the Balsillie School of International Affairs (BSIA) in Waterloo, Ontario, Canada. His areas of research expertise include: global politics, the politics of climate change science, the Anthropocene epoch, governmentality studies, and international political philosophy. He holds an M.Phil in International Relations (University of Oxford, UK), a Ph.D in International Relations (London School of Economics and Political Science, UK), and recently he was one of Canada's Banting Postdoctoral Fellows (2017–2019). A former editor of *Millennium: Journal of International Studies* (vol. 44), he has also published widely in such journals as *International Theory*, *The European Journal of International Relations*, *Review of International Studies*, and *Millennium: Journal of International Studies*.

**Hans-Martin Jaeger** is Associate Professor at Carleton University, Canada. His intellectual interests lie at the intersection of International Relations, contemporary political thought, and international political sociology. His work on governmentality and global governance has been published in *International Theory*, *European Journal of International Relations*, *International Political Sociology*, *Journal of International Relations and Development* and edited collections.

**Jonathan Joseph** is Professor of Politics and International Relations at the University of Bristol, UK. He has previously worked at the universities of Sheffield, Kent and Aberystwyth. Most of his recent work looks at the relationship between resilience and governmentality and he has published *Varieties of Resilience: Studies in Governmentality* (Cambridge 2018) and *Wellbeing, Resilience and Sustainability: The New Trinity of Governance* (with Allister McGregor, Palgrave 2020). Other recent work looks at critical realism, EU foreign policy, European integration and global governance.

**Nicholas Kiersey** is a Professor in the Department of Political Science at the University of Texas Rio Grande Valley, USA. His research addresses austerity, biopolitics, and the crises of the neoliberal capitalist state. He is currently working on a book about socialist governmentality, and the cultural political economy of the end of capitalism.

**Oscar L. Larsson** completed his PhD in Political Science at Uppsala University in 2015. The thesis concerned (meta-)governance and collaboration in Swedish crisis management. Oscar Larsson is since 2020, Assistant Professor in Military Studies at the Swedish Defence University, Sweden. He has previously done research on governance and collaboration as solution to various forms of social problems, such as segregated urban environments, integration in rural areas, in dealing with victims of trafficking, and to current crisis management and food security. For the past two years, research has focused on sovereign power and governmentality, national and social security and the role of civilian preparedness and population. Oscar Larsson has published articles on governmentality and civil preparedness in *Critical Policy Studies* and *Security Dialogue*.

**Halvard Leira** is Research Professor at the Norwegian Institute of International Affairs (NUPI), Norway. He has published extensively in English and Norwegian on international political thought, historiography, foreign policy and diplomacy. His work has appeared in e.g. *International Studies Quarterly, Review of International Studies, Millennium, Leiden Journal of International Law* and *Cooperation and Conflict*. Leira is co-editor of *International Diplomacy* (2013), *Historical International Relations* (2015) and the forthcoming *Routledge Handbook of Historical International Relations*. He is former section chair and programme chair of the HIST-section of the ISA and was programme chair of EISA PEC 2018.

**Iver B. Neumann** is Director of the Fridtjof Nansen Institute, Norway. He has previously served as professor at the University of Oslo and the London School of Economics and Political Science, and been an Associate Editor of the *International Studies Quarterly*. Neumann's areas of expertise are social theory, qualitative methods, diplomacy and Russian foreign policy. His latest books are (with Einar Wigen) *The Steppe Tradition in International Relations: Russians, Turks and European State Building, 4000 BCE-2018 CE* (Cambridge University Press, 2018); *Concepts of International Relations, for Students and Other Smarties* (University of Michigan Press, 2019) and *Diplomatic Tenses: Past, Present, Future* (Manchester University Press, 2021).

**Audrey Reeves** is an Assistant Professor of Political Science at Virginia Tech, USA and core faculty for the ASPECT doctoral program. Her research and teaching interests include feminist perspectives on international relations as well as the role of embodiment, emotions, and arts in world politics. Her work has been published in *Critical Military Studies, Mobilities*, and the *International Feminist Journal of Politics*, inter alia. She is currently working on a book manuscript on the governance of affect at war museums and memorials based on doctoral research funded by the Social Sciences and Humanities Research Council of Canada.

**Ole Jacob Sending** is Director of Research at the Norwegian Institute of International Affairs (NUPI), Norway. His research focuses on international organizations, diplomacy, the role of expert groups in global governance, and changes in state sovereignty. His research has appeared in, inter alia, *International Studies Quarterly, International Theory, Review of International Political Economy, Review of International Studies*, and *European Journal of International Relations*. He has been associate editor of *International Studies Quarterly* and the *Hague Journal of Diplomacy*. He is currently working on a book manuscript with Leonard Seabrooke on "The Market for Anarchy," and is serving as co-editor (together with Stacie Goddard and George Lawson) for the forthcoming Oxford Handbook of International Political Sociology.

**Stephan Stetter** is Professor of International Politics and Conflict Studies at the Bundeswehr University Munich, Germany. He holds an M.Sc. (LSE) in European Politics and Policy as well as a Ph.D. from the LSE. His research focuses on historical and sociological theories of world society and global modernity, politics and society in the Middle East, and EU foreign politics. He is co-editor of the leading German IR journal, *Zeitschrift für Internationale Beziehungen*. His last two book are *Modern Subjectivities in World Society: Global Structures and Local Practices* (with D. Jung, Palgrave, 2018) and *Middle East Christianity: Local Practices, Global Entanglements* (with M. Moussa Nabo, Palgrave, 2020). His work appears with leading publishing houses and journals.

**Andreas Vasilache** is Professor of European Studies at Bielefeld University, Germany and Director of the Centre for German and European Studies (CGES/ZDES). His research spans on International Relations, IR Theory, European Studies, and Political Theory, focussing i.a. on poststructuralist theory, governmentality approaches, borders and boundaries, migration, security studies, and Asian studies. He has published i.a. in *Security Dialogue, Zeitschrift für Internationale Beziehungen (ZIB), Migration Letters, Cambridge Review of International Affairs, European Journal for Security Research*, and *Politische Vierteljahresschrift (PVS) – German Political Science Quarterly*.

**Laura Zanotti** is Professor of Political Science at Virginia Tech, USA. Her research and teaching include critical political theory, international ethics as well as international organizations, UN peacekeeping and NGOs. Her most recent book, entitled *Ontological Entanglements, Agency and Ethics in International Relations – Exploring the Crossroads* (Routledge, 2018) explores the prevailing ontological assumption of international relations theories and the implications for ethics and political agency of embracing quantum physics' ontology of entanglements. In her previous monography, entitled *Governing Disorder: United Nations Peace Operations, International Security, and Democratization in the Post-Cold War Era* (Penn State

University Press, 2011), Zanotti uses Foucauldian theoretical tools to address the political imaginary and unintended consequences of peace-keeping in Haiti and in Croatia. Prior to becoming an academic Laura worked at the United Nations, where she served both in administration and as a political advisor for Peacekeeping Operations.

# Series editor's preface

For most of the twentieth century, attempts to establish the analysis of international relations as an independent field of study are usually depicted now as very much an Anglo-American activity. Indeed, a well-known article written by Stanley Hoffmann in 1977 entitled, somewhat provocatively, "International Relations: An American Social Science" seems to give some support to this idea. However, on closer inspection, the article provides a much more nuanced assessment. Hoffmann, born in Vienna and trained in France, although he spent most of his working life in the United States, traces the idea of international relations as a separate discipline to E. H. Carr's *Twenty Years' Crisis: 1919-1939*, subtitled as "An Introduction to the Study of International Relations", which is depicted as a realist response to what Carr saw as the "utopian" thinking of Arnold Toynbee, the world historian, who became Director of Studies in 1922 at the British Institute of International Affairs, founded in the aftermath of the First World War.

Hoffmann, however, goes on to make the point that even though the subsequent study of international relations was dominated by academics in the United States, it is not possible to ignore the role played by a large number of European emigres who ended up in American universities as the result of the rise of Hitler and the Second World War. He stresses, in particular, the role played by Hans J. Morgenthau, a German, who arrived in the United States in 1937. Like Carr, Morgenthau distinguished between realist and idealist approaches to international relations, and it is a distinction that continued to resonate in the field for the rest of the century. Morgenthau establishes the dichotomy at the start of *Politics Among Nations*, written as a textbook for American students to instruct them about the realities of power in the wake of the Second World War. It was an extraordinarily influential text for several decades, but it failed to illuminate how Morgenthau's ideas related to other significant European thinkers, such as Carl Schmitt, for example, who also wrote about power and despite his links with the Nazi party had a significant impact on other European thinkers.

Towards the end of the twentieth century, however, there was a growing recognition that Morgenthau was a much more sophisticated thinker than was generally acknowledged in International Relations. In the twenty-first century, interest in Morgenthau's thought and how it relates to the work of other European thinkers has continued to grow. This development, however, is only part of a much wider recognition that subsequent European thinkers, outside of the Anglo-American tradition, continue to have an important role to play in how the study of international relations does and should develop. This edited book makes a significant contribution to this move, drawing specifically on the work of Michel Foucault to enhance and expand our understanding of international relations and in particular the globalization of the contemporary world.

Foucault (1926–1984) was a French historian of ideas (although this designation considerably underplays the depth and range of his thinking), as well as a political activist, who has had an enormous impact across the social sciences. It is not possible to summarize Foucault's contribution to the social sciences but one of the central threads in his rich tapestry of thought is his argument that from the seventeenth century onwards sovereign power, associated with the "right to take life or let live," has been supplemented by new technologies or practices of power which he identifies as biopower and associates with biopolitics. Foucault identifies this development with the emergence of the modern world identified by key features such as liberalism and capitalism. From Foucault's perspective, in the modern world there is no central locus of power, instead, individuals are caught in complex networks of power which help to promote and protect the life of the whole population. In the first instance, he associated this development with the exercise of disciplinary power which he identified in terms of institutions such as schools and hospitals, on the one hand, and asylums and prisons on the other. In all these kinds of institutions, individuals are kept under constant observation and their behavior is carefully prescribed, regulated, and recorded. It follows that biopower is closely associated with experts and administrators.

At first sight, it might seem that Foucault is an unlikely candidate to enhance our understanding of international relations as he had relatively little directly to say about the subject. But as the contributors to this book make clear, Foucault began to think about government and he developed the conception of governmentality and it is argued these ideas, in conjunction with his earlier analyses of power, can be used very fruitfully to throw considerable light on the evolution of international relations. Government became Foucault's preferred term for a form of power which he traces back to Christianity and more specifically the relationship between the shepherd and his flock, hence his reference to pastoral power. Governmentality was the term he used to characterize and analyze the operation of power in the modern world.

Foucault died of AIDS in 1984 but a substantial body of his work has been published posthumously. His thinking about government and governmentality was developed in two series of lectures *Security, Territory, Population*, given in 1977–1978 and *The Birth of Biopolitics* given in 1978–1979. Despite Foucault's wish that none of his unpublished work should be published after his death, his estate decided that because the lectures were taped and the notes of the lectures were in his archives, edited versions of these lectures could be published. But these two sets of lectures were not published in English as complete sets until 2007–2008. However, a crucial lecture entitled Governmentality, given in 1978, was published in Italian, in the same year, and in an English translation the following year, although the best known and generally available English version did not appear until 1991. However, further unpublished work was available for researchers in Foucault's archives, but after 2013 when his partner, Daniel Defert, sold Foucault's archives to the Bibliothèque nationale de France, it was decided that it was unfair that work in the archives was not available more generally. So, the embargo on publication of material in the archives was removed. Several major publications have followed this decision.

Given this background, it is unsurprising that reactions to Foucault's work have continuously evolved and almost inevitably there are substantial disagreements about many aspects of his work and, in particular, on his writings on government and governmentality. By the same token, these debates have spilled over into the attempts to widen Foucault's discussion and encompass the international arena. Although the editor of this volume has his own clear views on the issue, he has wisely resisted the temptation to impose a template on his contributors. As a consequence, this book provides very clear expositions of some of the competing approaches to government and governmentality and how they impinge on international relations. The book advances in important ways the theoretical implications of Foucault's ideas as well as providing some fascinating case studies using Foucault's ideas to illuminate important aspects of international relations.

*Richard Little*
*Emeritus Professor*
*University of Bristol*

# Foreword

When scholars first began to debate governmentality within the Anglophonic social sciences, it was largely with reference to the domestic face of politics and power. A glance at the kind of research that initially took up concepts and analytics of governmentality reveals a focus on matters like the governance of cities, the formation of national economic policies, the regulation of poverty, the significance of civil society for liberal rule, and technologies of freedom and citizenship. Questions of relations between states, the power and violence of empires and colonies, the nature of global economies, or the force of great migrations did not feature prominently in Foucault-influenced research. Perhaps this was because such questions didn't appear all that prominently in Foucault's own work – at least not in those texts like *Archaeology of Knowledge* and *Discipline and Punish* that were amongst his most widely read works in the 1980s and 1990s. Or perhaps it reflected a view that the international was too "big," too distant from the world of microphysics; that the microphysics had much to teach us about power on the scale of a prison, workhouse, or town but not the rivalries of nations, or the great games of empire. Whatever the factors in play, the international and the global was for Foucault-inflected scholarship something of a *terra incognita*.

This picture has changed in the last two decades, the more that scholars in fields like International Relations, law, geography, and anthropology have engaged with themes of international governmentality, global biopolitics, and forms of sovereign power. It has shifted the more that research has recognized that the making of the international and the global can be grasped through apparently local or minor forms – whether the training of humanitarian experts or the administration of microcredit to entrepreneurial villagers – and heterogeneous networks of state and non-state actors. It has changed now that we have moved from a transcendental to an immanent and infrastructural view of globalization. In the former, the global features as a smooth space expanding above or across the world of states, whereas for the latter, the powers of control can be as global and as embedded as flows of people, money, or goods.

*The Globality of Governmentality* represents a timely and important contribution to these kinds of debates that are internationalizing governmentality and sharpening our understanding of power and politics. It seems to me the essays gathered here speak to this promise in at least three ways. First, many of them grapple with complex questions about relationships between heterogeneous powers. What governmentality means in relationship to sovereign powers, disciplinary practices, pastorates (not to mention the odd apostate) are questions that have long vexed Foucauldian scholarship. This book brings new understanding to those questions. Second, this volume continues the dialogue between governmentality and other critical traditions, especially Marxist political economy, poststructuralist feminist theory, postcolonialism, and new materialism. As such, it ensures that governmentality continues to be a lively zone of theoretical encounter rather than an inward-looking, parochial endeavor. What is especially appealing about *The Globality of Governmentality* is that its authors do not sing in unison. There is a lively and productive disagreement amongst some of the chapters not to mention the literatures they cite. Third, and perhaps most originally, this book puts the question of globality front and center. That is, it asks how totalities, universes, and wholes have been imagined and inscribed, and how they factor into strategies of rule and resistance. Given its microphysical, poststructuralist, and anti-substantialist inclinations, it would be easy for governmentality research to eschew such "big" objects. This book shows we can take big objects seriously without reifying them. As such, it can be read alongside the more recent work of scholars like Latour and Sloterdijk where one also finds an interest in the phenomenology of spheres, globes, and universes.

*The Globality of Governmentality* is being published precisely at a time when humanity finds itself in the grip of a new global crisis: the pandemic associated with the new coronavirus SARS-Cov-2. One of Foucault's most cited remarks is that political theory has still not cut-off the King's head. By this, he wanted to highlight the fallacy of looking at power in its most visible, centralized, and often spectacular manifestations, at power in the form of sovereignty, while neglecting the myriad devices, capillaries, and microphysics that flow through and actually construct bodies and societies. So, it is more than a little ironic that despite the microphysical turn which Foucault has inspired in the social sciences, we find ourselves locked in a struggle with a virus whose very name and molecular structure associates it with the crown, that ancient symbol of sovereignty.

There are other ironies. As I write this in the middle of August 2020, Russia has just announced it has developed a vaccine that is ready for mass production and inoculation. It is rather apt that the first country to make such a claim should be Russia. Now, it is true that the Bolshevik revolution did not cut-off the Tsar's head. Not literally. The great revolutions of the seventeenth and eighteenth centuries made a political spectacle out of the decapitation of their royalty, whereas the Bolsheviks killed and disposed of the Romanovs out of sight – a foretaste of the secret governmentality that was to follow. Nevertheless, it is surely fitting that a country that has form when it comes to the act of dethronement should now proclaim itself the leader in the global battle to defeat or tame the crowned virus.

But there is more to Russia's announcement that might deepen this line of reflection. It is not merely the fact that the virus resembles a crown that might get us thinking about the pandemic in terms of certain interactions between sovereign powers, biopolitical programs, and governmentality. What name has Russia given to this program of vaccine development? None other than Sputnik V. Let's leave aside the way in which that "V" makes Sputnik itself sound like the kind of mechanical monarch that might have impressed Thomas Hobbes! Let's concentrate instead on the implications of this act that inscribes the biopolitics of immunization within the historical geopolitics of the space race; that aligns it so closely with what commentators are now calling "vaccine nationalism." It was, after all, the space race, and more specifically the Apollo 17 mission, that gave us the "Blue Marble" photograph of Earth, one of the most iconic, beautiful, and powerful images of globality. One wonders what unexpected and unanticipated forms of globality might arise from the struggles to govern the coronavirus pandemic. For, there are emerging some very complex entanglements of sovereign power, biopolitics, governmentality, and capitalism (including the disaster and venture varieties). It would be foolish at this point to make predictions just as it would be unwise to regard Sputnik V as the last word in immunology. What we can say with a bit more confidence is that the open-ended, desubstantialized, and heuristic orientation of the essays in this book offers the kind of investigative ethos we will need to make sense of what is novel and what remains the same when it comes to power and globality in the age of the novel coronavirus.

*William Walters*
*Carleton University*

# Acknowledgements

As every book project, this volume is the conclusion of a long journey. A number of people played an important role along the way. I am particularly grateful to Scott Hamilton. For a very long time, he was a crucial companion and partner in this project, and I fundamentally regret that we could not finish together what we have jointly started back in 2014.

This volume benefited greatly from discussions at various conferences where initial versions of several chapters were originally presented. I am grateful to the participants of the panels and roundtables at the EISA Pan-European Conferences of International Relations 2015 in Sicily and 2018 in Prague, the ISA Annual Conventions 2015 in New Orleans and 2019 in Toronto, namely, besides the contributors themselves, Jens Bartelson, Olaf Corry, Debby Lisle, Eva Lövbrand, Andreas Aagaard Nøhr, Nikolas Rajkovic, and Mark B. Salter.

I am also grateful to Peter Miller and Nikolas Rose for being supportive of the overall idea of the volume.

The chapter co-authored by Mathias Albert and Andreas Vasilache was previously published in an altered form in the journal *Cooperation and Conflict* (Vol. 53 (1)), and I would like to thank the publisher Sage for granting permission to use the article in this volume. I am also indebted to the Bundeswehr University Munich for providing partial funding for the book project. Moreover, I am grateful to Alexander Heinze for compiling the index.

I also wish to thank Rob Sorsby and Claire Maloney at Routledge for their excellent work in accompanying this volume and the anonymous reviewers for their constructive comments on the project.

# 1 Introduction

## The globality of governmentality

*Jan Busse and Scott Hamilton*

## Introduction

Thirty years after the initial publication of Michel Foucault's governmentality lecture in English (Foucault 1991), this book sees good reason to reinvigorate the governmentality debate in International Relations (IR). In general, this book remedies a widening gap in the social sciences and humanities by reconciling Michel Foucault's concept of "governmentality" with global politics. Its novelty in comparison to the existing literature, and its contribution to the discipline of IR in general and to the field of governmentality studies in particular, lies in the volume's reinterpretation and expansion of Foucault's concepts to recent and contemporary global crises and events. It thereby builds on the increasing importance and popularity of governmentality studies, not only by updating Foucault's concepts at a theoretical level, but also by introducing novel empirical problems and practices of global governmentality that have not hitherto been explored in IR. As such, this volume makes an important contribution to growing debates over governmentality, globality, transnational events, and political crises, and to theoretically ambitious global governance research. It explores how the macroscales of politics and globality typically engaged in disciplines such as IR, intersect with the microscales of individual and group practice, sociality, and subjectivity that are interdisciplinary in their scope.

The volume's theoretical contribution moves beyond static and outmoded conceptions of both governmentality and global politics that are still widespread in IR and other social sciences, resting on a too selective reading of Foucault. Although IR and neighboring disciplines have witnessed an increased popularity and usage of governmentality analytics in recent decades, the use of governmentality as a tool of research into *global* concepts, problems, and crises discussed in IR, has not emerged in tandem. This is paradoxical when considering the widespread impact of Wendy Larner and William Walters's then path-breaking *Global Governmentality: Governing International Spaces* (2004c), and the recent upsurge in global discourses and crises such as environmental degradation, financial instability, the COVID-19 pandemic, nationalist and authoritarian populism, climate change, and fears

of global nuclear war. It seems that, with the decline of literature on globalization, global governmentality studies waned in tandem. However, the global
crises and problematics visible today are just as, if not more so, relevant for
diagnostics and analytics of governmentality than those included by Larner
and Walters (2004c). Hence, the need for an extensive reengagement with the
globality of governmentality and its relationship to IR and the social sciences
over 15 years after Larner and Walter's major contribution.

On the one hand, recent studies in IR addressing global politics from
critical or philosophical perspectives have adopted theoretical frameworks
embracing new materialism and Actor-Network Theory (ANT) (see Salter
2015). While these studies have clearly made important contributions to
the analysis of power relations beyond a state-centric framework, they risk
being preoccupied with what Foucault termed the "government of things"
(see Lemke 2015), while at the same time neglecting overarching dynamics
of political and societal order that go beyond such an object-oriented
ontology. On the other hand, research in IR addressing Foucauldian
concepts have not sufficiently addressed the concept of governmentality
(Bonditti et al. 2017), or they have maintained a familiar focus on the operation of security and liberalism within the overarching international system,
thereby interpreting the concept of governmentality from a too narrow
security perspective (de Larrinaga and Doucet 2010). This book also strives
to reequip the governmentality debate in IR with conceptual soundness.
In the past years, to a certain extent, governmentality has become a buzzword, used by many authors rather as an empty slogan than as an analytical tool. Thus, the present volume tries to remedy this deficiency by
explicitly pointing to the respective definitions of governmentality that are
being used.

In general, this volume moves beyond existing perspectives in two
ways: First, by confronting new materialism's and post-humanism's focus on
"flat" object-oriented ontologies through a governmentality lens, examining
new practices and concepts shaping power dynamics. Second, by providing
updated theoretical and philosophical readings of Foucault in relation to
these recent global crises and practices, the volume moves beyond a purely
"statist" or state-centric lens to act as a research "toolkit" or foundation for
students and scholars to use going forth. It is therefore applicable to any
scholars or students engaging the political relationship between individuals and groups, or analyzing relations of governmental power and practice
working at local and global scales. Accordingly, this volume highlights, that
in existing governmentality research, globality remains an underexplored
topic. As Martin Shaw puts it: "Even international relations, which has been
constituted as a discipline by interstate and political relations, has found it
difficult to conceive of globality except as the negation of statehood and politics" (2000: 81). This negligence is striking insofar as "the global" is a foundation of many common concepts in IR (see below). Put simply, when thinking
of globality, the entire world is regarded as a single place or a singular polity,

thereby being more inclusive and encompassing than a merely international dimension (Boli and Thomas 1997; Corry 2013; Shaw 2000).

As this volume will show, there are various ways of capturing this globality (see below). Here lie also interesting grounds of interconnection between Foucauldian research with other theoretical approaches which are interested in theorizing global order. Moreover, this volume suggests to treat the concepts of "globality" and "governmentality" as entangled, entwined, or constitutive of one another, so that one can ask how the globality of governmentality precedes, shapes, and provides the foundation for the forms of thought and subjectivity that comprise IR today. In other words, this volume is less interested in what the "global" is, but what it does to our thought and practices when it is invoked.

In addition, the volume steps back from the work and philosophy of Foucault to describe the strengths *and weaknesses* of governmentality and its application to international relations and global politics. The book deliberately makes use of governmentality instead of other Foucauldian concepts, such as discourse, discipline, or normalization. These Foucauldian notions are dependent upon the rigid and top-down structures Foucault discussed in his earlier work as well as upon patterns of thought delivered directly from sovereign and judicial authorities that establish clear lines of demarcation or confinement for subjects to follow. On the contrary, this volume views governmentality as fluid, bottom-up, and as a concept that cannot be "disciplined" per se. Accordingly, governmentality works well with the fluid global events and crises we see overlapping around us today, which, potentially, flow together and break apart in accordance with implicit and specific underlying rationalities of governance, rather than through any outdated or preordained top-down structures.

In general, the contributions to this volume do not necessarily adopt a unified understanding of globality and governmentality, but it offers room for debate and critical exchange of different perspectives on the globality of governmentality. Hence, the volume as a whole presents a diversity of engagements with these two dimensions; be it in their utilization of governmentality or the extent of engagement with it on the one hand, and the interpretation of globality on the other. The book, therefore, also represents a forum for critical and constructive engagement with the way governmentality is used in IR.

## The state of affairs: The governmentality debate in IR[1]

Before assessing the current state of governmentality in the discipline of IR, it is crucial to offer a clearer understanding of what "governmentality" actually is. This step is essential for three reasons. First, given the evolution of Foucault's writings over time and a certain lack of clarity in his work on governmentality. Second, and concomitantly, ever since governmentality has entered IR, there has been a tendency of using the term governmentality as a vague notion of a certain kind of political steering or manipulation that goes beyond governance by government, without actually offering a suitable definition (Walters 2012). Hence, governmentality is at risk of being relegated to a buzzword, losing its analytical clarity (Joseph 2010). Hence, by pointing to the importance of a clear definition, in this chapter we want to counter these developments. Third, defining governmentality also serves as a guidance for the contributors to this volume, helping them to explicitly refer to one or more of the suggested definitions, thereby furthering the book's conceptual coherence in the face of the existing and desired heterogeneity of its chapters.

According to William Walters (2012: 11–13), three different meanings of governmentality should be distinguished, and the volume's contributions relate to this distinction. First, governmentality is an analytical perspective aiming at examining specific modalities of governance. In the words of Laura Zanotti, governmentality utilized this way serves as a *"heuristic* tool to explore modalities of local and international government and to assess their effects in the contexts where they are deployed" (2013: 289, emphasis in the original). In this sense, governmentality refers to the analysis of "the way in which one conducts the conduct of men," thus serving as an "analytical grid for (...) relations of power" (Foucault 2008: 186). Governmentality is then understood as *conduct of conducts* (Foucault 1984: 314, see also 2007: 192–193), encompassing both the conduct of others and the conduct of oneself, or, in other words, *government of the self* and *government of others* (Foucault 2010).

Second, governmentality may be understood as the history of the art of government. This conceptualization refers to "the question how, at different times, in specific places, and always in connection with particular political issues, certain experts, authorities, critics and dissidents have come to reflect on the problem of *how* to govern the state" (Walters 2012: 20, emphasis in the original). The state in this perspective can be seen as a particular institutional manifestation of governmental rationalities and technologies. At the same time, this perspective takes into account that "government is in no way confined to or monopolized by the modern state" (Walters 2012: 19). In this sense, by referring to the "governmentalization of the state" (Foucault 2007: 109), Foucault "comprehends the state itself as a tactics of government, as a dynamic form and historic stabilization of societal power relations" (Lemke 2002: 58).

The third understanding of governmentality denotes a historical formation of a particular regime of power that first gained predominance in advanced liberal democracies since the 18th century. Governmentality, in this sense, serves as a *"descriptive* tool" in order to examine a "particular trajectory of global liberalism" (Zanotti 2013: 289). Therefore, it is often described as (neo-) liberal governmentality. This system of thought represents a specific, contingent form of governmental rationalities and technologies and is defined as:

> the ensemble formed by institutions, procedures, analyses and reflections, calculations, and tactics that allow the exercise of this very specific,

albeit very complex, power that has the population as its target, political economy as its major form of knowledge, and apparatuses of security as its essential technical instrument.

(Foucault 2007: 108)

Consequently, whilst territoriality is used as a tool of sovereignty, in (neo-) liberal regimes, it is the population that is the main target or reference point of governmentality and its related technologies of government. Rather than a top-down disciplinary form of power, here it is through political economy and its underlying forms of expertise as predominant forms of knowledge that is the base of liberal governmentality. In other words, economic calculations and the related idea of the *homo economicus* are the defining and limiting factors for political intervention. Solving liberal and economic problems becomes a *tool* for government, rather than its aim or purpose, as is traditionally understood. The rationalization of political problems is thus a characteristic feature of governmentality. To put it differently, "the population will be the object that government will have to take into account in its observations and knowledge, in order to govern effectively in a rationally reflected manner" (Foucault 2007: 106).

As the means to effectively govern the population, apparatuses (*dispositifs*) of security – i.e., mechanisms monitoring the condition of the population as a whole – are thus essential. These are the result of rationalized knowledge about the population and can be described as a "relatively durable network of heterogeneous elements" (Walters 2012: 36), such as "discourses, institutions, architectural forms, regulatory decisions, laws, administrative measures, scientific statements, philosophical, moral and philanthropic propositions" (Foucault 1980: 194) and are directed at the overall living conditions of the population.[2]

### *Governmentality and IR – The field of international governmentality studies*

While the ideas of Michel Foucault had been introduced to IR already since the late 1980s (see Ashley and Walker 1990; Bartelson 1995; Der Derian and Shapiro 1989; Edkins 1999), research on governmentality in IR is a rather recent phenomenon which has only emerged since the early 2000s. As Walters observes, it is striking that even though political science and political theory experienced a governmentality-related "Foucault Effect" early in the 1990s, this development was delayed by over a decade when it came to IR (2012: 82–83). In order to provide an overview of the existing governmentality research in IR, this chapter will distinguish it according to three main dimensions: (i) the question of how governmentality scholarship in IR addresses the relationship between the state and the international level, (ii) how it relates to liberalism, and (iii) how each variant conceptualizes political agency.

First, it is useful to examine how key contributions to global/international studies of governmentality perceive and conceptualize *the international*.

Explicitly designed as contribution to IR scholarship and as a critique of existing theories of International Relations (especially those associated with "global governance"), Iver B. Neumann and Ole Jacob Sending describe "the international as governmentality" in the sense that "[a] conceptualisation of the international as a socially embedded realm of governmentality sees the international as a structure (defined by relations of power) that generates different and changing practices of political rule (defined as governmental rationality)" (Neumann and Sending 2010: 68). While the authors are aware that this realm of governmentality not only affects states but also individuals (Neumann and Sending 2007: 699), their analysis primarily addresses the role of the state in a changing international sphere. Thereby, the authors remain within the boundaries of the discipline of IR as they consider the international as a distinct level of analysis which is situated "above the state" (Neumann and Sending 2010: 1). In this sense, Neumann and Sending explicitly reject the pervasiveness of international anarchy that is common in IR. Instead, they stress that "there does exist a rationality of government with matching principles that adds up to government over governments" (Neumann and Sending 2010: 164). This, in turn, has implications for state sovereignty as an ordering principle of world politics, because as a form of power, sovereignty is accompanied by a form of governmentality that exerts effects on states. At the same time, Neumann and Sending point out that the increasing importance of international governmental and non-governmental organizations (IGOs, INGOs) in world politics does not signify an "eclipse of the state" (Evans 1997) but rather a change in the mode in which power is globally exercised. Regarding the often constructed opposition between the state and the amorphous concept of "civil society," they argue that "the self-association and political will-formation characteristic of civil society and nonstate actors do not stand in opposition to the political power of the state, but is a most central feature of how power operates in late modern society" (Sending and Neumann 2006: 652). Furthermore, Neumann and Sending put an effort into identifying a Weberian ideal type of a global polity as "the relational practices of governing" (Neumann and Sending 2010: 172), characterized by the predominance of a liberal rationality of governmentality but accompanied by disciplinary and sovereign modes of power. It follows that, by deviating from Foucault's nominalist approach (Walters 2012: 37) in this regard, Neumann and Sending are guided by a notion of governmentality that is rather a descriptive tool than a heuristic device (Zanotti 2013). While utilizing the ideal type of a global polity might help embed their arguments into the discourse of IR, this happens at the expense of potentially limiting the analytical strength of their research perspective (see Corry 2013).

In a different manner, Wendy Larner and William Walters frame global governmentality "as a heading for studies which problematize the constitution, and governance of spaces above, beyond, between and across states" (Larner and Walters 2004b: 2). Thereby, they stress the different spheres of governmentality "in the global" (Latham 1999: 28) as opposed to an exclusively international macrolevel. As a result, Larner and Walters try to offer a "less *substantialized* account of globalization" (2004a: 496, emphasis in the original). To a certain extent at least, however, they share with Neumann and Sending a primary focus on the state as the main agent of global politics. Furthermore, there are several studies of governmentality with a global orientation that follow a Neo-Marxist interpretation of global order (Kiersey 2008, 2009; Weidner 2009). From such a perspective, global governmentality is equated with imperialism so that the state is both subjected to the forces of and a driving force of global imperialism.

By identifying a major limitation of governmentality which remains within the limits of national societies, Barry Hindess (2005: 405) introduces his conceptualization of international governmentality. He is critical of the focus on dynamics within states that result in a neglect of international politics. On this basis, Hindess argues that "[t]he modern art of government has thus been concerned with governing not simply the populations of individual states but also the larger population encompassed by the system of states itself" (Hindess 2005: 407). It follows that Hindess is aware of the importance of governmentality on the international level. At the same time, however, he treats governmentality within states and on the international as separate spheres. Thereby, his analytical perspective risks overlooking the interdependencies between both dimensions which instead reifies the difference between domestic and international.

Apart from these endorsements of global governmentality, the discipline of IR has yielded considerable criticism against such a "scaling-up" of governmentality to the international level. As part of this line of critique, Jan Selby (2007) stresses that Foucault was primarily engaged in the analysis of micropractices of power in domestic societies. Therefore, according to him:

> while the international arena is (...) a densely structured social space inhabited by all manner of discursive, bodily and material relations, it is nonetheless one in which these relations are in large part between powerful political and economic structures – whether states, international institutions, or large corporate actors – and where power thus tends to be more concentrated and centralised than within the domestic social arena.
> (Selby 2007: 338)

As a result, Selby rejects the idea of "scaling-up" governmentality research to the global as it represents an ontologically distinct level of analysis. In other words, what is going on at the international level cannot be compared to and equated with political dynamics in domestic societies. Similarly, Jonathan Joseph (2010, 2012) draws an ontological distinction between the global and the national level. He states that a key feature of governmentality is that it targets populations. On the international level, however, according to Joseph governmentality focuses on the state as the target of governmentality (Joseph 2010: 421–425). Therefore, he concludes that "the application of governmentality to the field of IR works best when it is attempting to explain the mechanisms of global governance" (Joseph 2012: 71). In turn, Joseph rejects utilizing governmentality beyond this very limited scope on the global level. Furthermore, David Chandler (2010) identifies a fundamental gap between Foucault's work and Foucauldian IR. This is the case as "[f]or Foucault, the contestation of governing rationalities (…) was the essence of politics" (Chandler 2010: 141). Therefore, according to Chandler, instead of criticizing the disconnection between politics and power on the global level, which is characteristic of the contemporary global order, Foucauldian IR contributes to its reproduction. Thus, in contrast to being a critical approach of existing global power relations, governmentality leads to their legitimation (Chandler 2009, 2010).

To counter these criticisms, we argue that such readings of Foucault seem problematic, in particular as they ontologize and essentialize the state, international organizations, or corporations in a way that entirely runs counter to a Foucauldian analysis of power relations. Neglecting its anti-essentialist research orientation and practically misreading Foucault, Selby, Joseph, and Chandler mistakenly treat governmentality as an *"onto-logically over-determined* theory" (Andersen 2003: XI). This is particularly surprising given that Foucault himself pointed to the utilization of governmentality below and beyond the state. Actually, Foucault was very explicit about the possibility of such a "scaling-up" of governmentality which is rejected by the above-mentioned authors. In this regard, Foucault observes

> the start of a new type of *global* calculation in European governmental practice. I think that there are many signs of this appearance of a new form of *global rationality*, of a new calculation on the *scale of the world.*
>
> (Foucault 2008: 56, emphasis added)

It is important to highlight that Chandler constructs a separation of politics from power in a way that locates politics, and thus political legitimacy exclusively on the state level and power, in turn, on the global level. As a result, Chandler not only ontologizes statehood but he also displays a normative bias towards the state as he perceives it as the genuine locus of politics, and thus political legitimacy (see Kiersey et al. 2010). By contrast, the specific strength of a Foucauldian analysis of power lies in its nominalist approach which makes it adaptable to different configurations of power relations. Therefore, if states or international organizations are understood as the contingent institutionalization of particular power relations, there is no plausible reason to exclude the analysis of international politics from a governmentality perspective. Such an approach also does not contradict governmentality's focus on populations. Rather, its emphasis on different political rationalities and technologies and underlying multifaceted power relations makes governmentality especially suitable for examining the international (see Walters 2012: 97–100).

Second, beside questions of the state and the international, it is important to assess the role liberalism plays in international/global studies of governmentality. While many researchers relate to Foucault's version of (neo-) liberal governmentality, they do so with different emphases. In some cases, often associated with a Neo-Marxist reading of Foucault and following the tradition of a repressive reading of governmentality referring to the works of Agamben (1998) as well as Hardt and Negri (2000), we can observe an over-emphasis of the global predominance of (neo-)liberal governmentality (Kiersey 2009; Weidner 2009). Such a perspective primarily utilizes governmentality in order to describe what is perceived as a totalizing vision of global liberalism. Hence, there is a focus on the supposed ubiquity and sophistication of liberal governmentality, resulting in an inescapabilty of liberalism. This, however, leads to an ontological reification of the forms of global order that these approaches intend to deconstruct (Chandler 2009). The main problem of such a reading of governmentality is therefore a "substantialist ontology" (Zanotti 2013) in which the diagnosis of global liberalism serves as the onto-logical starting point of analytical inquiries, as opposed to their outcome. At the same time, it is equally problematic that, from such a perspective, the result of the analysis, namely the imperial force of global liberalism, seems to be predetermined from the outset (see also Vrasti 2013). Wendy Brown (2005, 2015) offers a more nuanced discussion of the relationship between governmentality and neoliberalism by elaborating how a neoliberal ration-ality subjugates various spheres of society.

By contrast, we can observe a reflexive notion towards liberalism in other works on global governmentality. According to Neumann and Sending, global governmentality is characterized by the simultaneous tendencies to govern less (in the liberal sense) and to govern more if necessary. They attempt to show "how an increasingly effective liberal rationality of government is establishing itself worldwide, exerting structural pressure on the state to govern indirectly" (Neumann and Sending 2010: 157). Liberal governmentality, accordingly, exists as a guiding principle of global politics that clearly affects states' behavior. In this sense, in addition to the classic notion of liberal restraint of govern-ance, global governmentality also displays an expansive tendency to address ever new fields of intervention in order to contribute to the global spread of liberal rationalities of government (Neumann and Sending 2010: 174–176). Hence, as opposed to Neo-Marxist conceptions of governmentality, both Neumann and Sending as well as Hindess (2004) are aware of the limits of liberalism on a global scale. Neumann and Sending highlight that in order to facilitate the global spread of liberalism, international organizations, such as the IMF or the World Bank, tend to resort to rather illiberal mechanisms of governance. Therefore, Hindess argues that "[w]hat is required for the lib-eral government of populations, then, is a capacity to distinguish between what can be governed through the promotion of liberty and what must be governed in other [illiberal] ways" (Hindess 2004: 28, see also 2001). Despite many similarities, however, there is a difference regarding how Neumann and

Sending as well as Hindess perceive the relationship of liberal governmental rationalities towards the international and the domestic sphere. Neumann and Sending identify a qualitative difference of how governmentality works in the international sphere and within the state. They stress that internationally, governmentality is exercised through international organizations and primarily addresses states and that the expansive tendency of liberalism on the international level differs from the restrictive tendency on the domestic level (Neumann and Sending 2010: 156). Accordingly, they have a similar conception of governmentality in the international as Joseph, while they do not share with him the notion that this makes governmentality inapplicable beyond national societies (see below).

In a similar manner, Mitchell Dean (2010) makes a qualitative distinction between the international and the domestic level when he states that:

> [t]here is a social form of government concerned to govern the life and welfare of the populations that are assigned to certain states; and there is also a kind of international bio-politics that governs the movement, transitions, settlement and repatriation of various populations – including refugees, migrants, guest workers, tourists and students. This international bio-politics is a condition of the assignation of populations to states and thus of social government of any form.
>
> (Dean 2010: 119)

By contrast, Hindess does not draw the distinction between liberalism in the international and domestic sphere. Rather, he argues that the same liberal rationalities of governmentality are at play within and above the state since they eventually have the population as their target (Hindess 2004: 33).

In addition, there are studies that primarily subscribe to governmentality as an analytical perspective, or heuristic device as Zanotti (2013) puts it. Governmentality thereby does not serve as a means to describe global liberalism. Instead, analyzing political dynamics this way can lead to the conclusion that liberal rationalities of government are important in the global sphere. For instance, Larner and Walters make use of Foucault's concept of governmentality as an analytical perspective in order to make sense of the diverse phenomena subsumed under the label of globalization (Larner and Walters 2004b). Thereby, in contrast to many other studies, they do not limit their observations to "a particular ontology of power relations" (Walters 2012: 157, fn. 3) such as "liberal" governmentality. Hence, by emphasizing the contingency of power relations and governmental rationalities, they are not preoccupied with global liberalism but at the same time do not exclude its importance (Larner and Walters 2004a: 504).

As is the case with the relationship of the state and the international, Selby (2007) and Joseph (2010) reject using governmentality at a global level, as Foucault's ideas originated in the context of liberal western societies. In other words, governmentality is perceived as being inextricably intertwined with a specifically Western liberalism, and is therefore inappropriate for analyzing parts of the world that do not qualify as "liberal." As a result, as Joseph states, "because the international domain is highly uneven, contemporary forms of governmentality can only usefully be applied to those areas that might be characterized as having an advanced form of liberalism" (Joseph 2010: 224). In other contexts, however, governmentality can only be imposed, for instance through international organizations, and is therefore destined to fail or takes the shape of a "new type of imperialism" (Joseph 2010: 237, 2009: 418). A somewhat related criticism comes from Stephen Collier who points out that in governmentality studies, there is a problematic tendency to infer from individual cases a global logic of neoliberal power relations that do not hold out against empirical observations (Collier 2009: 97–98). As a consequence, Collier denies the usefulness of governmentality as it "is not a helpful tool for analyzing a topological field comprised of heterogeneous techniques, procedures and institutional arrangements that *cannot* be made intelligible through reference to common conditions of possibility" (2009: 98, emphasis in the original).

This criticism requires careful consideration as it raises some important points. In particular, we share the concern that a totalizing conception of global governmentality which leaves no room for variance and diversity of power relations is problematic. By utilizing governmentality in such a manner one would make the same mistake of determinism which a Foucauldian perspective is actually equipped to overcome. Both Selby and Joseph, however, fail to offer a satisfactory response to the shortcomings they identify in global governmentality research. By contrast, similar to Larner and Walters, it is useful to refer to Rose et al. (2006) who contradict a totalizing understanding of governmentality. Instead, they refer to its contingency and stress that the (re-)configuration of governmental power relations is a constantly ongoing process. Hence, according to such a dynamic conception of governmentality and power, "[r]ationalities are constantly undergoing modification in the face of some newly identified problem or solution, while retaining certain styles of thought and technological preferences" (Rose et al. 2006: 98).

How governmentality studies deal with the state and the international on the one hand, and liberalism on the other has important consequences for how these approaches conceptualize agency. Therefore, third, it is important to address the implications for political agency and subjectivity emanating from the different studies of international/global governmentality. Utilizing governmentality as a totalizing vision of global liberalism has important consequences for how these approaches understand agency. These approaches present the individual as a disenfranchised subject, totally subjugated to globally pervasive power relations. Due to the predominance that is ascribed to liberalism and its underlying power techniques, such a perspective risks dispossessing subjects of any sense of agency. Instead, individuals are merely subject to the superior forces of inescapable and all-embracing liberal forces (Kiersey 2008). According to these interpretations, capitalism fundamentally determines subjectivity (Weidner 2009). While scholars adhering to this perspective seem aware of this problem, they do not offer convincing solutions for it (Kiersey et al. 2010).

Equally problematic, however, are critiques that neglect Foucault's emphasis of freedom as an import dimension of governmentality and consequently limit their criticism exclusively to a repressive reading of governmentality. In this sense, Chandler (2009, 2010: 140–141) offers a distorted conception of Foucauldian power and a selective reading of governmentality studies that is only limited to conceptions that potentially deny agency in the face of global liberal predominance. Therefore, Chandler's critical engagement with governmentality only makes sense if it is directed towards a biopolitical reading of governmentality in the tradition of Agamben as well as Hardt and Negri, who themselves make use of Foucault's elaborations in a very selective manner (see Bruff 2009). Accordingly, even though Chandler is correct that certain authors tend to overemphasize the disciplinary potentials of biopolitics that result in a disempowered individual, he either misreads or neglects those authors who use governmentality in a way that takes into account the creative forms of agency that individuals are capable of.

As a result, both a repressive reading of governmentality as well as its narrow critique are problematic, as they misread a Foucauldian understanding of power for which the emphasis of freedom is crucial. In other words, it is crucial to highlight that governmentality rests on an understanding of power that clearly enables the agency of the individual. Governmentality thus depends on the idea of the free individual. In this sense, governmental rationalities and technologies have the potential to both simultaneously subjugate and empower the individual (Busse 2019). In this context, it is also worth stressing that there is good reason to extend Foucault's understanding of governmentality to the sphere of emotions. As Anne-Marie D'Aoust (2014: 269) has argued, by focusing on the body, it is possible to properly analyze the interplay of rationalities and emotions, as exemplified by what she terms as "technologies of love" (2013).

In contrast to a denial of agency or its blunt critique, Neumann and Sending are much more sensitive to the importance of freedom for governmentality, and they emphasize that "governing through freedom" (e.g. Neumann and Sending 2010: 9–15) is a defining feature of governmentality. By referring to Mitchell Dean's concept of "technologies of agency" (2010: 196–197), the authors point out that it is a typical feature of international governmentality that both governmental and nongovernmental organizations exercise agency and thus transform from a "passive object of government to be acted upon (…) into an entity that is both an object *and* a subject of government" (Neumann and Sending 2010: 115, emphasis in the original). In a similar manner, Larner and Walters highlight that concerning globalization, "the question of freedom as the modality of liberal power is central" (2004a: 507). What is more, since Larner and Walters operate on the basis of a non-substantialist ontology and utilize governmentality as a heuristic device instead of a descriptive one (Zanotti 2013), they do not display any analytical prejudices regarding the status of the subject but present "a view of agency in terms of contingent rather than fixed subjectivities" (Larner and Walters 2004b: 3; see Busse 2019).

### *From international governmentality studies to the globality of governmentality*

Despite the evident merits of existing governmentality research in IR, as this volume will highlight, both on a conceptual on an empirical level, it is necessary to advance the debate by fully taking into account the different quality of governmentality in a distinctively global context. Hence, there are multiple phenomena that cannot properly be captured by approaching them through the lens of the *international.* Rather, as we will elaborate in detail in the next section, they are of global scope with overarching implications which justify a focus on the *globality* of governmentality.

## Governmentality and globality: How can we make use of governmentality in the study of world politics?

What relevance does the concept of "globality" actually have for governmentality studies today? Has not Foucault's (supposedly) limited discussion of the international and "the global" been discussed *ad nauseum* before (see Dean 2010; Joseph 2012; Walters 2012)?

Contrary to many contemporary concepts of IR, such as the state, the international organization, and sovereignty (see Bartelson 1995), "globality" remains an underexplored topic. It is a buzzword or catchall phrase, used commonly – often in conjunction with the equally blurred notion of globalization – but rarely analyzed or explored in depth. This omission is surprising, considering that "the global" underpins a majority of the concepts that scholars now take for granted in the discipline. Equally important, examining the notion of globality should not be limited to IR, as it also resonates with developments in neighboring disciplines such Global History (e.g. Osterhammel 2014) and Global Historical Sociology (e.g. Go and Lawson 2015; see Rotger et al. 2019). Such a consideration of the global also helps overcoming a preoccupation with methodological nationalism (see Wimmer and Glick Schiller 2002) which often obscures a proper analysis of political dynamics which transcend clear-cut inside/ outside dichotomies.

Globality, or "the concept of the global and its cognates," argues Bartelson (2010: 219), "are commonly used to describe a condition characterized by the presence of a single sociopolitical space on a planetary scale." Among the first who conceptualized globality was sociologist Roland Robertson according to whom it "refers to the circumstance of extensive awareness of the world as a whole (...)" (Robertson 1992: 78). For van Munster and Syvest (2016: 1), globality or "oneness" is "reflected in a range of ideas and practices, including the ubiquitous use of global maps and iconography and the proclamation of planetary problems of security or ecology, as well as in omnipresent invocations of a common humanity." It can range from utopian aspirations towards a technological and environmentally and/or economically sustainable world state, to dire prognostications of a repressive or authoritarian global government. In other words, "there is not one, single globality, but multiple, at times even competing visions of globality across time and space" (van Munster and Sylvest 2016: 3). For instance, Pinar Bilgin criticizes from a postcolonial perspective the predominance of what she terms "colonial globality," narrowly denoting "Eurocentric understandings of the constitution of the global" (2019: 86). Historically, such an enduring colonial globality can be traced back to what can be termed "imperial globality" in a sense that European colonialism contributed to the above-mentioned oneness of the world:

> The era of high imperialism can be regarded as the first period in which a global order was seriously imagined as at least a possibility for the near future. Imperialism had not only made the globality of the world perceivable as an empirical reality, but also produced a whole range of theories and ideologies supposedly proving the irreversibility and quasi-natural character of imperial expansion.
>
> (Geulen 2007: 69)

Framed differently, as Buzan and Lawson have shown, the 19th century for the first time produced a state of globality described as "global modernity," which "pulled the world into a single system (...)" (2015: 2).[3]

Regardless of whether one chooses an optimistic or pessimistic consideration of globality, the concept embraces a planetary wholeness or scope. In other words, we do not conceive of globality as a normative concept as cosmopolitan research would do, but rather we emphasize the global scope of social relations and interactions on a structural and practical level. Simply speaking, globality means that the entire world is regarded as a single place (Corry 2013; Shaw 2000). Accordingly, as this volume highlights there are various ways of capturing this globality, be it through a theory of world society, as Stephan Stetter does in his chapter, or an emphasis on the inclusiveness of this globality in the sense of distinguishing it from the global as a mere level which would be situated above other ones. Here lie interesting grounds of interconnection between Foucauldian research with other theoretical approaches which are interested in theorizing global order. For instance, from the perspective of the Stanford School of Sociology, globality is described as a world polity, denoting the:

> conceptual vision of the world as a single social system, an encompassing "society" involving all of "humanity" in extensive webs of interaction

and flows of goods, ideas, money, values, and so on, among other social units (…).

(Lechner and Boli 2005: 20)

Taking the notion of globality in relation to governmentality seriously also means not to limit the scope of governmentality to western political contexts. Rather, referring to globality helps transcending such a limitation which is often inherent in *International Governmentality Studies*. Hence, there is good reason to also point to the validity of governmentality in the Global South, because despite evident variations all formations of centralized political authority are exposed to similar political dynamics within a singular global polity (Busse 2018). Such perspectives also help overcoming a potential Eurocentrism which is inherent in Foucauldian scholarship. This insight is, for instance, mirrored in the volume edited by Teo and Wynne-Hughes (2020a) which explores how governmentality is "reshaped in non-Western contexts" by engaging with postcolonial studies (Teo and Wynne-Hughes 2020b: 1). As a result, they identify what they term "postcolonial governmentalities" which basically acknowledges the importance to account for colonial historical legacies when utilizing a governmentality perspective (see also D'Aoust 2019; Legg and Heath 2018; Scott 1995).

We consider the concepts of "globality" and "governmentality" as entangled, entwined, or constitutive of one another. We take neither word nor concept for granted, but stress the need to explore how each now embraces and even engenders the other. In other words, rather than merely "scaling-up" Foucault to the international or global realm (Joseph 2010; Selby 2007), or making "the global" an epiphenomenal product of increased state interaction or globalization (Bartelson 2010), we suggest asking *how* the globality of governmentality precedes, shapes, and provides the foundation for the forms of thought and subjectivity that comprise IR today. This volume thus asks not only what "the global" is, but what it *does* to our thought and practices when it is invoked. As Foucault once remarked, alongside the emergence of the governmentalized state (2007) came corresponding forms of global governmentality: "a new type of global calculation in European governmental practice (…) a new form of global rationality, of a new calculation on the scale of the world. (…) [A] governmental rationality that has the entire planet for its horizon" (2008: 56). Governmentality, in other words, has *always* been global. Hence, we agree with Bartelson (2010) that neither is globality a mere extension of the international, nor was it preceded by it. Rather, as Bartelson has shown, globality as a way of imagining the world as a single unit on a planetary scale, has solid historical roots that even predate the international level. Even more so: "Conceptualizing the world as a spherical object was a precondition of the subsequent division of that globe into distinct portions by means of geometrical methods, but also for the subjection of these to exclusive sovereignty claims" (Bartelson 2010: 223). If governmentality, globality, and the state are all simultaneously co-produced and entangled – rather than existing as prepackaged separate scales or concepts to be combined, like puzzle pieces – then new approaches and conceptualizations of politics are required in order to reconsider the globality of conducts and actions. Indeed, as Bartelson stresses (2010), it is a mistake to consider "the global" as something secondary and epiphenomenal to subjectivity, the state, and the international. The global is not the aftershock of plural sovereignties. Rather, this order should be inverted, and our understanding of the global should be problematized anew: what if globality is as much *a part of* the state, as borders, governments, security, territory, and population? If governmentality has been global all along, then how might we rethink the concepts in IR that we have confined within the borders and boundaries of a statist governmentality that may now be transformed?

As the preceding section has shown, there are fascinating and erudite insights into global governmentality that this volume aims to expand upon. Although previous accounts have provided invaluable and pioneering analyses into the possibilities *and* limits of (global) governmentality, each stops short of conceptualizing globality on its own unique historical, ontological, and epistemological footing. Governmentality is analyzed, while "globality" remains assumed away as epiphenomenal. Echoing Bartelson, "the global" becomes another word for an excess of the international realm; an afterthought of the states and polities preceding it. Although the recent "global governmentality debate" has been reviewed elsewhere (Hamilton 2014; Vrasti 2013), it is worth noting that both critics and advocates of global governmentality studies succumb to this privileging of the state. Although Foucauldian IR has aimed to cut-off the King's head at the level of the state, at the level of globality, the King still subtly reigns. As Joseph (2009: 414) writes:

> An important theoretical issue concerns the difference between using the governmentality approach to understand what goes on at the local level in different places around the world ... and developing the idea that there is something substantially different operating at a higher level that deserves the name global governmentality.

The issue here, however, is the familiar one of scalar *extension*; scaling the local, national, and even international, upwards in scale, ontology, and epistemology. Similarly, although promoting the study of global governmentality, Sending and Neumann (2010) echo this narrative of extension, by arguing that changes of sovereignty, state, and society today, are moving upwards to new forms of power operating at the international level. In light of globalization and the emerging power of civil society groups, "[w]e would, therefore, expect that new practices of government emerge whereby civil society organizations on the global level are harnessed to the tasks of governing." (Sending and Neumann 2006: 656). However, although each side of the "global governmentality debate" might discuss the validity and accuracy of "scaling-up" rationalities and practices to the global realm, both sides share the underlying assumption that this globality proceeds *from*, rather than precedes, the state and the international. According to these authors, global governmentality is nothing new here; it has the same philosophical and conceptual meaning as statist governmentality. The form is the same, yet the scale is enlarged.

It is this common extension of governmentality *upwards to* the global realm that this volume wishes to problematize. Globality is not merely an extension of the state. Globality thus cannot be equated with the international level. Rather, it is constitutive, entangled, and deserving of an analyses unto itself. The conduct of global conduct is comprised of rationalities and subjectivities of a genuine character. As a result, one needs to overcome the methodological nationalism that is inherent both in IR theorizing and most governmentality research in IR.

## The need for global governmentality *redux*

The state and society cannot contain globality. If we are to truly consider the global, we cannot, should not, try to return the genie into its bottle. Rather, inevitably, the global is the horizon into which both are embedded and to which both therefore need to relate. As the chapters in this volume illustrate, there are many "global" rationalities, crises, and concepts that cannot be placed within, or limited to, a single state or polity. As noted above, these include a variety of discourses ranging from global financial flows and migration, to one of the most urgent, and obvious, which is anthropogenic climate change (see Hamilton 2018; Stripple and Bulkeley 2014). However, if we are seeking to analyze and diagnose practices and rationalities without succumbing to a "presentism" or "chronofetishism" (Hobson 2002), that asserts the history and essence of these concepts as things already known (Walters 2012), then a new type of analysis is required. If we view a global governmentality from the purview of the state, then critiques as brought forward by Joseph, Selby, or Chandler would indeed be justified in the sense that we are merely elevating statist concepts and limits upwards into a new level of analysis. So, the form of statist "governmentality" that IR has championed, which details the *security, territory, and population* of the state (Foucault 2007), can and should be reconceptualized if the global is not merely epiphenomenal to the national and international. Indeed, as Walters (2012) notes, a truly global governmentality cannot be conceptualized by focusing on inter- or transnational forms of liberal governance: Rather, a new variant of governmentality can here be established. It must be a form that is – as every form of governmentality should be – a careful diagnostic tool, that treats the "global" aspect of its thought and practices as foundational, and the state, society, municipality, etc., as either co-constitutive or concomitant, to the global, rather than primary. In other words, what is required for today's global concepts is an analytic of *global* governmentality that does not form a picture constructed from jigsaw pieces of the state and the international.

Rather, a global governmentality *redux* is required. In this sense, the *globality* of governmentality is not merely a new ontologized category that is replacing the state or the international. Rather, as advocated by Walters (2012), this particular *globality* of governmentality is constituted and performed in a historical nominalist sense. In other words, it is the technologies and rationalities of governmentality that materialize on a genuinely global level, that constitute this globality. Hence, globality is not ontologically preexistent but a particular constitution of power relations which materialize through governmentality. Accordingly, governmentality in this context is a social practice of the global as opposed to mere international practice (see Adler and Pouliot 2011).

How can this new global governmentality analytic emerge? Here, we must remember that governmentality is not a (grand) theory, in a classical sense. Rather, it can serve to make sense of global order, thereby being compatible to (de-)constructionist theories of global order that share similar epistemological underpinnings. In other words, as the contributions of this volume highlight, there are multiple manifestations of this globality in the practice of governmentality; be it as a world society, global entanglements, or through the emphasis of the specific features of globality in the chosen empirical case. Global governmentality, as understood in this volume, therefore, is not a roadmap outlining paths for subjectivity or political action to take, but is instead, the lens we may use to view how these roads are constructed and naturalized to form our everyday world. As our world inexorably changes and transforms in the vicissitudes of time, so too does the human experience of government. It behoves governmentality and IR alike to progress alongside these changes, analyzing the shifts and transformations of government and conduct that make citizens and subjects act the way they do, from the microscale to the macro.

## Outline of the volume

*The Globality of Governmentality* thus offers an in-depth conceptual and theoretical engagement with governmentality in IR, while at the same time emphasizing that this endeavor needs to be undertaken in the face of globality as a distinct sphere of the social which is not identical with the international level. The book, thereby, serves the two interlinked purposes of offering novel theoretical insights in relation to empirical phenomena that take into account the notion of globality in various forms. These two aims are also mirrored in the structure of the volume, since the first section "Governing Thought" encompasses chapters which put a relatively greater emphasis on theoretical and conceptual questions, while the second section "Governing Practice" addresses specific contexts of globality in their empirical manifestations.

In Chapter 2, Stephan Stetter offers an account of the evolution of international politics which links a governmentality perspective with sociological theories of modern society by Niklas Luhmann, Pierre Bourdieu, and John W. Meyer. Hence, by emphasizing Foucault's own sympathy for theoretical and conceptual eclecticism, Stetter develops an understanding of governmentality which is embedded in overarching dynamics of societal order. He thereby presents a discussion of the relationship of governmentality and international politics which is enriched by a sophisticated understanding of world society, rooted in the works of Luhmann and Meyer. In this way, Stetter's chapter succeeds in offering a thoroughly historically and sociologically informed framework for the analysis of international politics as a subsystem or field of power in the context of globality.

Jonathan Joseph in Chapter 3 explores different variations of governmentality in a global context by combining the concept of governmentality with a Gramscian account of hegemony. He does so by focusing on the case of resilience and argues that while being understood differently in different context, resilience is still informed by a certain hegemonic pattern of (neo-)liberal governmentality. Joseph's analysis thus differs from existing approaches to governmentality by assessing the material questions of its possibility instead of merely looking at governmentality as a rationality. Thereby, his contribution also critically engages with the concept of globality insofar as, in his view, it appears to be too homogenizing given the existing diversity.

In Chapter 4, from the perspective of Historical International Relations, and by making use of governmentality as an analytical perspective, Halvard Leira explores the potentials of governmentality in order to make sense of power dynamics before the early modern period. He, therefore, argues that the analytical toolkit provided by a governmentality perspective allows for the analysis of political dynamics in pre-modern history. Accordingly, what he describes as inter-governmentality denotes the analysis of the relations between polities before the emergence of modern statehood. In this context, Leira argues that governmentality has always existed in an entangled relationship to globality and that governmentality, understood as a heuristic device, can be utilized in order to analyze any kind polity and is thus not limited to a focus on states or interstate relations. Such a research perspective, as proposed by Leira, is capable of transcending temporal and spatial confinements, offering a framework for the analysis of a variety of power relations in different settings.

In Chapter 5, Mitchell Dean and Oscar L. Larsson present an alternative view of sovereignty and sovereign powers in global governmentality. They do so by offering a critical engagement with the ways governmentality has been used in IR, and they highlight the enduring importance of sovereignty. In this context, the chapter problematizes a certain disregard of sovereignty in favor of governmentality both in Foucault's own scholarship and subsequent studies. Dean and Larsson highlight that sovereignty needs to be understood as both a set of specific capacities as well as a form of authoritative rule over a certain domain. Thereby, they offer a nonreductive way of conceptualizing and analyzing the relationship between sovereignty and governmentality in a global context. In this relation, they also point to the need to focus on the entanglement of sovereign states as actors, sovereignty as a principle and sovereign powers as the functions of a state in a context of globality.

Laura Zanotti in Chapter 6 explores agency and resistance in the face of global entanglements. She does so by linking a governmentality perspective with complexity and quantum theories, the latter in particular based on the works of Karen Barad. Thereby, she examines how governmentality is deployed in contexts of uncertainty and complexity and how this affects political agency. As a result, she highlights that an increase of global complexity also yields further potentials for counter conducts. The concept of entanglements is relevant insofar in her chapter as it stresses the importance of micropractices as a central element of political agency. Crucially, Zanotti highlights that the combination of governmentality, quantum, and complexity theories helps going beyond deterministic understandings of power and instead focuses on uncertainty and contingency.

The volume's second section on "governing practice" starts with Chapter 7, in which Nicholas Kiersey takes a look at neoliberal rationalities in the context of European austerity policies in response to the 2008 financial crisis. He does so by employing a Marxist reading of governmentality and argues that a Foucauldian Political Economy can identify both the biopolitical and disciplinary functions of austerity. In this context, Kiersey points out that contrary to what is often assumed, Foucault's scholarship should not necessarily be seen as opposed to Marxism. Instead, Kiersey suggests that one needs to take into account that Foucault stressed that capitalism relies on a biopolitical regime. In this regard, he highlights that by being preoccupied with an emphasis on authoritarianism, Marxist critics of austerity neglect the importance of what he terms confessional biopolitics as a central feature of capitalism.

In Chapter 8, Audrey Reeves addresses the relationship of gender and global governmentality. She illustrates how the concept of "women" became a transnational category of persons worthy of gender-specific attention, support, and care on a global level. On this basis, as Reeves shows, a particular understanding of women's empowerment has become a frequent feature of development aid on a global level through various means which itself rendered acceptable only specific forms of knowledge about women as legitimate forms of expertise. As a result, the global governmentalization of gender expertise inhibited more subversive gender analyses of the androcentric bias of governmentalizing institutions and programs. In order to illustrate her arguments, she refers to statebuilding endeavors in the Global South between 2000 and 2010.

Hans-Martin Jaeger, in Chapter 9, makes an innovative connection of the BRICS (Brazil, Russia, India, China, South Africa) group and governmentality. He does so by arguing that BRICS represents a project of post-neoliberal global governmentality which responds to the dual crisis of neoliberalism and US hegemony. According to Jaeger, crisis is a central feature of this governmentality as it fundamentally shapes the outlook of international order. For that purpose, Jaeger makes use of Mitchell Dean's "signature of power," (2013) leading to a deconstructive reading of BRICS' signature of power. As Jaeger shows, BRICS makes use of crisis in order to bring forward reforms of international financial organizations towards a quasi-ordoliberal direction, while at the same time promoting a state-capitalist understanding of economic development. In this way, the chapter argues, BRICS contributes to a vision of globality which relies on a mixture of governmental–economic and sovereign–multipolar rationalities and practices.

In Chapter 10, Mathias Albert and Andreas Vasilache assess the importance of the Artic as an international region by making use of a governmentality perspective. Based on a discussion of multiple visions of the Artic – as a region to be explored or a region of economic opportunity – they argue that the perception of the Artic as an international region fundamentally relies on the emergence of related practices of governmentality. They show that in certain respects the Artic fundamentally differs from other regions. In this sense, the chapter points out that in order to make sense of the future of the Artic, it is crucial to take into account patterns of Arctic governmentality, which is constituted by patterns constitutive of the Artic as a social and political space. Albert and Vasilache thereby highlight that this Artic governmentality affects the region's spatial, figurative, and political reconfiguration.

The concluding chapter, authored by Iver B. Neumann and Ole Jacob Sending offers a critical and constructive engagement with the volume's contributions. In their critical appraisal they, first, point out why they consider Marxist approaches unfit to a governmentality perspective. Moreover, while expressing some disagreement with the notion of globality, Neumann and Sending stress that the discussion about "scaling-up" governmentality is not useful insofar as the concept focuses on social relations, making questions of levels of analysis irrelevant. In addition, the authors suggest that approaches from processual sociology – in particular, the works of Norbert Elias – might turn out useful in combination with governmentality in order to yield greater insights about global politics.

## Acknowledgments

We wish to thank Stephan Stetter for his helpful feedback to a draft version of this chapter.

## Notes

1  This sub-section draws on Busse (2018): 48–65.
2  On that matter, see also Lisle, who discusses the "biopolitical apparatus of public health and social hygiene" (2016: 51) in the context of the British colonial endeavor in Egypt.
3  Note that Martin Albrow explicitly contrasts globality and modernity. According to him, "the Global Age involves the supplanting of modernity with globality and this means an overall change in the basis of action and social organization for individuals and groups" (1996: 4).

# References

Adler, Emanuel and Pouliot, Vincent (eds) (2011) *International Practices* (Cambridge: Cambridge University Press).

Agamben, Giorgio (1998) *Homo Sacer: Sovereign Power and Bare Life* (Stanford, CA: Stanford University Press).

Albrow, Martin (1996) *The Global Age: State and Society Beyond Modernity* (Cambridge: Polity Press).

Andersen, Niels Åkerstrøm (2003) *Discursive Analytical Strategies: Understanding Foucault, Koselleck, Laclau, Luhmann* (Bristol: The Policy Press).

Ashley, Richard K. and Walker, R. B. J. (eds) (1990) 'Speaking the Language of Exile: Dissident Thought in International Studies', *International Studies Quarterly* 34:3, 259–416.

Bartelson, Jens (1995) *A Genealogy of Sovereignty* (Cambridge: Cambridge University Press).

Bartelson, Jens (2010) 'The Social Construction of Globality', *International Political Sociology* 4:3, 219–235.

Bilgin, Pinar (2019) 'Colonial Globality, Postcolonial Subjectivities in the Middle East' in Dietrich Jung and Stephan Stetter (eds) *Modern Subjectivities in World Society: Global Structures and Local Practices* (New York: Palgrave Macmillan), 85–103.

Boli, John and Thomas, George M. (1997) 'World Culture in the World Polity: A Century of International Non-Governmental Organization', *American Sociological Review* 62:2, 171–190.

Bonditti, Philippe, Bigo, Didier and Gros, Frédéric (eds) (2017): *Foucault and the Modern International: Silences and Legacies for the Study of World Politics* (New York: Palgrave Macmillan).

Brown, Wendy (2005) 'Neoliberalism and the End of Liberal Democracy' in *Edgework: Critical Essays on Knowledge And Politics* (Princeton: Princeton University Press), 37–59.

Brown, Wendy (2015) *Undoing the Demos: Neoliberalism's Stealth Revolution* (New York: Zone Books).

Bruff, Ian (2009) 'The Totalisation of Human Social Practice: Open Marxists and Capitalist Social Relations, Foucauldians and Power Relations', *British Journal of Politics & International Relations* 11:2, 332–351.

Busse, Jan (2018) *Deconstructing the Dynamics of World-Societal Order: The Power of Governmentality in Palestine* (London: Routledge).

Busse, Jan (2019) 'The Everyday Production of Modern Subjectivity in World Society: Global Structures meet Local Practices in Palestine' in Dietrich Jung and Stephan Stetter (eds) *Modern Subjectivities in World Society: Global Structures and Local Practices* (New York: Palgrave Macmillan), 105–124.

Buzan, Barry and Lawson, George (2015) *The Global Transformation: History, Modernity and the Making of International Relations* (Cambridge: Cambridge University Press).

Chandler, David (2009) 'Critiquing Liberal Cosmopolitanism? The Limits of the Biopolitical Approach', *International Political Sociology* 3:1, 53–70.

Chandler, David (2010) 'Globalising Foucault: Turning Critique into Apologia—A Response to Kiersey and Rosenow', *Global Society* 24:2, 135–142.

Collier, Stephen J. (2009) 'Topologies of Power: Foucault's Analysis of Political Government beyond 'Governmentality'', *Theory, Culture & Society* 26:6, 78–108.

Corry, Olaf (2013) *Constructing a Global Polity: Theory, Discourse and Governance* (New York: Palgrave).

D'Aoust, Anne-Marie (2013) 'In the Name of Love: Marriage Migration, Governmentality, and Technologies of Love', *International Political Sociology* 7:3, 258–274.

D'Aoust, Anne-Marie (2014) 'Ties that Bind? Engaging Emotions, Governmentality and Neoliberalism: Introduction to the Special Issue', *Global Society* 28:3, 267–276.

D'Aoust, Anne-Marie (2019) 'Liberal Estrangements and Global Intimacies: Making the Connections', *Geopolitics* 1–6 (online first).

De Larrinaga, Miguel and Doucet, Marc G. (eds) (2010) *Security and Global Governmentality: Globalization, Governance and the State* (New York: Routledge).

Dean, Mitchell (2010) *Governmentality: Power and Rule in Modern Society*. Second Edition (London: Sage).

Dean, Mitchell (2013) *The Signature of Power: Sovereignty, Governmentality and Biopolitics* (London: SAGE).

Der Derian, James and Shapiro, Michael J. (eds) (1989): *International/Intertextual Relations: Postmodern Readings of World Politics* (New York: Lexington Books).

Edkins, Jenny (1999) *Poststructuralism and International Relations: Bringing the Political Back In* (Boulder: Lynne Rienner).

Evans, Peter B. (1997) 'The Eclipse of the State? Reflections on Stateness in an Era of Globalization', *World Politics* 50:1, 62–87.

Foucault, Michel (1980) *Power/Knowledge: Selected Interviews and Other Writings 1972-1977* (New York: Pantheon Books).

Foucault, Michel (1984) 'Deux essais sur le sujet et le pouvoir' in Hubert Dreyfus and Paul Rabinow (eds) *Michel Foucault: Un pacours philosophique* (Paris: Gallimard), 297–321.

Foucault, Michel (1991) 'Governmentality' in Graham Burchell, Colin Gordon and Peter Miller (eds) *The Foucault Effect: Studies in Governmentality* (Chicago: The University of Chicago Press), 87–104.

Foucault, Michel (2007) *Security, Territory, Population: Lectures at the Collège de France 1977-1978* (New York: Picador).

Foucault, Michel (2008) *The Birth of Biopolitics: Lectures at the Collège De France, 1978-1979* (New York: Picador).

Foucault, Michel (2010) *The Government of Self and Others: Lectures at the Collège de France, 1982–1983* (New York: Palgrave Macmillan).

Geulen, Christian (2007) 'The Common Grounds of Conflict: Racial Visions of World Order 1880–1940', in Sebastian Conrad and Dominic Sachsenmaier (eds) *Competing Visions of World Order: Global Moments and Movements, 1880s–1930s* (Basingstoke: Palgrave Macmillan), 69–96.

Go, Julian and Lawson, George (eds) (2017) *Global Historical Sociology* (Cambridge: Cambridge University Press).

Hamilton, Scott (2014) 'Add Foucault and Stir? The Perils and Promise of Governmentality and the Global', *European Review of International Studies* 1:2, 129–141.

Hamilton, Scott (2018): 'The Measure of All Things? The Anthropocene as a Global Biopolitics of Carbon', *European Journal of International Relations* 24:1, 33-57.

Hardt, Michael and Negri, Antonio (2000) *Empire* (Cambridge, MA: Harvard University Press).

Hindess, Barry (2001) 'The Liberal Government of Unfreedom', *Alternatives: Global, Local, Political* 26:2, 93–111.

Hindess, Barry (2004) 'Liberalism - What's in a Name?' in Wendy Larner and William Walters (eds) *Global Governmentality: Governing International Spaces* (London: Routledge), 23–39.

Hindess, Barry (2005) 'Politics as Government: Michel Foucault's Analysis of Political Reason', *Alternatives: Global, Local, Political* 30:4, 389–413.

Hobson, John M. (2002) 'What's at Stake in 'Bringing Historical Sociology Back into International Relations'? Transcending 'Chronofetishism' and 'Tempocentrism' in International Relations' in Stephen Hobden and John M. Hobson (eds) *Historical Sociology of International Relations* (Cambridge: Cambridge University Press), 1–41.

Joseph, Jonathan (2009) 'Governmentality of What? Populations, States and International Organisations', *Global Society* 23:4, 413–427.

Joseph, Jonathan (2010) 'The Limits of Governmentality: Social Theory and the International', *European Journal of International Relations* 16:2, 223–246.

Joseph, Jonathan (2012) *The Social in the Global: Social Theory, Governmentality and Global Politics* (Cambridge: Cambridge University Press).

Kiersey, Nicholas J. (2008) 'World State or Global Governmentality? Constitutive Power and Resistance in a Post-Imperial World', *Global Change, Peace & Security* 20:3, 357–374.

Kiersey, Nicholas J. (2009) 'Neoliberal Political Economy and the Subjectivity of Crisis: Why Governmentality is Not Hollow', *Global Society* 23:4, 363–386.

Kiersey, Nicholas J. Weidner, Jason R. and Rosenow, Doerthe (2010) 'Response to Chandler', *Global Society* 24:2, 143–150.

Larner, Wendy and Walters, William (2004a) 'Globalization as Governmentality', *Alternatives: Global, Local, Political* 29:5, 495–514.

Larner, Wendy and Walters, William (2004b) 'Introduction - Global Governmentality: Governing International Spaces', in Wendy Larner and William Walters (eds), *Global Governmentality: Governing International Spaces* (London: Routledge), 1–20.

Larner, Wendy and Walters, William (eds) (2004c): *Global Governmentality: Governing International Spaces* (London: Routledge).

Latham, Robert (1999) 'Politics in a Floating World: Toward a Critique of Global Governance', in: Martin Hewson and Timothy J. Sinclair (eds.), *Approaches to Global Governance Theory* (Albany: State University of New York Press), 23–53.

Lechner, Frank J. and Boli, John (2005) *World Culture: Origins and Consequences* (Malden: Blackwell Publishing).

Legg, Stephen and Heath, Deana (eds.) (2018) *South Asian Governmentalities: Michel Foucault and the Question of Postcolonial Orderings* (Cambridge: Cambridge University Press).

Lemke, Thomas (2002) 'Foucault, Governmentality, and Critique', *Rethinking Marxism* 14:3, 49–64.

Lemke, Thomas (2015) 'New Materialisms: Foucault and the 'Government of Things'', *Theory, Culture & Society* 32:4, 3–25.

Lisle, Debbie (2016) *Holidays in the Danger Zone* (Minneapolis: University of Minnesota Press).

Munster, Rens van and Sylvest, Casper (2016) 'Introduction' in Rens van Munster and Casper Sylvest (eds) *The Politics of Globality Since 1945* (London: Routledge), 1–19.

Neumann, Iver B. and Sending, Ole Jacob (2007) ''The International' as Governmentality', *Millennium - Journal of International Studies* 35:3, 677–701.

Neumann, Iver B. and Sending, Ole Jacob (2010) *Governing the Global Polity: Practice, Mentality, Rationality* (Ann Arbor: University of Michigan Press).

Osterhammel, Jürgen (2014) *The Transformation of the World: A Global History of the Nineteenth Century* (Princeton: Princeton University Press).

Robertson, Roland (1992) *Globalization: Social Theory and Global Culture* (London: Sage).

Rose, Nikolas, O'Malley, Pat and Valverde, Mariana (2006) 'Governmentality', *Annual Review of Law and Social Sciences* 2, 83–104.

Rotger, Neus, Roig-Sanz, Diana and Puxan-Oliva, Marta (2019) 'Introduction: Towards a Cross-Disciplinary History of the Global in the Humanities and the Social Sciences', *Journal of Global History* 14:3, 325–334.

Salter, Mark B (ed.) (2015) *Making Things International 1: Circuits and Motion* (Minneapolis: University of Minnesota Press).

Scott, David (1995) 'Colonial Governmentality', *Social Text* 43, 191–220.

Selby, Jan (2007) 'Engaging Foucault: Discourse, Liberal Governance and the Limits of Foucauldian IR', *International Relations* 21:3, 324–345.

Sending, Ole Jacob and Neumann, Iver B. (2006) 'Governance to Governmentality: Analyzing NGOs, States, and Power', *International Studies Quarterly* 50:3, 651–672.

Shaw, Martin (2000) *Theory of the Global State: Globality as an Unfinished Revolution* (Cambridge: Cambridge University Press).

Stripple, Johannes and Bulkeley, Harriet (2014) *Governing the Climate: New Approaches to Rationality, Power and Politics* (New York: Cambridge University Press).

Teo, Terri-Anne and Wynne-Hughes, Elisa (eds) (2020a): *Postcolonial Governmentalities: Rationalities, Violences and Contestations* (London: Rowman & Littlefield).

Teo, Terri-Anne and Wynne-Hughes, Elisabeth (2020b) 'Introduction: Postcolonial Governmentalities' in Terri-Anne Teo and Elisa Wynne-Hughes (eds) *Postcolonial Governmentalities: Rationalities, Violences and Contestations* (London: Rowman & Littlefield), 1–42.

Vrasti, Wanda (2013) 'Universal but Not Truly 'Global': Governmentality, Economic Liberalism, and the International', *Review of International Studies* 39:1, 49–69.

Walters, William (2012) *Governmentality: Critical Encounters* (London: Routledge).

Weidner, Jason R. (2009) 'Governmentality, Capitalism, and Subjectivity', *Global Society* 23:4, 387–411.

Wimmer, Andreas and Glick Schiller, Nina (2002) 'Methodological Nationalism and Beyond: Nation-State Building, Migration and the Social Sciences', *Global Networks* 2:4, 301–334.

Zanotti, Laura (2013) 'Governmentality, Ontology, Methodology Re-Thinking Political Agency in the Global World', *Alternatives: Global, Local, Political* 38:4, 288–304.

# Part I

# Governing thought

# 2 Global governmentality and Foucault's toolbox

## Reflections on international politics as a social system and field of power relations

*Stephan Stetter*

## Introduction

International Relations (IR) can learn from Michel Foucault to be skeptical about a specific type of theorizing. Namely one that narrows down the complexities of society as a whole, or the realm of international politics, in specific, to a few "explaining" variables – such as anarchy, Western hegemony, neoliberalism, contestations or postcolonial inequalities. Foucault-inspired scholarship in IR can be conceived of as an alternative approach, namely one that does, as Doerthe Rosenow (2008: 497) forcefully states, not follow the "tendency to solidify and take for granted certain paradigms of global political rule, which lead to the problematic impression that 'the international' is determined by a single overarching project." In that context, it is paramount to bear in mind that Foucault famously rejected notions about his oeuvre being a holistic theory (see Section 3 below). Although it might precisely be just that, paradoxically, because Foucault builds his way of theorizing on a certain fuzziness of concepts – a fuzziness that arguably matches quite well with the heterogeneity and poly-contextuality of modern society.[1] With a view to this theoretical ambivalence and its relevance for IR, Andrew Neal (2009: 542) thus rightly observes that "Foucault does not allow us to give ontological or epistemological priority to any object, concept or category, including 'the international' and 'capitalism.'" Following this line of reasoning, I will resort in this chapter to a key concept from Foucault, namely the concept of governmentality, as a devise from a much broader Foucauldian conceptual toolbox. These tools can be deployed in a flexible manner, depending on the issue addressed. Thus, not all Foucauldian concepts have to be used simultaneously. For some research questions devoted to the study of modern society, in general, and IR-related topics, in specific "biopolitics" is your hammer, for others "genealogy" is the right screwdriver, while for a different set of questions "governmentality" plumbs well – and, to further complicate things, it has to be highlighted from the outset that Foucault refrained from offering specific definitions for these concepts, including governmentality. But what is even more important: not everything you need for the study of modern society might necessarily be in Foucault's toolbox – including the realm of international politics as an element of modern society, a system and field as explained below. Thus, the box can, and in many cases should be, filled up with tools purchased at your local Social Sciences DIY-store. And at this store – the "Theories-of-Modern-Society-Store," if you will – one shelf is reserved for Foucauldian tools, the other sells Luhmannian appliances, other aisles offers Bourdieusian kits or drilling machines by John W. Meyer, while – although not withdrawn from their shelves for the purpose of this chapter –-Marxian, Durkheimiam, Habermasian and Simmelian items are stored there too.

Based on this kind of reasoning, I explore in this chapter the evolution of international politics from the vantage point of theories of modern society, focusing on governmentality understood as a pervasive form of power that hinges on technologies of indirect rule "from above" and technologies of the self "from below." This is a form of power that became pronounced in modern society as a whole, in general, and within the international system that emerged therein in particular since the 19th century, in specific. Again recalling here the eclectic nature of Foucault's reasoning, one is well advised to heed to Neal's (2009: 542) advice that also in the realm of international politics Foucauldian concepts such as "'governmentality' can only be used to problematise diverse techniques of power, not to systematize." Departing from this understanding, the main purpose of this chapter then is to discuss the relationship between governmentality and international politics. Taking Foucault's toolbox argument serious, I will enrich the concept of governmentality through theoretical inspirations drawn from alternative, yet related research traditions that have modern society and its indirect forms of political power as a main focus of observation too. This allows me to resort in particular to the concepts of world society associated with modern systems theory championed by Niklas Luhmann and sociological neoinstitutionalism associated with John W. Meyer and to Pierre Bourdieu's concept of social fields. The core objective then is to account for how international politics emerged and evolves as a distinct subsystem – or field – within an encompassing system of (modern) world society. I argue in particular that such a conjoined reading of Foucault and related theories of modern society offers a historically and sociologically informed framework for the study of the evolution of international politics as a social system and field of power relations under the condition of "globality" (see Busse and Hamilton's introductory chapter). The core argument being that within the modern international system governmentality and its core feature of indirect power is a central operating feature. After a general introduction into the overarching topic of the evolution of international politics as a subsystem (Section 2), I take a closer look into Foucault's toolbox in Section 3, exploring here the concept of governmentality – thereby highlighting its double dimension of constraining and engendering individual conduct through indirect power – while in Section 4, I explore how this can be enriched through insight from the aforementioned theories of modern society on offer at your local Social Sciences DIY-store.

## International politics as a social system and field of power relations

Before discussing how tools from Foucault, and in particular the concept of governmentality, can contribute to the study of international politics, some comments on how international politics is understood in this chapter are paramount for such an analysis. Central here is the notion of politics as an evolving social system and the fundamental function of politics in ensuring that power-related communications and practices become institutionalized, defended, and contested with a given society in permanent feedback-loops. This is important because in Sections 3 and 4, I will identify governmentality as a key trigger for the evolution of the modern international system, thereby highlighting both continuity and differences to pre-modern forms of organizing international spheres. Viewing politics as a social system and field of power relations is, hence, more than observing how single instances of power materialize, that is A making B do something that B would not do otherwise, to cite a particularly famous definition. This A–B relationship in its purest, one-shot form, surely is about power (on different conceptions of power in IR, see Berenskoetter 2007). But it is only the repeated and institutionalized use of power – and struggles over the legitimacy of such "impositions" as Luhmann (2008) calls it – that renders its plausible to talk about politics as a social system and field of recursively related power relations. Ultimately, and in order to become *political* power (see Luhmann 2012, 2013), the sedimentation of manifold single instances of power impositions into rules, norms, principles of governing, practices, forms of authority, and habitus is required, leaving open here the question of whether a narrow (focusing on a however defined political system that needs to be distinguished from other spheres of society) or wide notion of politics, that traces the political across social spheres, is from a theoretical perspective more fruitful (see for this discussion Stäheli 2000). Over time, the entanglement of single power-related instances with each other can lead to the build-up of political fields or, in systems–theoretical parlance, a system of politics in which power as the field-specific form of communication is constantly traded and in which various forms of legitimacy of rule are defended, altered, and contested. In short, a system in which political rule is constantly renegotiated (ibid.). Yet, political rule is by definition distributed unevenly, while the ontological status of legitimacy of resulting orders lies in their constantly contested nature. That is why politics as a social field is fundamentally based on the hierarchical consolidation of power relations that stay "in power" for as long as claims on legitimacy can be upheld – by coercion as well as non-violent means. Once specific hierarchies implode, they are then replaced by new power-related inequalities that become, in one way or another, contested too. In this unavoidability of inequalities and contestations lies the trigger of the constant social evolution of politics (Stetter 2014).

Scholarship in global history and IR draws attention to these deep historical roots related to the emergence of this field or system, of politics in human society (see Buzan and Little 2000; Osterhammel 2014). Such an evolutionary perspective can be told from different conceptual angles, but the basic story line is that changes in human organization have led to the emergence of politics, at the dawn of civilization, as a distinct social sphere. Over time, such changes have led to more complex forms of organizing political power, including the advent of (modern) governmentality (see Section 3; see Leira's chapter in this volume). Without going into detail, the storyline unfolds as follows: prior to the Neolithic revolution, roughly 10,000 BCE, human groups lived in territorially scattered hunter-and-gatherer-gangs or, in systems theoretical terminology, segments (Luhmann 2013). These segmentary societies were small, egalitarian clusters of usually a few dozen people, with no permanent or strongly differentiated internal hierarchies in form of a political, military, or religious elite. Individual gangs entertained contacts with the outside world, for example, they engaged in early forms of international relations through the exchange of mating partners, (luxury) goods, rituals, and technologies, even across large distances. As within segments, there were no permanent hierarchies involved in these external relations between them. In other words, politics as a social sphere in which the consolidation and contestation of power-relations is organized, had not yet emerged neither within nor between groups.

Seen from this perspective, the Neolithic revolution – that is, the emergence of sedentary societies – was not only a major change in social organization but also signaled an adaptive advance by reorganizing social relations in hierarchical terms. In Foucauldian terminology, this period witnessed the rise of sovereign power understood as a system based on obedience towards a ruler installed and legitimized by God, possessing the ultimate power to "take life or let live" (Foucault quoted in Erlenbusch 2015). Concretely, the emergence of sedentary villages led, over time, to both the differentiation of initially quite unstable, nonhereditary political roles for successful warrior-chiefs and, if specific chiefs proved to be successful over time, the integration of other communities into the orbit of a specific chief: chiefdoms got established and in each of them the accumulation of political capital in the hands of specific leaders – military strongmen and religious elites – over time saw the shift from segmentary to stratified societies. This trend then accelerated following the emergence of script. This technological advance was central to the rise of knowledge/power nexuses that engendered a permanent centralization of power within larger empires (but also Steppe-polities; Neumann and Wigen 2018) – such as Sumer, China, Mesopotamia, or Egypt – and a stratification of society into a permanent, and self-reproducing ruling class (nobility) and subjects within these societies, on the one hand, and hierarchical core–periphery relations between empires and suzerain entities, on the other. Thus, already before the establishment of modern states, script empowered bureaucracies. It also revolutionized external relations with other polities by establishing diplomacy as an institutionalized and formalized social undertaking, as for example, the

Amarna letters from the third millennium BCE attest. From the first sedentary civilizations to early modernity, empires faced many challenges from
nonsedentary polities, which organized in similarly stratified patterns. These
"steppe polities" (see Neumann and Wigen 2018) – from the Scythians during
the ninth century BCE to the Golden Horde in the 13th century CE – became
at times powerful competitors to settled empires. They posed, *inter alia* due
to their capacities in effective warfare, a severe challenge to sedentary polities but also often merged with them, as the advance of the Goths into the
late Roman Empire or the Mongols into Western Eurasia, India, and China
during the "Middle Ages" indicate.

The invention of the printing press then became a decisive factor for a fundamental transformation of politics. It underpinned the shift to new forms
of political organization, which in Foucauldian terms can be understood
as a shift from sovereign to disciplinary and governmental power (Foucault
2006a, 2006b). Thus, the technology of mass printing – and the gradual emergence of mass media – enabled not only a major increase in the activities
and rationalities of governance that characterized the absolutist and in particular the modern, bureaucratic-legal state, but also provided for new forms
of voicing and amplifying political dissent – Martin Luther's challenge to
the authority of the Roman-Catholic church profited from this new technology, as did anticolonial movements in the 19th and early 20th century.
As systems theory highlights, segmentary and stratified forms of organizing
political authority were in that context enriched by an amplified functional
differentiation of society, with different sectors such as law, economy, science,
mass media, and others gaining increasing self-complexity as connected, yet
separated social fields (Luhmann 2013). Thus, also the mutual dependence
between these systems accelerated in what can be called modern world society,
exemplified *inter alia* by the ambition, unique to modern societies, to regulate
an ever wider scope of what now became "public" affairs, such as through disciplinary practices enacted in schools, the health system, police, the criminal
justice apparatus, taxation, environmental regulation, and so on. Entrenched
forms of organizing politics based on sovereign power did not disappear.
Thus, stratified forms of legitimizing political rule as a divine, quasi-eternal
order that is based on an undisputable distinction between a ruling class and
the rest gave way to a greater awareness (not just practice) of the contingency
of political rule and social order. This, in turn, gave rise – in both democratic
and authoritarian contexts – to modern mass society in which resistance and
contestation become part and parcel of political practice.

Seen from this perspective, the advent of modern politics is characterized
by two dimensions of power stressed by Foucault: the emergence of modern
politics in its disciplinary form – that is, direct power, on the one hand, and
the more subtle mechanisms of "securing" society through means of modern
governmentality, an often indirect form of power, on the other. What has
to be added though is the observation that politics in the context of functional differentiation is characterized by a dual transformation. The first

one is related to the specifically *modern* form of politics, including the afore-mentioned shift to what can termed discipline-cum-governmentality, as expressed in an increasing ambition to "regulate" society "effectively" as a whole through a combination of direct and indirect power. The other one relates to its planetary reach and ensuing globality-effects (on the concept of globality, see the volume's introduction). Thus, whereas even the most powerful civilizations prior to the 15th century were spatially contained, technological advances such as in navigation and communication technology led to what globalization scholars refer to as time–space compression (Harvey 1990). The fact that it was Europeans – and not, say, Arabs or Chinese – that ventured first in that global enterprise was a contingent affair, but had real power-related effects, namely the gradual subjugation of most parts of the world into a European- (and later Euro-American) dominated global polit-ical, economic, and cultural system.

A world societal perspective is helpful here. Thus, the pre-modern world knew, in a sense, several world societies, meaning that territorial boundaries constituted rather strict physical horizons beyond which no meaningful political power projections could pass. Political systems were thus spatially contained. This changed in modernity, which has been global from the outset. The poten-tial or actual reach of political power, as in particular colonialized polities had to realize, proved to be of global nature. In this setting, mainly Western metropolitan centers and territories ruled directly over large parts the world, only to be transformed in the 19th century into a global system characterized by a mix of direct colonial rule, indirect rule through semi-autonomy of colo-nial spaces and, finally, standards, organizations, and global bureaucracies that were set up in the context of international cooperation, often dominated by the hegemons of the day – such as the British Empire in the 19th and the US in the 20th century. This simultaneity of global integration, on the one hand, and stark global power differences, on the other, is well captured by the concept of world society in modern systems theory (see Albert 2016; Stetter 2008): a single, now global system characterized by internal diversity, fragmentation, and inequality. However, and notwithstanding the manifold power inequal-ities that shape the (waning?) age of Western hegemony, this global outreach also enables new forms of contesting power, for example, through processes of individualization or through new forms of political actorhood that *inter alia* draw their power from scandalizing these very inequalities or marginaliza-tion: from nongovernmental organizations such as antislavery campaigns, to populist political movements of different strains, to decolonization movements starting with Haiti in 1804 to present-day human rights activism and to resist-ance against actual or perceived marginalization that has brought to power populist leaders such as Donald Trump (the loser of the 2020 US presidential elections though), Narendra Modi, Boris Johnson, Jair Bolsonaro, Benjamin Netanyahu, Evo Morales, and others.

**Load: Global governmentality and Foucault's toolbox**

Concepts from Foucault's toolbox, and related approaches from the Social Sciences DIY-store do a good service in further improving our theoretical understanding of these broad historical processes. Rather than substituting the historical–sociological narrative set out above, they enrich it. In the case of the concept of governmentality, this enrichment comes through its inherent distinct theory of (indirect) political power. It then also sheds light on the constitution of international politics as a distinct (sub-)system in world society and the role indirect power plays in maintaining and contesting hierarchies within this social field. Before getting to this though, a few conceptual clarifications need to be set out, highlighting: (1) what Foucault had in mind when referring to his work as a toolbox and (2) specifying what, in that context, the concept of governmentality entails.

One of the attractions of Foucault's theory – in particular in relation to self-proclaimed "critical" scholarship – is this theory's (paradoxical) emphasis on the very lack of an encompassing theoretical perspective resorting instead, as Walters (2012: 36) highlights based on Michel Sellenart, on what can be termed "methodological nominalism."[2] Thus, Foucault (1996: 149) states provocatively, thereby playing with the DIY-analogy, that:

> all my books [...] are, if you like, little tool boxes. If people want to open them, use a particular sentence, idea or analysis like a screwdriver or wrench in order to short-circuit, disqualify or break up systems of power, including eventually the very ones from which my books have issues [...] well, all the better.

In other words, the main purpose is not to set out a comprehensive theory of society, so claims Foucault, but to provide tools for the analysis of society and the deconstruction of power relations.

This rejection of theoretical comprehensiveness has to be read with caution though. As Gary Gutting (2005) notes, this alleged modesty might tell us more about Foucault's tactics, rather than his broader intellectual ambition. Thus, at closer inspection

> Foucault does not hesitate to construct theories and methods, but the constructions are always subordinated to the tactical needs of the particular analysis at hand. They are not general engines of war that can be deployed against any target

> (ibid., 4)

but "temporary scaffoldings, erected for a specific purpose" (ibid., 16). Foucault's work on power/knowledge nexuses and how they operate in as diverse fields as sexuality, education, prisons, hospitals, or state bureaucracies offers, from an ontological perspective, a comprehensive understanding of modern society, in all its heterogeneity and diversity. They are – to use Luhmannian terminology here – building blocks for the study of society as a polycontextual setting and Foucault can indeed be understood as a "cartographer of modernity" (Pasha 2010: 214). A Foucauldian perspective on society, and one that shows many overlaps with the concept of world society, refrains from the widespread tendency of viewing society as something integrated by norms, consensus, or rules. What is emphasized instead is the observation that society is constituted by difference, diversity, inequality, conflict, fragmentation, and heterogeneity. So, it is from a methodological – and as Gutting rightly notes tactical – viewpoint that Foucault puts forward his toolbox approach. It is tactical because it allows adjusting theoretical concepts to diverse empirical contexts, and because it highlights that searching for a single paradigm through which to understand society or specific sectors of society such as the realm of international politics, is futile. But precisely by doing so, a Foucauldian perspective works well in order to understand better how complex and fuzzy social spheres that defy a single operating logic work – one of these fuzzy spheres being international politics.

It is important to highlight this here, not least because a widespread reception of Foucault's writings in IR, and in particular the appropriation of the concept of governmentality, has often been one-dimensional, thereby underestimating the ontological status, which the fuzziness of concepts has in Foucault's reasoning. More specifically, and in particular, in the context of self-proclaimed "critical" research traditions in IR that aim at deconstructing hegemonic, usually Western security-imperatives in international politics, Foucault's original concept of governmentality often gets misrepresented and misunderstood – for example, by focusing more on direct than indirect power or not stressing technologies of the self in a sufficient manner (see also Rosenow 2008). This is problematic insofar as this results in a way too executive-focused and state-centered understanding of what governmentality entails (a good example is Chandler 2009). This runs counter to what Foucault had in mind when discussing governmentality as a distinct, pervasive, and immensely productive form of power, different from disciplinary power. A widespread bias in IR is to unduly boil governmentality down to strict notions of security, enforced by mainly Western decision-makers and security professionals and serving the larger purpose of "neoliberalism" (see for example, Barnett et al. 2008). This stems from a narrow focus on Foucault's famous attempt of defining governmentality as a social context in which "apparatuses of security" are the "essential technical means," while neoliberal political philosophy is its ideological foundation (Foucault 2006a: 564). To be clear, there is no doubt that "critical" IR scholarship has done a great job in deconstructing modern security paradigms and neoliberal underpinnings of political practice and this can certainly be well addressed in Foucauldian terms; but arguably more in terms of disciplinary than governmental power. In other words, there is a lot of use for studies that detect entrenched hierarchies and structural forms of violence inherent in security policies, such as Foucault-inspired studies on airport security (Salter 2007), policies *vis-à-vis* asylum seekers (Puumala and Pehkonen 2010), the role of fear in the biopolitical production of terror and how states of emergency are used in governing terror (Debrix and Barder 2009; Dillon 2007). But, this quite dominant reception of Foucault in much IR scholarship misses out on the actual clue of his concept of governmentality, namely its contribution to understanding the very complexity in which modern society and power operates in an *indirect* manner as well as through a dialectic interplay between executive impositions *and* individual subjectivities.

Central for adopting such a wider focus on indirect power, on the one hand, and individual subjectivities in power relations, on the other, is the aforementioned insight that the unity of modern society lies in particular in its heterogeneity. The dialectics between different dimensions of indirect power – such as the interplay between power from below and above – are a central factor for how modern society, in general, and in distinct spheres, such as international politics, in specific, operate. As Jonathan Joseph (2009) rightly observes, the focus in much IR scholarship on what can be termed "governmentality from above" obscures these dialectics and gives way to a much too static and state-centric understanding of international politics that ultimately conflates governmentality with disciplinary power. In contrast, and in line with what Busse and Hamilton highlight in the introductory chapter to this volume, governmentality is not primarily about direct power or about securing permanent hegemonies by further marginalizing the already powerless. While such forms of disciplinary power that go hand in hand with strong hierarchies are important in modern society, and not least in the international political system (Zarakol 2017), governmentality as a distinct form of power rather is about the equally important, yet indirect ways social order is defended, maintained, and challenged. Governmentality then, of course, involves security, but in a much wider understanding of the term than often deployed in IR. Thus, the aforementioned "apparatuses of security" do not only include security professionals in what could be termed hard security fields – such as state diplomacy, police, military, private security providers, etc. – the core focus of much IR scholarship on the topic. They also include bureaucracies and professionals in manifold sectors – and levels from the local to the global – that have as its objective to render society and its population more "secure" in (at times also emancipatory) policy-areas such as the health system, education, developmental assistance, climate protection, race and gender equality, pension and unemployment schemes, infrastructure regulations, workplace safety, nutrition regulations, patents, and statistical offices etc. In other words, governmentality is about a deeply held belief in global modernity that politics, understood as the interplay between executive action and individual empowerment, is about bettering life, making it ever more secure and orderly – well expressed by the modernist narrative of (inner-worldly) progress – *ordem e progresso* which the Brazilian flag famously sets out as its motto since 1889.

It is not the place here to outline in detail the nuances, and the intended fuzziness, of the concept of governmentality (see again the introduction by Busse and Hamilton). But for the purpose of this chapter, two of its main dimensions should stand out. There is firstly what can be described as governmentality from above. And this relates, in contrast to disciplinary power, to the mainly indirect forms of ensuring political acquiescence by setting parameters of "expected" and socially orderly behavior. This corresponds with the modern ambition – shared by former colonizers and colonized as well as many liberal, leftist, and rightist political ideologies – to regulate society in all its niches. A mere imposition in form of disciplinary power would not render modern politics possible for it requires not only acquiescence but active participation of those governed – the pervasiveness of governmental power thus lies in its subtle and productive nature. As Michael Dillon and Julian Reid (2001: 41) observe, governmentality can be located in the "varied and complex regime of power, whose founding principle lies in the administration and production of life, rather than in threatening death." This should, therefore, be read as a plea to move beyond the study of state apparatuses, and overcoming the quite state-centered reception of Foucault in large parts of IR. In contrast, it is important to highlight that global governmentality from above has what can be termed a twofold international dimension. The first dimension relates to the global spread of this general belief in governmental power. Thus, the forms of ordering and securing society that Foucault had studied with a view to France, the US, and Germany have become part of global governmentality insofar as indirect power is, in addition to disciplinary modes, a tool and worldview that is pervading techniques of government and statehood more or less anywhere on the globe. This becomes particularly visible when studying different regional and national state-building processes throughout the 19th and 20th centuries. Thus, it is no coincidence that a state in the Global South, such as Brazil, has chosen the notion of ordering society as its state motto, as mentioned above. And, neither is it surprising then that today's independence movements that aim to legitimize their capacity for running a state, such as the Palestinian Authority or the Kurdish government in Northern Iraq had as one of their first authoritative decisions the establishment of a statistical office, that is an office that has the creation and ordering of knowledge across a wide range of parameters about the population to be governed as its core objective (see for the case of Palestine Busse 2018). There is a specific type of legitimacy associated with modern governmentality, namely the expectation that "knowledge" about different policy-areas needs to be collected in order to improve life of populations with a view to health, education, participation in the labor market, etc. Central then is, of course, to refrain from a Eurocentric reading that restricts governmentality to an allegedly Western modernity. Thus, as also historical–sociological debates in IR show, modernity is a global phenomenon that has multiple origins, both in the West and the Global South (see Hobson 2004). And, it is for that reason, that indirect power and the normative expectations that shape reform-projects of leaders and expectations of masses has been a powerful social force not only in polities that more or less successfully resisted Western colonial ambitions – such as the Ottoman Empire, Persia, Egypt, Turkey, Japan, or Siam – but also shaped the progress-oriented and modernist state-building projects in the context of decolonization in as diverse places as Latin America, the Caribbean, South-East Europe, Asia, Africa, and the Middle East.

The second international dimension that allows speaking of global governmentality then relates to the international system as a whole. Two aspects stand out here. First, during the 19th century, in which the idea of great power management became the dominant paradigm around which power relations in the international system were structured, the so-called "standard of civilization" gradually emerged as a guiding parameter for European and American colonial powers in how to rule over their possessions overseas (Buzan 2014). Central here is the observation that while direct, disciplinary methods of imperial politics endured, notions of indirect rule that allowed for a gradual semi-autonomy of colonized polities gained ground. Being based on the dominant racist thinking of the time (Bhabha 2000; Busse and Stetter 2018), Western powers argued that for the time being, they had to ensure the proper governance of colonized territories. But there was a growing recognition in metropolitan centers – triggered by both resistance from colonized subjects and support for greater colonial independence from parts of the Western public – that at some, of course undefined moment in the future, also non-Western societies can transform into truly modern societies. And until then, they should remain under the tutelage of their European and American overlords. As a result, governmental power, understood as indirect rule, gained importance in that context. Thus, as Julian Go (2011) and George Steinmetz (2013) highlight, imperial rule was not only defined by direct rule of metropolitan centers but was supplemented, during the 19th century, by what is coined in this literature as semi-autonomous rule. Direct power executed by imperial agents was gradually accompanied by indirect forms of power that were characterized by joint governance through newly empowered (often ethnoreligiously defined) local elites and resident colonial officers on the ground. The so-called standard of civilization, as a founding idea of the League of Nations, then even became part, as late as with the Paris Peace Treaties after the end of World War I, of mandate territories that existed well into the middle of the 20th century, and thereby became firmly anchored in international law. Fundamental here was the notion that the requirement to comprehensively govern a given polity the modern way, must be viewed as a prerequisite for legitimate statehood in the international realm – somewhat ironically echoing the provisions of the legal norm of "responsibility to protect" that became part of international law in the early 2000s and that renders the failure of a government to ensure the well-being of its population a potential case of external military intervention. Secondly, and again since the 19th century, the international level also witnessed the emergence and rapid growth of countless international organizations (IOs) founded by nation-states on both global and regional scales. The tasks of these IOs closely resemble key aspects of what modern governmentality is about: issuing guidelines and benchmarks, collecting information, and advising state authorities on a wide scale of issue-areas relevant for the administration and protection of life. Direct executive power – that would mix disciplinary and governmental power as common in nation-states – is mostly missing; the World Trade Organization (WTO) with its dispute settlement body and in particular the EU, that has evolved into a fully fledged polity of its own, being exceptions here. While one should not downplay the role of states and in particular of hegemonic powers in the way IOs were set-up and operate until today (see Mazower 2012; Ikenberry 2001) – well reflected in the fierce global debate in 2020 about the independence of the World Health Organization (WHO) during the Covid-19 pandemic – IR would be well advised to take this governmentality perspective on IOs more into focus. This would add a much-needed sociological and power-related perspective in addition to liberal institutionalist and realist perspectives on this topic (see also Joseph's chapter on this matter).

As highlighted above, the concept of governmentality has a two-faced nature. It is about the different forms of government from above, as discussed in the previous paragraphs. But the pervasiveness and productive force of indirect power can only be fully appreciated if it is complemented by an equally strong focus on government from below, arguably not a stronghold in IR theorizing and classical IR perspectives that often ignore the relevance of the everyday and individual subjectivities, more generally speaking (see Jung and Stetter 2019). This focus on governmentality from below requires addressing people not only as subjects to be ruled, but as co-participants in maintaining social order both as individuals and in the form of associations formed by individuals within a given political setting – in other words, it is about the way individual subjectivity based on individual action or forms of association individuals entertain, contribute to social order by enacting what Foucault (1998) calls technologies of the self. As Iver B. Neumann and Ole Jacob Sending (2007: 699) maintain, global governmentality can therefore be conceived of as a "global system of indirect forms of power that operates to guide, shape and foster specific types of not only states, but also other polities, as well as individuals" (ibid., 699). I cannot elaborate here in detail on the manifold fields in which individual subjectivities shape international realms (see Jung and Stetter 2019), but one should point here to the incremental rise of notions of individual and human rights in international law as well as in manifold state-building processes since the 19th century. There would have been no decolonization process if this fundamental notion of individual subjectivity and the way this mobilized intellectual and political elites and, later on, wider masses, had been absent. It also underlines the always-already modern outlook of colonial societies and the multiple, non-Western origins of human rights and individual subjectivity (Reus-Smit 2011). Technologies of the self are of paramount importance to international relations at large, from the first associations in the West and colonial territories that opposed slavery, to nationalist movements from Syria to Serbia and Greece in the 19th and 20th century, to the protest movements at Cairo's Tahrir square in 2011 and the Fridays for Future movement, to contemporary right-wing militias in the US that oppose liberal identity politics, to the more subtle, and often at first apolitical ways in which everyday actions might or might not, have emancipatory or conservative effects – for example, on gender norms in Turkey (for the latter example, see Yüksel et al. 2017).

In sum, addressing global governmentality within the international sphere allows understanding the complexity of organizing political spaces that results from the interplay between governmentality from above and below as its two indispensable elements. The dialectics at play here also increase the contingency of political orders, and highlight the productive side of power, at local, national, and international scales due to the widened scope of legitimized actors that engage in struggles over the shape of political and social orders. As Foucault has nicely put it, thereby highlighting the autonomy of authorities and individuals in the maintenance of modern social order, governmentality is about the conduct of conduct – *conduire des conduits*. It is a double empowerment or in the words of Michael Merlingen (2008: 273), a "daemonic [force] because of its capacity to mold people's subjectivities and bodies that they nevertheless consider to be uniquely their own." Governmentality from above thus works in complex interdependencies with everyday conduct from below and if properly studied cannot be viewed in isolation from the latter. This includes the various forms through which individuals legitimize, enact, or contest social orders, both through everyday action but also the manifold forms of modern social association that are at their core based on the belief in the legitimacy, rationality, and necessity, of technologies of the self. Subjectivity, in short, is a core feature of modern political orders, including international politics (see also Kiersey 2009; Neumann and Sending 2007), and IR would be well advised to focus on the dialects of government from above and below when studying key developments in this specific social sphere that complement the undoubtedly enduring forms of disciplinary power that shape this realm of practice too.

## Re-load: Taking global governmentality to the theories-of-modern-society DIY-store

As the previous section has shown, the concept of global governmentality offers important theoretical insights into the way power operates in international politics – thereby "unraveling" (Calkivik 2010: 208) some of the key features that render it necessary to study the "international as governmentality" (Neumann and Sending 2007: 690). In this section, I will now offer some suggestions as to how these insights can be further sharpened. This will be based on a linkage of the Foucauldian perspective presented above with other theories of modern society, readily available at the Theories-of-Modern-Society DIY-store. Doing so, I will discuss in the following, in particular, the concepts of world society in modern systems theory and socio-logical neo-institutionalism in the traditions of Niklas Luhmann and John W. Meyer respectively, on the one hand, and social fields as well as inclusion/exclusion dynamics in Bourdieusian field theory and modern systems theory, on the other. Rather than discussing these complex theories in detail, a task that would be impossible on a few pages, the purpose in this chapter is of a more limited scope. Thus, the objective of this discussion is to suggest the basic contours of possible research foci global governmentality approaches could, and probably should, relate to when studying international politics. A certain problem here is, that Foucault's own excursions into the realm of international politics have suffered from certain Eurocentric biases (the same could be said about Luhmann, Meyer and also to some extent Bourdieu). This is particular visible in Foucault's rather unimaginative Orientalist inter-pretation of the revolution in Iran in 1979 (see Jabri 2007). But, this does not render the objective to have an understanding of governmentality beyond the "territorialised state" (see Merlingen 2006: 184–188), if properly translated into the context of global modernity, less important.

In the previous section (3), I have highlighted two main elements that define the global dimension of governmentality, namely the way this specific type of power shaped state-building processes and state policies throughout the world in global modernity, on the one hand, and in the policies of IOs and nonstate actors, on the other. Both dynamics point to the embedding of governmentality within broader structures of world society – a key concept in both sociological neoinstitutionalism and modern systems theory. This also includes addressing the specific, global culture of modernity that shapes modern social orders. This relates, for example, to the cultural belief in mod-ernity that society can and should be organized rationally, a belief underpin-ning the knowledge/power nexuses that sustain governmental power. Modern world culture – a key concept from the notion of world society in sociological neo-institutionalism – is thus not only characterized by the global diffusion of the nation-state (Meyer et al. 1997), but also by a global spread of the spe-cific type of power relations engendered in that context. Next to disciplinary power – which is until today a central source of power in autocratic and demo-cratic polities as well as the international system at large – governmentality can, in the terminology of sociological neoinstitutionalism, be understood as a "program" that is implemented throughout the world, based on simultaneous processes of diffusion and diversity-in-practice described as decoupling in this theoretical tradition. This reproduction occurs in an isomorphic manner and with manifold variations and hybrid ways of merging this program with local contexts and knowledge (see also Krücken and Drori 2010), resulting in connected global histories and multiple modernities (Subrahmanyan 1997; Eisenstadt 2000). Organizing society rationally, by means of governmentality from above, in as diverse sectors such as the school system, health regulations, taxation, economic planning, and others is a technology of rule that pervades nation-states throughout the world – and at other scales, such as the level of IOs. This is based on specific knowledge/power nexuses that have the "security" and "ordering of life" as its main form of knowledge generation and indirect power as its main technology of government. This should in no way lead to underestimating the centrality of disciplinary power – but it offers a broader conceptual understanding of the multiple origins of global modernity, such as in the Ottoman Empire, Czarist Russia, or Imperial China and of how such projects were not only characterized by local, privileged elites "modernizing" their allegedly "traditional" societies, but by a much broader notion of legitimized "actorhood" that relied on the active participation and agency, of the individual actors in pursuit of this program (see Fox and Ward 2008). Nineteenth-century Prussia, France, or the US are in that regard not different from non-Western polities.

In the context of modern systems theory, the notion of world society then is closely related to the forms of differentiation I have highlighted above in Section 2. Thus, as Luhmann (2012, 2013) has forcefully argued, societies are characterized not by integration, shared normative and cultural underpinnings, or shared identity. In fact, what defines societies are continuously changing forms of differentiation, that is, the increasing internal complexity and structural independence of social systems, such as politics, religion, economy, art, science, etc. in relation to each other that shape social orders in modernity. As the discussion in the previous section has suggested, modern politics is characterized by the interplay between disciplinary (direct) power and indirect power known as governmentality. Such interplays are, however, usually not spatially confined and have an essentially planetary reach. The distinction between actual and potential global reach is of importance here. Thus, power can have a global dimension in actual terms, for example, when Russia aims to secretly influence, through trolls, bots, and other means political debates in the context of US presidential elections, thereby attempting to impact on individual voters' decisions. But the global dimension can also be of a potential nature. This is well reflected in the attempt by leaders such Aljaksandr Lukashenka or Hosni Mubarak to limit interaction between local protest movements and the outside world, or, as in the case of North Korea or Albania under Enver Hoxha, when a leadership tries to radically minimize the knowledge about domestic politics for outside actors and about political processes abroad for the local population.

Viewing politics as a (global) system characterized by the interplay between these different forms of modern power should, finally, be combined with a study of how power is distributed in that system. As highlighted above, politics fundamentally is about struggles over the distribution of power between different actors. That is what Nick Fox and Katie Ward (2008: 519) have in mind when arguing that international politics is a "social context imbued with cultural values and in which power is distributed unevenly and dynamically." The reference to cultural values in this quote fits well with the view that governmentality from above and below can be understood, in the tradition of sociological neoinstitutionalism, as a specific (cultural) program of political rule in global modernity. However, it would be a stark mistake to think that governmentality would somehow be a magic formula to produce equality and to magically reduce power differences. One might be inclined to think so due to the importance of "objective" knowledge about populations to be governed (in relation to statistical factors such as age, gender, education, health, etc.) in this specific form of power and due to its indirect character that triggers an empowerment of a wide range of actors, not least due to legitimized status of individual subjectivities. However, as Luhmannian systems theory reminds us, politics always is about the constant renegotiation of the border between power and powerlessness, resulting in the dynamic distribution of power, as Fox and Ward term it. This constant renegotiation not only relates to struggles over the hegemony of distinct dominant ideologies (such as neo-liberalism, communism, fascism, democracy, and populism) but also to the uneven distribution of power amongst concrete social groups (for a utilization of a Neo-Gramscian of hegemony in conjunction with governmentality see Joseph's chapter in this volume) .

This is where the study of (international) politics as a distinct social system can be brought into discussion with Bourdieusian field theory. Thus, (international) politics can be understood as a social field in which social positions are constantly defended and contested. Such a "world-making" (Bourdieu 1989) is defined not only by actors' habitus and the types of (social, cultural, economic) capital they can mobilize, but also by the distinct dynamics within different social fields, namely the history and specific modes of observation, traditions, and customs unique to specific fields. As Yingyao Wang (2016: 364) notes, this allows studying, within and across fields, "the uneven agentic and structural conditions of diffusion and herein explain the uneven outcomes" of social positions of concrete social groups across different fields. Bourdieu (1988: 174) has pointed to a "conjunctural alliance" between different social fields, in which the specific positioning of actors in one field (for example, the economy) has repercussions for the position in other fields, such as international politics. This dynamic, called homology in Bordieusian field theory, reveals interesting overlaps with the notion of inclusion/exclusion as a distinct form of societal differentiation in modern systems theory (see Stetter 2008). Thus, homologies can result in relatively enduring patterns of inclusion/exclusion and "frozen" social positioning across social fields and can be well studied when looking at the status of states – for instance, the relative dominance throughout the 19th and 20th century of mainly Western states in the world economy and the international political system. It also relates to the supportive and impeding factors for enabling technologies of the self, for example, how extreme poverty goes hand in hand with political exclusion, lacking access to health services and education in many parts of the world – understood as chain exclusions (ibid.). The key point though is to inquire, in a Bourdieusian tradition, to which extent governmentality functions as "a mechanism of producing social inequality" (Wang 2016: 354), "narrowing down the 'space of possibilities'" in the context of the "historical formation of a field" (ibid., 358). What are then the power-differences between social groups, engendered by global governmentality? The balance sheet is certainly mixed and hardly one-dimensional. The reference to a narrow space of possibilities that relates to the founding conditions of a field certainly works well in explaining how the dominant position of the West in the emerging international system of the late 18th/early 18th century somewhat cemented Western hegemony in that system into the present (Buzan and Lawson 2015). However, as highlighted above, international politics is simultaneously shaped by a complex empowerment of manifold actors through technologies of the self. This then is a quite dynamic factor for the manifold contestations to Western hegemony. More generally speaking, it also injects a great deal of dynamism into international politics by making this system/field sensitive to political demands and actions from below – paraphrasing Foucault, resistance is always possible, and often successful.

## Conclusion

A systematic mapping of power relations and the (shifting) social positioning of actors in the field of international politics is far beyond the purview of this chapter, but one thing seems clear: such a mapping would produce a complex picture of hegemonies and contestations that could hardly be narrowed down to a single factor explaining power differences. To state it clearly, neither Western hegemony or the security dilemma, nor neoliberalism or postcolonialism are catch-all concepts that could account for the complexity – and contingency – of international politics as a distinct system and field of power relations. In that sense, a mapping of the power relations resulting from the interplay between disciplinary power and governmentality in the field of international politics, enriched through key concepts from related theories of (global) modernity such as world society and social fields (readily available at the Theories-of-Modern-Society DIY-store), appears as a useful tool in order to further develop the concept of global governmentality. In the words of Mathias Albert and Peter Lenco (2008: 266), on that basis Foucauldian governmentality is an intriguing tool that "surveys the power structure of the heterogeneous elements [of that field], rather than succumbing to the binarisms of hegemony."

This is precisely what this chapter has attempted to suggest. Take Foucault seriously by distinguishing meticulously between disciplinary power and governmentality, both highly relevant contexts of power in modern world society. And then enriching this analysis with insights from related theoretical traditions. My suggestion, on that basis, was to explore the potential of the concept of world society (in modern systems theory and sociological neoinstitutionalism) in order to account for the planetary and interconnected nature of political spaces and how the role this has played for the spread of governmentality to polities throughout the world and in the context of the emergence of a distinctively modern international political system since in

particular the 19th century. Drawing from Luhmann's concept of inclusion/
exclusion and Bourdieu's theory of social fields then enriches governmentality
theory by allowing to systematically address the concrete forms of hierarchies
in different social spheres such as international politics, and in particular the
means of defending and contesting such hierarchies. Taken together these
approaches thus add an important dose of "globality" (see the introductory
chapter to this volume) to the concept of governmentality.

## Notes

1  A comment on terminology is at place here. Thus, this chapter draws from a range
   of theories that fundamentally deal with the key concern of, to paraphrase from the
   famous sociologist Georg Simmel, how society becomes possible. This question is
   at the core of Foucault's theorizing, but also shapes the ambition of other theorists
   resorted to in this chapter, such as Luhmann, Meyer, and Bourdieu. These theories,
   in essence, do not deal with human societies throughout the history of civilization, but mainly with modern societies. Modernity should not be confused with
   Western societies, though, and therefore, the notion of a distinctively global mod-
   ernity/modernities has taken ground in social theorizing, shaped by the immense
   global interconnectedness that took hold of erstwhile more separated regional societies over the course of the last centuries. In many ways, the term global modernity
   and world society, a core concept in this chapter, are interchangeable terminologies
   and, at least as the core arguments of this chapter are concerned, can and will
   be used accordingly below (for a discussion of both concepts see also Jung and
   Stetter 2019).
2  I thank Jan Busse for alerting me to the concept of "methodological nominalism."

## References

Albert, Mathias (2016) *A Theory of World Politics* (Cambridge: Cambridge University
    Press).
Albert, Mathias and Lenco, Peter (2008) 'Introduction to the forum: Foucault and
    International Political Sociology', *International Political Sociology* 2:3, 265-266.
Barnett, Clive, Clarke, Nick, Cloke, Paul and Malpass, Alice (2008) 'The elusive
    subjects of Neo-liberalism: Beyond the analytics of governmentality', *Cultural
    Studies* 22:5, 624-653.
Berenskoetter, Felix (2007) 'Thinking about power', in Felix Berenskoetter and
    Michael J Williams (eds) *Power in World Politics* (London: Routledge), 1–22.
Bhabha, Homi K (2000) '"Race" time and the revision of modernity' in Les Back and
    John Solomos (eds) *Theories of Race and Racism: A Reader* (London: Routledge),
    354–368.
Bourdieu, Pierre (1988) *Homo Academicus* (Stanford: Stanford University Press).
Bourdieu, Pierre (1989) 'Social space and symbolic power', *Sociological Theory*
    7:1, 14–25.
Busse, Jan (2018) *Deconstructing the Dynamics of World-Societal Order: The Power of
    Governmentality in Palestine* (London: Routledge).

Busse, Jan and Stetter, Stephan (2018) "'Face the thing that should not be': Rassismus in Theorie und Praxis der Internationalen Beziehungen" in Ina Ulrike Paul and Sylvia Schraut (eds) *Rassismus in Geschichte und Gegenwart: Eine interdisziplinäre Analyse. Festschrift für Walter Demel* (Berlin: Peter Lang), 361–394.

Buzan, Barry (2014) 'The "Standard of Civilisation" as an English School concept', *Millennium: Journal of International Studies* 42:3, 576–594.

Buzan, Barry and Lawson, George (2015) *The Global Transformation: History, Modernity and the Making of International Relations* (Cambridge: Cambridge University Press).

Buzan, Barry and Little, Richard (2000) *International Systems in World History: Remaking the Study of International Relations* (Oxford: Oxford University Press).

Calkivik, Asli (2010) 'Why not to choose a secure "we" in a security-obsessed world', *International Political Sociology* 4:2, 207-209.

Chandler, David (2009) 'Critiquing liberal cosmopolitanism? The limits of the biopolitical approach', *International Political Sociology* 3:1, 53-70.

Debrix, François and Barder, Alexander D (2009) 'Nothing to fear but fear: Governmentality and the biopolitical production of terror', *International Political Sociology* 3:4, 398-413.

Dillon, Michael (2007) 'Governing terror: The state of emergency of biopolitical emergence', *International Political Sociology* 1:1, 7-28.

Dillon, Michael and Reid, Julian (2001) 'Global liberal governance: Biopolitics, security and war', *Millennium: Journal of International Studies* 30:1, 41-66.

Eisenstadt, Shmuel N (2000) 'Multiple modernities', *Daedalus* 129:1, 1-29.

Erlenbusch, Verena (2015) 'From sovereignty to war: Foucault's analytic of power', *e-international relations*, www.e-ir.info/2015/12/12/from-sovereignty-to-war-foucaults-analytic-of-power/, accessed 26 September 2020.

Foucault, Michel (1996): 'From Torture to Cellblock' in Sylvère Lotringer (ed) *Foucault Live: Collected Interviews, 1961-1984* (New York: Semiotext(e)), 146–149.

Foucault, Michel (1998) 'Technologies of the Self' in Luther M Martin, Huck Gutman and Patrick H Hutton (eds) *Technologies of the Self: A Seminar with Michel Foucault* (Amherst: University of Massachusetts Press), 16-49.

Foucault, Michel (2006a) *Sicherheit, Territorium, Bevölkerung: Geschichte der Gouvernementalität I* (Frankfurt: Suhrkamp).

Foucault, Michel (2006b) *Die Geburt der Biopolitik: Geschichte der Gouvernementalität II* (Frankfurt: Suhrkamp).

Fox, Nick J and Ward, Katie J (2008) 'What governs governance, and how does it evolve? The sociology of governance in action', *British Journal of Sociology* 59:3, 519-538.

Go, Julian (2011) *Patterns of Empire: The British and American Empires, 1688 to the Present* (Cambridge: Cambridge University Press).

Gutting, Gary (2005) 'Michel Foucault: A user's manual' in Gary Gutting (ed) *The Cambridge Companion to Foucault* (Cambridge: Cambridge University Press), 1-28.

Harvey, David (1990) *The Condition of Postmodernity: An Enquiry into the Origins of Cultural Change* (Malden: Blackwell).

Hobson, John M (2004) *The Eastern Origins of Western Civilization* (Cambridge: Cambridge University Press).

Ikenberry, G John (2001) *After Victory: Institutions, Strategic Restraint, and the Rebuilding of Order After Major Wars* (Princeton: Princeton University Press).

Jabri, Vivienne (2007) 'Michel Foucault's analytics of war: The social, the international, and the racial', *International Political Sociology* 1:1, 67-81.

Joseph, Jonathan (2009) 'Governmentality of what? Populations, states and international organisations', *Global Society* 23:4, 413-427.

Jung, Dietrich and Stetter, Stephan (eds) (2019) *Modern Subjectivities in World Society: Global Structures and Local Practices* (New York: Palgrave).

Kiersey, Nicholas J (2009) 'Neoliberal political economy and the subjectivity of crisis: Why governmentality is not hollow', *Global Society* 23:4, 363-386.

Krücken, Georg and Drori, Gili S (eds) (2010) *World Society: The Writings of John W. Meyer* (Oxford: Oxford University Press).

Luhmann, Niklas (2008): *Die Politik der Gesellschaft* (Frankfurt: Suhrkamp).

Luhmann, Niklas (2012) *Theory of Society*, Volume 1 (Stanford: Stanford University Press).

Luhmann, Niklas (2013) *Theory of Society*, Volume 2 (Stanford: Stanford University Press).

Mazower, Mark (2012) *Governing the World: The History of An Idea* (London: Penguin).

Merlingen, Michael (2006) 'Foucault and world politics: Promises and challenges of extending governmentality theory to the European and beyond', *Millennium: Journal of International Studies* 35:1, 181-196.

Merlingen, Michael (2008) 'Monster studies', *International Political Sociology* 2:3, 272–274.

Meyer, John W; Boli, John; Thomas, George M and Ramirez, Francisco O (1997) 'World society and the nation-state', *American Journal of Sociology* 103:1, 144–181.

Neal, Andrew W (2009) 'Rethinking Foucault in International Relations: Promiscuity and unfaithfulness', *Global Society* 23:4, 539–543.

Neumann, Iver B and Sending, Ole Jacob (2007) '"The International" as governmentality', *Millennium: Journal of International Studies* 35:3, 677–701.

Neumann, Iver B and Wigen, Einar (2018) *The Steppe Tradition in International Relations: Russians, Turks and European State Building 4000 BCE-2017 CE* (Cambridge: Cambridge University Press).

Osterhammel, Jürgen (2014) *Transformation of the World: A Global History of the Nineteenth Century* (Princeton: Princeton University Press).

Pasha, Mustapha Kamal (2010) 'Disciplining Foucault', *International Political Sociology* 4:2, 213–215.

Puumala, Eeva and Pehkonen Samu (2010) 'Corporeal choreographies between politics and the political: Failed asylum seekers moving from body politics to bodyspaces', *International Political Sociology* 4:1, 50–65.

Reus-Smit, Christian (2011) 'Struggles for individual rights and the expansion of the international system', *International Organization* 65:2, 207-242.

Rosenow, Doerthe (2008) 'Decentring global power: The merits of a Foucauldian approach to International Relations', *Global Society* 23:4, 497–517.

Salter, Mark B (2007) 'Governmentalities of an airport: Heterotopia and confession', *International Political Sociology* 1:1, 49–66.

Stäheli, Urs (2000) *Sinnzusammenbrüche: Eine dekonstruktive Lektüre von Niklas Luhmanns Systemtheorie* (Weilerswist: Velbrück).

Steinmetz, George (2013) *Sociology and Empire: The Imperial Entanglements of a Discipline* (Durham: Duke University Press).

Stetter, Stephan (2008) *World Society and the Middle East: Reconstructions in Regional Politics* (New York: Palgrave).

Stetter, Stephan (2014) 'World politics and conflict systems: The communication of a "no" and its effects', *Horizons of Politics* 12:4, 43–67.

Subrahmanyan, Sanjay (1997) 'Connected histories: Notes towards a reconfiguration of early modern Eurasia', *Modern Asian Studies* 31:3, 735–762.

Walters, William (2012) *Governmentality: Critical Encounters* (London: Routledge).

Wang, Yingyao (2016) 'Homology and isomorphism: Bourdieu in conversation with New Institutionalism', *British Journal of Sociology* 67:2, 348–370.

Yüksel, Gökçen, Stetter, Stephan and Walter, Jochen (2017) 'Localizing modern female subjectivities: World society and the spatial negotiation of gender norms in Turkey', *Alternatives: Global, Local, Political* 41:2, 59–82.

Zarakol, Ayşe (ed) (2017) *Hierarchies in World Politics* (Cambridge: Cambridge University Press).

# 3 Variations of governmentality across the globe

## The case of resilience

*Jonathan Joseph*

## Introduction

This chapter seeks to go beyond previous discussions of global governmentality that often divide into the possibility of governmentality on the one hand and the limits of governmentality on the other. Instead, it looks at the different options for governmentality, its variation, tensions, and calculations. To demonstrate this, the chapter looks at the spread of resilience-building policies across different European countries and then considers the promotion of resilience as part of the system of global governance (or global governmentality). This suggests that resilience is understood somewhat differently in different countries and different contexts, but that its usage in global governance is still dominated by a strong neoliberal dynamic that is informed by the hegemonic Anglo-Saxon form of governmentality. In doing this, we can see the limits of both governmentality and its hegemonic form, but also the essential connection between the two.

This has a strong ontological component inasmuch as the differences or variations of governmentality and resilience derive from the terrain on which these must operate and the sociohistorical context these find themselves in. The argument presented below differs from most poststructuralist approaches to governmentality which tend to emphasize governmentality as a rationality and set of practices while avoiding questions of its material conditions of possibility. The two ought to be seen together, with the more discursive element enabled and constrained by the context and conditions within which it must operate. Some of this element is brought into the discussion below by combining a theory of governmentality with the arguments about hegemony.

The chapter proceeds by looking at the context of governmentality and its essentially liberal or neoliberal character. It looks at governmentality alongside a theory of hegemony as one way of introducing a more strategic – and ultimately materialist – element. It also introduces some discussion about the role of the state and the relation between the macro and micro. An examination of the promotion of resilience-building is used as a means to illustrate the variations in governmentality and to show that, despite these differences, global governance (or governmentality) still takes a hegemonic Anglo-Saxon form.

## Liberal governmentality in wider context

For some contributors to the governmentality debates, the beauty of the concept lies in its analytical purchase (Death 2013). But describing the concept as an "analytics of governance" (Dean 1999: 20) means a conscious rejection of a more ontological view of governmentality as something "out there," in a wider world. By contrast, emphasizing that governmentality is also shaped by the context within which it finds itself and that it must operate across a complex social and historical *terrain* of fortresses and earthworks (Gramsci 1973: 238–239) means that different varieties of governmentality can emerge based on a combination of different social and historical dynamics – as well as the emergence of different rationalities of governance. This chapter is partly concerned, therefore, with how the complexities of the international terrain create varieties of governmentality (and resilience). This shows the limits of starting with the idea pursued in this volume, of the "globality of governmentality" (see introduction) given the unevenness of the actually existing terrain "out there." The notion of terrain is both ontological – in the sense of being social and historical conditions and context – and strategic – in the sense of being the location for, and continually reworked outcome of, different hegemonic projects and struggles for power and leadership. Combining hegemony and governmentality is therefore useful in getting at the materiality of the context, rather than seeing governmentality more in terms of an underlying rationality or as a kind of wider "globality" (see Kiersey's chapter for a similar approach). Terrain also indicates the strategic element to governmentality, revealed as it goes through processes of pushing and pulling by different forces with its integration into different hegemonic projects leading to certain adaptations and variations (Li 2007: 264).[1] A materialist approach would therefore look at how the character of governmentality is conditioned by the nature of the hegemonic projects on the one hand and the stratification of governmentalities across a differentiated, multilevel terrain on the other. This means that governmentality's ability to enable and constrain is itself enabled and constrained.

Most governmentality scholars, particularly in IR, are of course quite skeptical of such an approach, and there are three possible responses to my argument. One would be to say that posing something underlying governmentality undermines Foucault's main insight that governmentality itself is an underlying and constitutive force that frames the world in a certain way and allows for the emergence of governable objects (Corry 2013). Another would be to say that there is nothing formative or determinative of the governmentalities that emerge, no deeper, underlying social force – whether conceived of as social structure or rationality (Hamilton 2014). A third view would be to admit that there are underlying forces and causes, but to leave these to one side. The third approach would seem the least consistent since, if these other forces exist, they surely enter into the equation of what governmentality is and how it develops. However, it forms part of the influential view of global governmentality developed by Larner and Walters who go so far as to argue that "What we have called global governmentality entails a move of 'bracketing' the world of underlying forces and causes, and instead examining the different ways in which the real has been inscribed in thought" (Larner and Walters 2005: 16). Walters, following Rose (and probably Latour), calls for an "empiricism of the surface," with emphasis placed on "the differences in what is said, how it is said, and what allows it to be said and to have an effectivity" (Walters 2005: 157; Rose 1999: 57;).

Some critical Marxist engagements with Foucault (Jessop 2016; Marsden 2003; Selby 2007; Sum and Jessop 2013) would respond that this leaves out "why" it is said and the conditions that make what is said both possible and intelligible.[2] Looking at social structure is one way of exploring those possibilities and limitations while a focus on the terrain of civil society and the state links this to concrete political projects, social practices, and institutions.[3] For this line of argument an examination of these social and material conditions better allows us to account for why governmentality takes a particular form and character, why liberal and neoliberal types of governmentality have risen to prominence in certain parts of the world.

While both Gramsci and Foucault are keen to stress the importance of microtechnologies and everyday practices in shaping human conduct, they also emphasize the essential role of the state in the strategic codification of power relations (Jessop 2007: 39) and as a "site at which power condenses" (McKee 2009: 476). The combination of microtechnologies of conduct and strategic intervention of the state helps get at something of the distance involved in the process of governing, now seen as a "multi-scalar ensemble of governing rationalities and technologies that facilitate the governance of social relations at a distance" (Sum and Jessop 2013: 210). However, as Sum and Jessop note, while Foucault provides a better account of the mechanisms involved in capitalist societalization and stabilization, Gramsci better helps us understand the tensions in governmentality that might arise from the contradictions and crisis tendencies in the objects of governance as well as from the resistance of subjects (2013: 213).

Another main issue that came out of the last round of governmentality debates was whether governmentality is an inherently liberal/neo-liberal approach or whether there are non-liberal and other alternative governmentalities. For example, Death (2013: 777) questions my arguments that governmentality cannot properly regulate populations themselves when faced with challenging social conditions, while Walters (2012: 94–95) believes that I equate governmentality with liberalism, ignoring other governmentalities such as those of a colonial or postcolonial character. My response would be that to give ontological primacy to social conditions and context (rather than relying on a genealogy of governmentality or an analytics of governance) requires us to examine which forms of governmentality rise to prominence in particular times and places as well as offering some explanation of why this should be so. Foucault undoubtedly provides some alternative accounts of governmentality in his genealogy, but most of his writing focuses on the rise to prominence of Western, liberal forms of governmentality. My suggestion is that this relates to the issue of which forms of governmentality become dominant or hegemonic, leading eventually to the idea of globality. This clearly goes against a poststructuralist reading of Foucault because it presupposes some prior hierarchy, selectivity, and condition of possibly – something considered by many in IR to be Marxist and old-fashioned (Jaeger 2014; Joseph and Corry 2014).[4] However, this seems clearly evident in Foucault's work and would also, in my view, be a crucial issue in understanding the dominant forms of global governance as well as the leading role of the state in the "strategic selectivity" of particular forms of governance. We will address this latter issue in the next two sections and concentrate on the liberal character of governmentality in the following paragraphs.

Foucault writes that governmentality is not a permanent thing, but is a product of a particular era which in his view can be traced back to the 18th century and the transformation of the state through new techniques of government. For Foucault, these new forms of government contributed to the transformation of the state – or its "governmentalization" (Foucault 2001: 220). Governmentality is thus neither a short-term phenomenon nor a permanent feature, but a long-term process that has a clearly identifiable genealogy and is linked to the development of capitalism, the state and bourgeois society (Foucault 1980: 41, 203). This wider sociohistorical context is what gives governmentality its distinctively liberal character and which fosters and encourages certain rationalities of governance.

It is no surprise, therefore, that the majority of Foucault's arguments about governmentality are concentrated on a specifically liberal form of rule that is based on the *laissez-faire* principles of political economy which finds its expression in civil society and is legitimated through a concern not to "govern too much" (Foucault 2008: 319). Instead, the exercise of power "consists in guiding the possibility of conduct" (Foucault 1983: 220). As Hindess argues, liberalism is distinctive from other approaches to the government of the state by "its commitment to governing as far as possible through the promotion of certain kinds of free activity and the cultivation among the governed of suitable habits of self-regulation" (Hindess 2005: 26), while Busse adds (2015: 172) that modern governmentality "is unthinkable without the freedom of the individual." This modern governmentality, in contrast to more directly coercive forms of power, works from a distance, is thus always concerned with its own limits and follows a rationality of governance that aims to respect the freedom of the governed by allowing things to take their "natural course." In particular, governing well comes to be understood as respecting the freedom of social and economic processes, that is, the spheres of civil society and the market (Foucault 2008: 10).

However, this freedom is socially constructed. As Foucault argues, liberalism works "not through the imperative of freedom, but through the social production of freedom" (Foucault 2008: 65). Foucault goes on to argue that: "Liberalism is not acceptance of freedom; it proposes to manufacture it constantly, to arouse it and produce it, with, of course, [the system] of constraints and problems" (Foucault 2008: 65). Liberal governmentality requires political economy as its main form of knowledge and security as an essential technique for the protection of interests in the workings of freedom. In other words, it requires the support of an economic "regime of truth" and accompanying processes of policing and security. In fact this recognition of the need for intervention to "construct" freedom is a strong characteristic of *neo*liberalism that distinguishes it from classical liberalism's faith in the autonomous subject.

Looking at the social situatedness of governmentality and the wider sociohistorical context allows us to see how it assumes today's dominant form as a neoliberal intervention. Neoliberalism's rise to prominence in the 1980s was due to its ability to offer a reflexive critique of the postwar institutional settlement and the failures of socioeconomic regulation. Although the genealogy of liberal governmentality is traced back to the 18th century, Foucault's approach is particularly well suited for describing current strategies of rolling back direct state involvement in various social and economic matters, bringing the state into cooperation with a complex network of other social institutions and giving the state more of a managerial role as an overseer of different social processes. Neoliberal thinking is concerned with matters of "what should or should not fall within the state's domain, what is public and what private, what is not within the state's competence, and so on" (Foucault, 2007: 109). A Gramscian argument would suggest that this critique gained coherence due to the crisis of the postwar settlement, with new things now allowed "to be said." Neoliberal approaches may have emerged at the microlevel, but they were supported and promoted by active state intervention in response to the crisis of the postwar mode of regulation. Neoliberal governmentality becomes the hegemonic variant of governmentality when a specific set of neoliberal micropractices are adopted by or coalesce into a particular macrostrategy of governance. Nikolas Rose might be correct that neoliberalism emerged in the 1980s without any clear strategy or overall logic behind it, but as a loose assemblage, a "contingent lash-up" of thought and action (Rose 1999: 27). However, these techniques and practices were gradually colonized at the macrolevel and given the coherence of a neoliberal rationality in relation to the exercise of state power. Once "translated," these practices could be redirected to a number of domains like the welfare system which had previously been resistant to such a logic. Just as Foucault argues that the 19th-century bourgeoisie came to realize the advantages of medicalization to the interests of capitalist development,[5] so the Reaganites, Thatcherites, and associated groups of the 1980s came to realize the usefulness of various neoliberal techniques that could be utilized by the state and other institutions and international bodies in response to underlying socioeconomic pressures and the ensuing failure of postwar regulation. For Foucault, such techniques are "incorporated into the social whole" once the dominant groups grasp their political utility and economic advantages (Foucault 1980: 101).

Cohered into a mode of governance, neoliberalism strives to promote the norms and values of the market across different areas of social life, seeking to govern through the dynamics of competition and enterprise. Models of competitive or entrepreneurial conduct must reach not just to institutions and social practices, but right down to the self-understanding and self-governance of individuals. These individuals are appealed to as active citizens or consumers or, best of all, entrepreneurs (Bröckling 2016), who are expected to show awareness, enterprise and initiative. We will see how this is characteristic of the neoliberal approach to resilience as well as other policies that encourage greater self-reliance.

However, this focus on the resourcefulness of individuals is often, paradoxically, a state-driven process. In this sense, we might support McKee's view that:

> Whilst the state no longer claims to have all the answers to solving all of society's problems, and may be increasingly reliant on non-state actors, including individuals, to secure its objectives it still remains a pivotal actor in shaping both the conceptualization of the "problem" and the proposed solution.
>
> (McKee 2009: 471)

This is certainly the case when we look at how states promote resilience-building policies. It is also the case that states are the key actors – and targets for intervention – when it comes to the operation of global governmentality.

## The dominant form of global governmentality

Now we can make a distinction between domestic and global governmentality (which, despite the expression, is actually a form of international governmentality that reflects the unevenness of the international system rather than the realization of a truly global society). We saw how Foucault sees governmentality gradually evolving in the West over a number of centuries. It is driven by the development of the economy, a liberal rationality, and transformation of the state and its means of governing. International governmentality is a more conscious affair, driven by the political rationality of liberal states and used by them to shape international institutions, and to promote a particular type of conduct among states, particularly in relation to those that are developing and conflict-affected (Ejdus 2018: 32).

There has been a lot of discussion about the usefulness of a governmentality approach to IR and whether governmentality can be "scaled-up" to account for what goes on at the international level. Likewise, we might also raise a question of whether governmentality can be "scaled down" – that is to say, taken by international organizations and applied to local context. The title of this chapter draws attention to the different "varieties" this may generate as governmentality comes up against different social conditions and contexts.

Global governmentality is a more conscious process because it is largely something that is applied to "others." It thus forms part of a postcolonial set of power relations and inequalities. Given what Foucault says about the dominant liberal form of governmentality, this is what we would expect to dominate at the international level. However, the international is a complex and uneven terrain. Different social contexts, historical conditions, political processes, and institutional frameworks all place significant limits on the transfer of a liberal form of governmentality. There has been some discussion of whether distinct local forms of governmentality might exist, although arguments on this (e.g., Death's views on different African forms of governmentality (2013)) are unconvincing.[6] For us, the issue is really what the hegemonic form of governmentality is at the global level and how this might (or might not) get implemented locally.

This is again an issue of the social conditions of possibility for governmentality, something that requires a wider social ontology than most poststructuralists are prepared to allow for. It is to go beyond discursive and extradiscursive practices to deal with underlying social structures, sociocultural conditions and the political and institutional forms that enable and constrain such practices – for example, level of integration into the global economy, type of class structure and social groups, nature of civil society, and institutional structure of the state.

Whether these conditions allow for governmentality might in any case be a secondary issue. We might in fact ask the opposite question – whether governmentality allows for a process of intervention that tries to change these conditions – and in particular, the nature of the state and its relation to the populations it seeks to govern. For this reason, I tend to the view that global governmentality differs in its intended object even if it uses a similar discourse of responsibilization and local empowerment. Indeed, this discourse can work in favor of the larger effect, even when it fails in achieving its purported aims in relation to local self-governance. For the main aim of global governmentality, whatever stated aims it might claim to have, is not to responsibilize individual conduct, but to responsibilize states and governments and lock them into an international system of monitoring and regulation. This is governmentality as the reality of power relations in the international system, not governmentality as a romanticized expression of subaltern groups. This would also be my argument in relation to the promotion of resilience, despite its obvious appeal in claiming to help people survive in the face of adversity.[7]

If we look at current approaches to international interventions such as peacebuilding, poverty reduction, development strategy and disaster risk reduction, then the notion of governmentality certainly helps explain the general trend of trying to appeal to the freedom of the governed to behave in a responsible way. However, while the discourse of global governmentality makes such liberal appeals, the actual mechanisms of governance involve a far stricter approach that enforces a system of monitoring and regulation that takes performance, capacity and competitiveness as its indicators (Busse 2018; Löwenheim 2008). This appears as governance from a distance, through empowering local actors, incentivizing good conduct and enhancing human, social and institutional capacities. However, this conceals the exercise of hegemonic power of the dominant groups in the dominant states whose concern with local populations is less of an end goal than the means by which the main governmentality effect is achieved – which is to govern the behavior of states and ensure their compliance with a set of international norms and regulations. The World Bank, the United Nations Development Programme (UNDP) and other international organizations recognize that the most effective way to promote global governance is to target states and their governments, using the wellbeing of their populations as a means to legitimate this. I would call this, following Michael Merlingen's work, "the international conduct of the conduct of countries" (2003: 367). In such cases, we get a better picture by looking at the wider issues of power politics in the international system, rather than focusing in on specific micropractices on the ground.

All of this requires both a study of governmentality and its specific techniques and an account of hegemony in the international system. It means examining the forms of hegemony that emerge within particular states – for example, the advanced techniques of governmentality that have emerged in Europe and other parts of the world – and the forms of hegemony that are imposed on other states as the exercise of power relations in the international sphere. It means explaining how governmentality emerges in different parts of the world in relation to certain states, institutions and dominant groups, and how it is forced upon others by the dominant forces in international politics. When it comes to looking at the dominant rationality behind intervention, we might contrast the liberal rationale that responsibilizes populations domestically and the rationality driving those countries to govern insecurities beyond their own borders which, as Ejdus notes, (2018: 44) often echoes the colonial principle of indirect rule.

This exercise of hegemony can involve the use of governmentality, as suggested above and in the next section, but it is important to carefully analyze who or what is being subjected to the techniques of governmentality and what its overall effects are. In many cases, it can be that some sort of alternative governmentality or hybrid system develops as a result of governmentality combining with sovereign and disciplinary power, and local conditions combining with the aims and intentions of international organizations. As Gupta and Sharma (2006) argue, in a postcolonial context, the state remains obliged to look after marginal groups, limiting the ability of neoliberal governmentality to fully push through its agenda of self-help and personal responsibility. Moreover, as Neumann and Sending suggest, there are a variety of prototypes developing, where the limits of a neoliberal form of intervention may generate a diversity of combinations and hybrid forms (Neumann and Sending 2010: 44).

In this respect, the advantage of combining governmentality with hegemony is that it allows us to account for varieties of governmentality as global dynamics come up against different social conditions that both enable and constrain governmentality in its various manifestations. Studying this is not, therefore, about denigrating local agency by suggesting that poorer countries lack the rationality to do governmentality (Death 2013: 782), but about insisting on the structural context that makes various forms of agency possible and which leads to strategic selectivity in relation to who gets whom to do what. In fact, it is indeed about highlighting varieties of governmentality, but this is based on social relations rather than just rationality. Consequently, there are indeed problems translating the Anglo-Saxon form of governmentality, not only to poorer parts of the world, but, as the next section will show, across Europe as well. In each case, whether it is about European approaches to resilience, poverty reduction strategies, or promoting good governance, it is accounting for the hegemonic form of governmentality that is the key issue.

## Varieties of resilience and global governmentality

This section provides a brief examination of different approaches to building resilience in different countries before showing how this works in relation to humanitarian and development concerns. While some IR scholars have provided a more balanced account of the positive and negative aspects of the resilience approach – for a sophisticated account, see Bourbeau (2018) – the majority of understandings in IR are overwhelmingly critical of resilience discourse and practices and have largely expressed this through connecting resilience to a neoliberal form of global governmentality.

Resilience has been described as governmentality because of such features as governing from a distance, with the population as its target, and encouraging reflexivity and adaptability among subjects (Joseph 2018; Walker and Cooper 2011; Zebrowski 2016). These subjective features include reflexivity, resourcefulness and ability to cope with adversity. It can also be described as neoliberal because of its promotion of individual initiative and enterprise and support for market solutions (Joseph 2018). In contrast to classical liberalism, it takes a more pragmatist and "best-fit" approach to complex, often irresolvable problems. Indeed resilience and associated ideas like wellbeing and sustainability do not so much break with neoliberal governance as enhance its ability to measure and evaluate human resources, capacities, and behavior.

However, in different countries we find significant tensions and contradictions between neoliberal views and alternative approaches. Certainly, the neoliberal approach is the hegemonic form of governmentality, but we find significant variations, some of which rearticulate the meaning and practice of resilience. This section will therefore distinguish between the hegemonic Anglo-Saxon approach to resilience, and alternative European understandings. This focuses on such questions as whether other countries accept the Anglo-Saxon view of resilience as based on individuals and communities, what kind of roles are given to the state, the market and civil society, and whether different countries fully embrace the transformative notion of resilience with its emphasis on learning and adaptation, or whether they place greater emphasis on protection, resistance, and robustness.

Resilience reinforces governmentality through support for a system of governing from a distance, particularly in relation to enhancing capacities – claiming to help local communities through support and advice that will enable them to deal with risks and crises themselves. This is presented as facilitative – for example, using benchmarks to assess business continuity plans – but there is often no opt-out possibility. Those who are governed from a distance must conduct themselves in a responsible way, or be held to account. The devolution of powers to individuals and communities is backed up with the use of indicators and monitoring tools as well as various coercive measures (see also Löwenheim (2007) and Shamir (2008) for examples).

Despite the rhetoric, such an approach, as evident in something like the UK's Civil Contingencies Act, still represents a form of top-down state intervention. Nevertheless, other European countries, notably France and Germany, see the UK approach as more oriented to civil society and the private sector (Francart 2010). There is far less mention of individual or community resilience and more mention of both the responsibilities of the state (to protect the population) and the need for what in Germany is called a "whole of society approach" (Federal Ministry of Defence 2016: 60). These approaches introduce an element of governing from a distance, but remain focused on the role and responsibilities of the state, the legal system, and society as a whole.

Differences in approach are indicated by how far down resilience is meant to travel. Domestic approaches in the US and UK develop facilitative practices targeted at individuals and communities with the government operating in "partnership" with the private and voluntary sectors, communities and individuals (Cabinet Office 2016: 43). Government guidelines are frequently addressed to individuals, encouraging them to be more aware of the risks they face, to know how they can get involved in community planning and how they might better help themselves in an emergency – in the US this is formalized through the National Preparedness Goal (FEMA 2015: 2). By contrast, Germany talks of a "whole of society" approach while the French political culture continues to emphasize the themes of solidarity and national cohesion with little encouragement for communities to be engaged in resilience-building. In the French context, the state tends to operate through decrees and legally binding guidelines, with private companies showing little interest in taking over key state responsibilities. Indeed, there is a degree of distrust in devolving such powers and encouraging local initiative and a much more passive relationship prevails (Bourcart 2015).

Whereas the Anglo-Saxon discourse positively promotes governance though the market as the best way of getting things done, the discourse from

France, Germany and the EU has more of a tone of inevitability based on the recognition that areas like critical infrastructure are shifting to the private sector. In contrast to the UK and US, there is more emphasis on the need for the state to intervene to deal with market failures and inadequate provision and protection, but there is also recognition that privatization is changing the role of the state as well as its ability to intervene. Resilience plays an important role in justifying this situation by promoting such things as business continuity and financial risk management (Joseph 2018).

Differences again emerge in domestic interpretations of resilience as an innovative approach that encourages self-management and initiative. Resilient subjects are those who are able to learn from their experiences and adapt their behavior in appropriate ways. Something like the UK Civil Contingencies Act should be seen as an approach aimed at keeping populations in a constant state of preparing for a range of possible emergencies (Anderson and Adey 2011: 29). This encourages the population to be always alert to their situation, to the risks that they face and to the choices that they might make. Now intensified with fiscal entrenchment, this should allow for the creation of more pragmatic subjects. This is different in France and Germany despite some talk of creating a "novel risk culture" (Federal Ministry of the Interior 2009: 11). Germany maintaining an emphasis on protecting the "whole of society" and French emphasis on social solidarity in France is at odds with the Anglo-Saxon appeal to specific enterprising groups and individuals.

In the UK and US, a transformative view of resilience has developed whereby crises are seen as opportunities to embed neoliberal norms of behavior. Resilience is about "seiz[ing] the opportunities to transform and revitalize" the neighborhood and to improve such things as commercial activities, skills, and people's aspirations (Cabinet Office 2004: 83). This neoliberal notion of transformation is largely absent from domestic policy in countries like France and Germany. In Germany, the dominant view of resilience is that it is a "resolute approach" that emphasizes robustness and resistance rather than adaptation (Federal Ministry for Education and Research 2016: 51). The French understanding similarly views resilience as the restoration of the capacity to function (Présidence de la République 2008: 60). Resilience is based on a formal and centralized relationship between state, local government and strategic businesses sectors.

If the varieties of resilience across Europe show quite different degrees of devolving power and responsibilities, then in overseas policy we find European governments more willing to discuss devolution to local actors. The most obvious reason is that this less directly affects national interests and domestic consensus. It is in keeping with the approach of international organizations like the World Bank, IMF, UNDP and OECD, all of which talk about encouraging countries to take responsibility for their own resilience-building. There is still some tension in the discourse – the German approach places more emphasis on the need to consider social context and "people's real needs" (BMZ 2009: 15). However, the general pattern is for European countries to support the system of global governance that is shaped by the hegemonic Anglo-Saxon understanding of the major international organizations and US and British development agencies (it is worth noting, for example, how much the UK's Department for International Development (DFID) has influenced the discourse of the EU and Germany's overseas strategy (BMZ 2013: 7; Joseph 2017)). The EU's approach to resilience, while failing to have much impact in EU policymaking despite the more active attempts by the European Commission to promote such a culture across its member states, is more prominent in overseas policy. Here, the EU approach more openly encourages innovation in risk management and, following DFID's lead, sees the stimulation of enterprise as the best way to encourage human development while attracting foreign investment (Joseph 2018: 179). We also find organizations like the United States Agency for International Development (USAID) free to promote innovation as allowing people the chance to think more critically and challenge their existing structures and ways of life, while drawing on their human attributes in order to develop better coping mechanisms and deal pragmatically with deficiencies in service delivery (Bujones, Jaskiewicz, Linakis, and McGirr 2013: 13).

Hence in the international domain all organizations, including French and German development agencies as well as the EU promote resilience as a distant form of governance. In particular, a process of responsiblization of local states and actors is taking place so that poor countries must develop their own adaptive capacities in response to shocks and disasters and make themselves less vulnerable and prone to poverty (DFID 2011a: 1; European Commission 2013: 3). The international community, now in retreat from liberal universalism, will make less direct interventions, preferring instead to play a facilitating role – although again, as with domestic resilience, this is backed up with disciplinary mechanisms of monitoring and surveillance (see Fougner 2008). In contrast to domestic policymaking, German and French approaches to global governance largely follow an Anglo-Saxon model whose neoliberal character would encounter significant social and political obstacles at home, but which can more easily be applied to populations overseas (see Joseph 2018).

This model adopts a transformative view of resilience that eschews trying to preserve and resist in favor developing adaptive capacities and of looking to take advantage of the opportunities crises provide (DFID 2011b: 8). The Anglo-Saxon approach to building resilience overseas takes the free market as its model, arguing that traditional coping mechanisms are unable to deal with new, complex challenges and that it is necessary to engage more with the global market and show greater individual and community adaptability (Headey and Kennedy 2012: 5).

In conclusion, our finding is that there are variations of resilience across the globe, some more and others less governmentalizing, particularly if considered in relation to neoliberal approaches. This can be seen in the discourse of UK, US, French and German policymaking, particularly at the domestic level. Here, the Anglo-Saxon model is more developed in its consideration of such things as the role of civil society and the private sector, devolution of responsibilities and promotion of innovation and initiative among individuals and communities. By contrast, European approaches remain wedded (rightly or wrongly) to the idea of resilience as resistance or robustness, lacking the emphasis on building adaptive capacities and seeking transformative opportunities for individuals and communities. Rather than saying that these European approaches stand as clear alternatives to the Anglo-Saxon approach, we can say that they reveal the limits of Anglo-Saxon governmentality. The failure of the neoliberal understanding of resilience to fully travel, particularly in domestic policymaking is due to the wider sociopolitical context – different national and cultural characteristics, political traditions and policy objectives, a less individualistic approach to society, and a greater emphasis on the role of the state. Consequently, resilience lacks deeper substance outside of its Anglo-Saxon context, but it is also fair to say that little by way of a coherent alternative to resilience has emerged either.

In terms of global governmentality, however, the picture is different. Here, the Anglo-Saxon view has long predominated and countries like France and Germany as well as the EU are willing to let the UK and US take the lead on resilience initiatives. This explains the significant influence of DFID and USAID over other countries' overseas strategies alongside the established Anglo-Saxon thinking of the World Bank and the International Monetary Fund (IMF). In recent years, a trend has developed to see previous international interventions such as statebuilding and development strategy as failures. Resilience, alongside the local and the hybrid, can be presented as a radical critique. However, (and in contrast to arguments such as Chandler's (2014)) it actually reinforces rather than challenges existing governmentalizing trends, using the perceived failure of state intervention to promote greater devolution of responsibility to those being governed. In this way, resilience has risen to prominence as a hegemonic form of governmentality at the international level, even though we have seen that domestically it lacks such legitimacy outside its Anglo-Saxon heartlands.

## Conclusion

In the last section, I sought to contribute to an understanding of resilience as a form of neoliberal governmentality, while adding some nuance to this argument. In so doing, this illustrates how governmentality may take a dominant form, but is also unevenly developed in different countries. While this only looked at differences in three European countries and the EU, such differences are significant given that governmentality is sometimes taken as a homogenous Western development. We can certainly expect forms of governmentality in non-Western parts of the world to vary significantly from these cases. However, we can also conclude that there is a dominant Anglo-Saxon approach to governmentality (and resilience) that does enjoy considerable influence even if this is not as widespread as critical scholars of governmentality sometimes suggest. My findings from a study of resilience is that while the influence of the dominant Anglo-Saxon approach is much more varied in domestic approaches across Europe – civil protection, counterterrorism, infrastructure protection and disaster risk reduction – it is much more pronounced in the sphere of global governance. Here, Western states and international organizations like the EU or World Bank seek to export a particular model of resilience to poorer parts of the world. This model has a stronger Anglo-Saxon character with prominent neoliberal liberal assumptions about the role of markets, privatization, "modernization," capacity building, seizing opportunities, and encouraging initiative within communities and individuals. It works as a form of governmentality from a distance, devolving responsibility to local actors while locking them into a system of global monitoring and surveillance. There is no longer talk of "protecting" those populations made vulnerable by the effects of capitalist development and the global market. Instead, the populations are encouraged to develop their own resilience in the face of such challenges and to see their vulnerability to crises as an opportunity to transform and adapt. This is reinforced by the now universal discourse of global complexity and uncertainty. This would seem to render states and their governments impotent in the face of radical challenges, yet, paradoxically, these very same states are the main targets of the interventions, while concern with their populations serves as a pretext for regulating and monitoring state behavior.

The argument presented here, while focused on resilience, is intended to sharpen our understanding of the global character of governmentality. In particular, the way that it is unevenly spread, but picked up in its dominant form, with a neoliberal rationality at its core. A more Gramscian approach to governmentality suggests that certain forms of governmentality become hegemonic, albeit not in a permanently established way. We use a more materialist approach to ask about the conditions under which governmentality itself comes into being, to look at how it is enabled and constrained by deeper social conditions, and to look at the strategic selectivity and agential opportunities that might arise from this. Hegemony helps us understand the terrain across which governmentality must operate and the relationship between governmentality and such things as institutional context, the role of social and class forces, how particular interests are represented and how political projects are constructed. These are all things that we saw Foucault hints at in some of his writings, without further developing the argument.

The main finding is that there are varieties of governmentality due to such things as social, historical and political context, different hegemonic projects and political interests as well as forms of opposition and resistance, but not really substantial alternatives to the dominant neoliberal form of governmentality. When it comes to global governmentality, approaches like resilience-building definitely assume a more Anglo-Saxon, neoliberal form. We might say, following a well-known Gramscian in IR, that governmentality does tend to reflect the strategies of the dominant strata in the dominant states (Cox 1996: 151).

## Notes

1  For Li, using an assemblage approach emphasizes the "the hard work required to draw heterogeneous elements together, forge connections between them and sustain these connections in the face of tension… of how the elements of an assemblage might – or might not – be made to cohere" (Li 2007: 264). Assembling is "a continuous work of pulling disparate elements together" (Li 2007: 264) and requires an agential focus that looks at the "situated subjects" who do the pulling without attributing to them some kind of master-plan (Li 2007: 265). While the emphasis on "pulling" is important, this is an argument in need of a deeper, more embedded, and more collective notion of how agency works.

2  See Nicholas Kiersey's contribution on to this volume for a Marxist take on global governmentality.

3  See Stephan Stetter's chapter to this volume for a connection of governmentality with an overarching structuralist framework rooted in sociological theorizing on global modernity.

4  Olaf Corry opposes the idea that governmentality expresses some underlying ontology, arguing that Marxist readings of Foucault, such as mine, reduce governmentality to the implementation of liberal capitalist development, denying that practices, mentalities, and discourses are constitutive in their own right. Instead, governmentality is seen as something similar to the concept of ideology that relies on underlying social configurations of power. He wonders "what is ultimately gained by referencing Foucault whose project was precisely to explore the constitutive role of discourses, their role in resistance and in relation to multiple rationalities" (Joseph and Corry 2014: 128). Scott Hamilton argues that a Marxist approach to Foucault "is antithetical to the basic notion that governmentality is a nominalist mode of inquiry into fluid, unpredictable, and historically-contingent relations of power and thought" (2014: 138), although he also critiques Corry for having an *a priori* pictorial model of discourse that is determinative of the governmentalities emanating from it. Jaeger, like Corry, laments the failure to engage with Foucault on poststructuralism's terms, in fact I move backwards from any insights governmentality might offer – "Joseph not only resurrects a number of dichotomous distinctions (between structure and process, reality and discourse, the material and the ideational), which governmentality seeks to transcend" (Jaeger 2014: 236).

5  Hence Foucault deliberately focusses on the "infinitesimal mechanisms of power" while asking how these might be useful to the bourgeoisie. He argues that, in the case of madness, the bourgeoisie found a use for the techniques of exclusion, the surveillance apparatus and the mediacalization of sexuality, madness, and delinquency (Foucault 1980: 101).

6  Here governmentality, employed as an analytical framework, is expanded far beyond the idea of governing through freedom and responsibilization to include a wide range of colonial and postcolonial practices without a convincing case being made for deploying the term governmentality rather than, say, biopolitics or disciplinary techniques. Where more convincing examples of governmentality are

provided – for example, aid partnerships (Death 2013: 778–781) – these tend to be examples of what I have called the governmentalization and responsibilization of *states*, not of individuals and populations.
7 See for example, Lindroth and Sinevaara-Niskanen (2019) for how resilience romanticises indigenous populations.

## References

Anderson, Ben and Peter Adey (2011) 'Governing Events and Life "Emergency" in UK Civil Contingencies', *Political Geography* 31:1, 24–33.
BMZ [Federal Ministry for Economic Cooperation and Development] (2009) *Promoting Resilient States and Constructive State-Society Relations – Legitimacy, Transparency and Accountability* (Bonn: BMZ).
BMZ (2013). *Strategy on Transitional Development Assistance: Strengthening Resilience – Shaping Transition* (Bonn: BMZ).
Bourbeau, Philippe (2018) *On Resilience: Genealogy, Logics and World Politics* (Cambridge: Cambridge University Press).
Bourcart, Léo (2015) ' "The State Can't do Everything Any More": Understanding the Evolution of Civil Defence Policies in France', *Resilience: International Policies, Practices and Discourses* 3:1, 40–54.
Bröckling, Ulrich (2016) *The Entrepreneurial Self: Fabricating a New Type of Subject* (Thousand Oaks: Sage).
Bujones, Alejandra Kubitschek, Katrin Jaskiewicz, Lauren Linakis, and Michael McGirr (2013) *A Framework for Analyzing Resilience in Fragile and Conflict-Affected Situations* (Washington: USAID and Columbia University).
Busse, Jan (2015) "Theorizing Governance as Globalized Governmentality: The Dynamics of World-Societal Order in Palestine," *Middle East Critique* 24:2, 161-189.
Busse, Jan (2018) *Deconstructing the Dynamics of World-Societal Order: The Power of Governmentality in Palestine* (Abingdon: Routledge).
Cabinet Office (2004) *Emergency Response and Recovery Non Statutory Guidance Accompanying the Civil Contingencies Act* (London: Cabinet Office).
Cabinet Office (2016) *Community Resilience Framework for Practitioners*, (London: Cabinet Office). Available from: www.gov.uk/government/publications/community-resilience-framework-for-practitioners/the-contextfor-community-resilience [Accessed 18 April 2017].
Chandler, David (2014) *Resilience: The Governance of Complexity* (Abingdon: Routledge).
Corry, Olaf (2013) *Constructing a Global Polity: Theory, Discourse and Governance* (Basingstoke: Palgrave).
Cox, Robert (1996) *Approaches to World Order* (Cambridge: Cambridge University Press).
Dean, Mitchell (1999) *Governmentality: Power and Rule in Modern Society* (London: Sage).
Death, Karl (2013) 'Governmentality at the Limits of the International: African Politics and Foucauldian Theory, *Review of International Studies*, 39:4, 763–787.
DFID (2011a) *Defining Disaster Resilience: A DFID Approach Paper* (London: Department for International Development).

DFID (2011b) *Defining Disaster Resilience: What Does It Mean for DFID?* (London: Department for International Development).

Ejdus, Filip (2018) 'Local Ownership as International Governmentality: Evidence from the EU Mission in the Horn of Africa', *Contemporary Security Policy*, 39:1, 28-50.

European Commission (2013) *Action Plan for Resilience in Crisis Prone Countries 2013–2020* (Brussels: European Commission).

Francart, Loup (2010), 'What Does Resilience Really Mean?' Available from: www.diploweb.com/What-doesresilience-really-mean.html [Accessed 29 July 2012].

Federal Ministry for Education and Research (2016) *Research for Civil Security 2012 – 2017: Framework Programme of the Federal Government* (Bonn: Bundesministerium für Bildung und Forschung/ Federal Ministry for Education and Research (BMBF)).

Federal Ministry of Defence (2016) *White Paper on German Security Policy and the Future of the Bundeswehr* (Berlin: Federal Ministry of Defence).

Federal Ministry of the Interior (2009) *National Strategy for Critical Infrastructure Protection (CIP Strategy)* (Berlin: Federal Ministry of the Interior).

FEMA (2015) *National Preparedness Goal* Second Edition (Washington DC: FEMA).

Foucault, Michel (1980) *Power/Knowledge: Selected Interviews and Other Writings 1972–1977*, ed. Colin Gordon (New York: Pantheon Books).

Foucault, Michel (1983) 'The Subject and Power' in Paul Rabinow (ed) *Michel Foucault: Beyond Structuralism and Hermeneutics* (Chicago: University of Chicago Press), 208-226.

Foucault, Michel (2001) 'Governmentality', in J. D. Faubion (ed) *Michel Foucault: Power*, (Harmondsworth: Penguin Books), 200–222.

Foucault, Michel (2007) *Security, Territory, Population* (Basingstoke: Palgrave Macmillan).

Foucault, Michel (2008) *The Birth of Biopolitics* (Basingstoke: Palgrave Macmillan).

Fougner, Tore (2008): "Neoliberal Governance of States: The Role of Competitiveness Indexing and Country Benchmarking." *Millennium - Journal of International Studies* 37 (2), 303–326.

Gramsci, Antonio (1973) *Selections from the Prison Notebooks* (London: Lawrence and Wishart).

Gupta, Akhil and Aradhana Sharma (2006) 'Globalization and Postcolonial States', *Current Anthropology* 47:2, 277–307.

Hamilton, Scott (2014) 'Add Foucault and Stir?', *European Review of International Studies* 1:2, 129–141.

Headey, Derek and Adam Kennedy (2012) *Enhancing Resilience in the Horn of Africa* (Washington, DC: USAID and International Food Policy Research Institute).

Hindess, Barry (2005) 'Liberalism – What's in a Name?', in Wendy Larner and William Walters (eds), *Global Governmentality: Governing International Spaces* (London: Routledge), 24–29.

Jaeger, Hans-Martin (2014) 'Book Review, The Social in the Global: Social Theory, Governmentality and Global Politics', *Acta Politica* 49, 234–237.

Jessop, Bob (2016) *The State: Past, Present, Future* (Cambridge: Polity).

Joseph, Jonathan (2018) *Varieties of Resilience: Studies in Governmentality* (Cambridge: Cambridge University Press).

Joseph, Jonathan (2017) *The Resilience Turn in German Development Strategy and Humanitarian Intervention* (Global Cooperation Research Papers 20).

(Duisburg: Käte Hamburger Kolleg/Centre for Global Cooperation Research) (KHK/ GCR21).

Joseph, Jonathan and Olaf Corry (2014) 'Jonathan Joseph and Olaf Corry Review Each Other's Books on Governmentality and Global Politics and Then Respond to Each Other's Reviews', *European Political Science*, 13, 124–130.

Li, Tania Murray (2007) 'Practices of Assemblage and Community Forest Management', *Economy and Society*, 36:2, 263–293.

Lindroth, Marjo and Heidi Sinevaara-Niskanen (2019) Colonialism Invigorated? The Manufacture of Resilient Indigeneity, Resilience, 7:3, 240–254.

Löwenheim, Oded (2007): "The Responsibility to Responsibilize: Foreign Offices and the Issuing of Travel Warnings." *International Political Sociology* 1 (3), 203–221.

Löwenheim, Oded (2008): "Examining the State: A Foucauldian Perspective on International 'governance Indicators.'" *Third World Quarterly* 29 (2), 255–274.

Marsden, Richard (2003) *The Nature of Capital: Marx After Foucault* (London: Routledge).

McKee, Kim (2009) 'Post-Foucauldian Governmentality: What Does It Offer Critical Social Policy Analysis?', *Critical Social Policy*, 29:3, 465–486.

Merlingen, Michael (2003) 'Governmentality: Towards a Foucauldian Framework for the Study of NGOs', *Cooperation and Conflict* 38:4, 367.

Neumann, Iver B. and Ole Jacob Sending (2010) *Governing the Global Polity: Practice, Mentality, Rationality* (Ann Arbor: University of Michigan Press).

Présidence de la République (2008) *The French White Paper on Defence and Security: Press Kit* (Paris: Présidence de la République).

Rose, Nikolas (1996) 'Governing "Advanced' Liberal Democracies;' in Peter Osborne, Andrew Barry, and Nilolas Rose (eds) *Foucault and Political Reason* (London: UCL Press), 37-64.

Rose, Nikolas (1999) *Powers of Freedom: Reframing Political Thought* (Cambridge: Cambridge University Press).

Selby, Jan (2007) 'Engaging Foucault; Discourse, Liberal Governance and the Limits of Foucauldian IR', *International Relations*, 21:3, 324–245.

Shamir, Ronen (2008): "The Age of Responsibilization: On Market-Embedded Morality." *Economy and Society* 37 (1), 1–19.

Sum, Ngai-Ling and Bob Jessop (2013) *Towards a Cultural Political Economy: Putting Culture in Its Place in political Economy* (Cheltenham: Edward Elgar).

Walker, Jeremy and Melinda Cooper (2011) 'Genealogies of Resilience from Systems Ecology to the Political Economy of Crisis Adaptation', *Security Dialogue* 42:2, 143–60.

Walters, William (2012) *Governmentality: Critical Encounters* (Abingdon: Routledge).

Zebrowski, Chris (2016) *The Value of Resilience: Securing Life in the Twenty-First Century* (Abingdon: Routledge).

# 4 Inter-governmentality

## A framework for analysis

*Halvard Leira*

## Introduction

Even though it was primarily developed to make sense of developments within the central European states over the last four centuries, the analytical concept of governmentality has proved to be fruitful for explorations beyond this spatiotemporal framework.[1] As demonstrated in this volume and a growing literature over the last two decades, governmentality yields important insights when applied to that which goes on between, above and beyond the states; to the international and the global (e.g. Larner and Walter 2004; Neumann and Sending 2010; Kiersey and Stokes 2011). The concept has also been put to good use in regions beyond Europe (e.g. Corbridge et al. 2005; Death 2013; Busse 2018) and to periods well before the emergence of the self-reflective state discussed by Foucault (Chatterjee 2013; Jobe 2015). It has been argued that governmentality might also yield important insights when applied to the history of inter-state relations from the early modern period and onwards (Leira 2009). An important question still remains unexplored: whether governmentality provides any added analytical purchase when applied to interactions between polities before the early modern period.

This chapter is dedicated to an exploration of this question. The topic might seem counterintuitive, since Foucault himself did not have much to say about relations between polities. However, as stressed in the introduction to this volume and as one can observe in some of Foucault's own comments, there is no inherent reason to assume the state as the basis for the study of government. The modern state is a central expression of government, but not the only possible one. The introduction points out how "governmentality, globality, and the state are all simultaneously co-produced and entangled." (p. 15) This understanding of intertwinement is logically connected to an understanding of governmentality as a "history of the art of government," in particular, in the European context. It nevertheless seems worthwhile exploring if and how earlier, nonstate centered forms of government were also entangled in forms of "globality" (understood as a way of conceptualizing the totality of the known world). To be a bit more specific, assuming that: (1) governmentality (historically understood) was always entangled with globality and (2) that governmentality (heuristically understood) can be studied in polities other than the modern state, it makes sense to establish a form of heuristic analytical apparatus for the study of the relation between nonstate governmental apparatuses.

My conclusion is that the analytical tools of governmentality are indeed applicable beyond Europe and the last four centuries. By being explicitly *analytical*, the conceptual vocabulary of governmentality allows us to make sense of logics and practices of government across time and space, without assuming sameness. More specifically, I argue that these analytical tools can enhance our understanding of what I will here term *inter-governmentality*, even before the emergence of the modern state and state-system. I conceive of inter-governmentality as a heuristic tool for investigating the history of government which takes place in between governmental apparatuses, how relations between governmental apparatuses can be understood as a form of conduct of conduct, an orchestration without an orchestrator. To maintain analytical distance, I specifically want to avoid the term "international governmentality" for phenomena predating states and nations. The term "inter-governmentality" has been used sporadically in the academic literature, typically to denote current governmental logics in situations of multiple and overlapping levels and fields of authority (Sheptycki 1999; Lee 2012). My usage is somewhat similar. I want to focus on the logics and techniques we can find in relations between different governmental apparatuses. Whether they are located on different levels or not, is, however, an empirical question. I also want to be clear that I do not think that governmentality above and beyond governmental apparatuses is a prerequisite for analytics of government to be fruitful; inter-governmentality applies as much (if not more) to relations between governmental apparatuses.[2]

To be specific – the point is not to explore global governmentality before the state, but forms of relations between apparatuses of government which need not be states. The conceptual apparatus of governmentality (or the analytics of government) provides three clear and interrelated benefits. First, and most importantly, it provides an explicitly analytical framework to the academic subfield of Historical International Relations, where the distinction between analytical and practical concepts is central, but often hard to get around. Second, it can direct attention at overlooked issues, such as gift-giving and marriage practices, and help bring meaning to practices which do not make sense to the modern eye. Third, it offers potential coherence to already ongoing research, by suggesting an overarching and integrative analytical framework.

This chapter is exploratory. I am trying to gauge the usefulness of a new conceptual framework. Thus, I provide illustrations for my arguments, rather than in-depth arguments. I will make suggestions and illustrate them with available secondary data, with the hope that they make enough sense for others to pursue them further in explorations of inter-governmentality.

The argument is made in three steps. First, I revisit Foucault and Foucauldians on governmentality and the international suggesting that there is intellectual room for an analytical framework of inter-governmentality. Second, I very briefly discuss the relationship between analytical and practical concepts in historical studies of the relations between polities and highlight the need for a strictly analytical concept. This is followed by the main part of the chapter, the elaboration of how the study of what went on between, above and beyond polities can be enriched by the application of an inter-governmentality perspective. Finally, a conclusion ties the chapter together, and suggests a way forward, pointing also to how inter-governmentality can help decenter the state in studies of contemporary government.

## Governmentality between, above and beyond

As discussed in the introduction to this volume and other commentaries, Foucault (2007: 108–109 *et passim*) developed the concept of governmentality in both a general and a more specific sense. Generally (or heuristically, as described in the introduction), it is concerned with "how we think about governing, with the different mentalities of government," with "the art of government" (Dean 1999: 16, 18). The specification concerns the historical emergence of one concrete form of governing; the one developing in Europe from the 16th century and onwards. As Foucault saw it, "the general problem of 'government' suddenly breaks out in the sixteenth century with respect to many different problems at the same time and in completely different aspects" (Foucault 2007: 88, cf. 231). This can again be further specified with governmentality being seen as a descriptive tool used to explore the trajectory of modern liberal forms of government. For the sake of exploring the usefulness of the concept before the 16th century and on a global scale, the general conception is clearly the one we need to focus on in the context of this chapter, although the exploration also implies expanding on the historical notion of governmentality. Nevertheless, for the sake of example and inspiration, it makes sense to revisit briefly how relations between polities figured into Foucault's more specified framework.

Foucault clearly did not spend much time on interpolity relations, even though he considered the "diplomatic-military technique" (or apparatus) (Foucault 2007: 289, 295–297) to be one of the key features of governmentality, and even though he clearly saw an interconnectedness between government at the level of the state and at the interstate level. Foucault's take on international relations shows a family resemblance to the one Hedley Bull (1977) presented at the same time, with an emphasis on a "society of nations," where balance of power upheld by the great powers allowed for the development of international law and where great power management was crucial to maintenance of the system. Foucault's take here lacks much of the critical distance found in his take on domestic developments. His take on state-formation provides a distinct historical sociology of the emergence of European states

(Valverde 2007; Devetak 2008), displacing the key concepts of political science (Bigo 2017; Dean 2017), but his take on the international, at least of the 16th to 18th centuries, is decidedly more traditional. In their questioning of established terms, later historically oriented analysts following the paths suggested by Foucault, like Jens Bartelson (1995) and David Campbell (1998), have in a sense been truer to a logic of inter-governmentality than Foucault was.

The main thrust of governmentality scholarship has been directed at current affairs domestically as well as internationally (Neumann and Sending 2010), typically with a focus on the supernational; on global governmentality (Larner and Walter 2004). Critics who accept the validity of Foucauldian analysis for domestic contexts, but question the value of scaling-up (Selby 2007; Joseph 2010) have argued that Foucault's account primarily works for liberal domestic settings, and that scaling governmentality-concepts up and applying them beyond the specific European context is problematic, at least without coupling them with more structural accounts. Others disagree and have argued that this critique prioritizes the specific understanding of governmentality over the general one. Substantiating the usefulness of the more general approach, researchers have for instance demonstrated how governmentality can be applied fruitfully to nonliberal settings outside of Europe (Death 2013). I have elsewhere (Leira 2009) argued that an analytic of governmentality which goes beyond what Foucault originally offered can add important insights to our understanding of interpolity relations from the 16th century and onwards. Even though these different studies indicate an analytical value-added by applying governmentality before and beyond, we should pause to consider if such a push makes the analytical concept meaningless. Foucault (2007: 247) considered governmentality (or at least government, his usage was ambiguous) to be related to self-reflective government, and thus closely related to the emergence of something which could be described as "political science"; reflections on statecraft which went beyond the "mirror of princes"-tradition.[3] He dated this to the years around 1600, and we would be hard-pressed to find something like this for relations between, above and beyond polities, before the 17th century emergence of the first guide-books for negotiations aimed at ambassadors (Berridge et al. 2001).

But the emphasis on the early-modern "self-consciousness of government" (Senellart 2007; 387, cf. Foucault 2008: 2) might be unnecessarily restricting, particularly when we consider how Foucault himself saw governmentality drawing on earlier forms and techniques of power, in particular the pastoral one. As discussed by Jobe (2015), and contra Foucault, it might be possible to distinguish a political pastorate in ancient Greece, centered on military–pastoral technologies. Discussing the intersection of law and other forms of regulation, Kendall and Wickham (1999) make a similar point for the government of urban life in antiquity. This would seem to imply that even within the original Foucauldian framework, it makes sense to explore governmentality before the early modern period. And looking more specifically at the changes during the early modern period, on the one hand, there is no denying that major changes took place in how the emerging states started governing around 1600, particularly with regards to reflections on population and territory (Elden 2007; de Carvalho 2016). On the other hand, it is not as obvious that these changes were mirrored in inter-governmentality, where it might well be argued that self-reflectiveness did not develop until much later. One alternative for a later dating would be the treaty of Utrecht from 1713, when self-reflective discussions about the balance of power emerged for the first time. Another alternative would be the treaty of Vienna from 1815, when diplomatic conduct and ceremonial was first jointly codified.

The discussion so far suggests that it does not constitute conceptual violence to study inter-governmentality before the early modern period. It is also possible to find support for an open approach to governmentality in Foucault's own work, when he suggested that governmentality "is no more than a proposed analytical grid," and that he had wanted to explore if it was "not confined to a precise domain determined by a sector of the scale, but should be considered simply as a point of view, a method of decipherment which may be valid for the whole scale, whatever its size" (Foucault 2008: 186). More generally, as Nick Onuf (2017) has recently pointed out, the figure of "Foucault" has already become many different things to many different people, just as Foucault himself seems to have intended when describing his work as a toolbox for others to utilize (see Stetter's chapter in this volume). In an exploration like this, the goal should thus be less about match than about being somehow "loyally unfaithful" (Dean 2017: 97) to the concepts. The further exploration of the fruitfulness of inter-governmentality must therefore proceed first to the question of whether inter-governmentality adds anything of value, then to the specific analytics, and what we would look for when studying pre-modern inter-governmentality.

## Concepts of the past

Having now established that it does make analytical sense to apply the analytics of government and inter-governmentality to the pre-modern world, it remains to be seen what the value-added of such application might be. In this section, I outline a key set of problems besetting many analyses of the past. Subsequently, I suggest that this is a problem which inter-governmentality can help us rectify.

A key challenge for any historical analysis of the pre-modern period, but perhaps particularly analyses of political history, concerns how the past can be conceptualized. Put very briefly, most of our political vocabulary was either invented or transformed during the 18th and 19th centuries (Koselleck 1985; Palonen 2006). When analyzing the past using our current terms, the risk of anachronism is ever-present. This general challenge of historical analysis is compounded in analyses of political history by the fact that so many of the concepts put to use are both analytical concepts and practice concepts. They have a specific analytical meaning and are intended to establish some sort of critical analytical distance between researchers and their objects of research, but they are also steeped in the practices of everyday life (cf. Brubaker and Cooper 2000: 4–6). A central example of this is "the state," which can easily be given a strict analytical form, but where it is very hard to avoid reading our experience of the state into the past. For that exact reason, researchers have come up with other alternatives. Some have suggested that empires have historically been much more prevalent than states, and that we should thus understand former political units as empires more generally. This nevertheless just sidesteps the problem, since empire itself has a distinct conceptual history (Jordheim and Neumann 2011). Another alternative, popularized in International Relations by Ferguson and Mansbach (1996), is to refer to political units more generally as polities.

Moving on to the relations between polities, conceptual usage becomes even more problematic. When discussing such relations, scholars have had few qualms describing diplomacy, foreign policy and international relations in ancient Egypt (Cohen and Westbrook 2000; Hoffmeier 2004), antiquity (Chittick and Freyberg-Inan 2001; Wolpert 2001) or any other period up until our own. But "international" was famously coined by Bentham in the late 18th century, and both "foreign policy" and "diplomacy" were 18th-century innovations as well (Leira 2016, 2019). Reading past practices analytically through these modern analytical *and* practical concepts invariably leads to an understanding of the past in terms of the present.[4] Foreign policy as a current practical concept is associated, for instance, with ministries of foreign affairs, embassies and ambassadors, as well as ideas such as national interests, rational utility-maximization and bureaucratic politics. These are all modern phenomena and using the term "foreign policy" in periods during which they did not exist can lead the analyst to interpret past actions through terms which made little or no sense to past actors. Typically, as soon as one starts delving into the empirics in any detail, the (seemingly) tidy categories of our present dissolve. This is obvious for instance in Wolpert's (2001) study of what he refers to as diplomacy in classical Greece, where he stresses the discontinuities between antiquity and our current age, but *still* insists on using our current terms to analyze the past. He refers repeatedly to terms like foreign policy and balance of power, and reads the empirics as an assertion of domestic factors over structural forces (and thus contra the realist reading). A more reasonable interpretation, divested of International Relations preconditions, would seem to be that the very concepts Wolpert applies, make very little sense, and that any distinction between what we would call domestic and foreign policy have to be understood in a completely different way in ancient Greece.

Before we move on, we should note that despite the obvious attention Foucault paid to conceptual (or epistemic) change in politics and science, he remained fairly conservative in his usage of terms relating to the international. He referred repeatedly to diplomacy in centuries where the term never existed, never problematized war (contra Bartelson 2018), read balance of power in a standard 20th-century way (contra Little 2007; Andersen 2016) and saw a diplomatic-military technique as central to the emergence of governmentality, two centuries before the concept "diplomacy" was coined.

## The possibilities of inter-governmentality

From the previous section follows that there is a distinct room for a strictly ana-lytical concept which covers relations between what is now often (analytically) referred to as polities. And this is where I suggest that inter-governmentality has a lot to offer. Rather than referring to foreign policy and diplomacy of states and empires in times where no such concepts existed, we can analyze what can be called *regimes of inter-governmentality* in the relations between governmental apparatuses. A starting point for studying such regimes can be Foucault's ([1979] 2000: 312) description of the pastoral dimension of governmentality as "government of individuals by their own verity." In Dean's (1999: 18–19) understanding (cf. also Foucault (2010), regimes of government concern "practices through which we are governed and through which we govern ourselves," and "involve practices for the production of truth and knowledge, comprise multiple forms of practical, technical and calculative rationality, and are subject to programmes for their reform."

It should be stressed though, that what constitutes "we" will necessarily vary across time and place; that the "individuals governed by their own verity" are variable.[5] From the 18th century and onwards, "foreign policy" can for instance be understood as a regime of government concerned with the establishment and perpetuation of distinctions between both inside and outside and state and society, producing the "truth" of foreign policy as a distinct and separate field of policy, to be kept away from popular scru-tiny and control (Leira 2011, 2019). Here, the "we" which is governed and governs itself is probably best understood as civil society, and the individuals as citizens. Conversely, in the work of Justus Lipsius in the late 16th cen-tury, "prudence" can be read as a regime of government concerned with "an understanding and discretion of those things which we ought either to desire or refuse, in publicke, and in privat" (Lipsius [1594] 1970: 11–12). Directed as it was towards those governing, the "we" which is governed and governs itself is the royal we – the sovereign individual (cf. Leira 2008). More gener-ally, sometimes the governmental apparatus which engages in what we will call inter-governmental practices will work on and on behalf of a population, at other instances, particularly before the discovery (or invention) of "popu-lation," it will work on its own behalf or on the behalf of the leader of the apparatus.[6] Even before "population" in a Foucauldian sense was discovered, governmental apparatuses were seeking to govern themselves and others.

A focus on governmental apparatuses has the further benefit of allowing us to overcome the unwarranted (and anachronistic, when applied to pre-modern history) dichotomies between domestic and foreign, and public and private. Death's (2013: 764–765) argument along these lines in favor of applying the analytics of government beyond Europe, are equally applicable to the world before modernity. Death (2013: 768) suggests that a benefit of the analysis of government is that it draws attention to "similarities between power relations that cut across perceived binaries," and this is clearly the case for historical analyses of inter-governmentality as well. However, I would suggest that the opposite also holds, namely that the analytics of government sensitizes us to difference – how seemingly parallel practices at different times might best be understood in light of different regimes of practice. Two key practices of inter-governmentality can serve as general examples. Both "diplomacy" (Der Derian 1987) and "war" (Bartelson 2018) have been constituted through different understandings of the phenomena and different regimes of practice. More specifically, the regimes of practice governing diplomacy changed quite dramatically in the decades around 1815. Until the late 18th century, diplomacy was not an established term, but the multifarious practices feeding into what became diplomacy were associated with the salons, with kinship, with active roles for both men and women and with fleeting hierarchies. After the revolutionary and diplomatic wars, with the establishment of "diplomacy" as a term in its own right and its codification in the treaty of Vienna (1815), and with thoroughgoing changes in how gender and civilization was conceptualized, diplomacy became masculinized, hierarchical and formal. A further advantage of locating governmental apparatuses as the object of study and cutting across the dichotomies is that it allows us to study both horizontal and vertical relations, avoiding the anachronistic presupposition that the only "relevant" relations for International Relations were the ones between the state-like units.[7]

## Analyzing regimes of inter-governmentality

Having established the object of analysis, the next step becomes to specify how to study it. Here, it makes sense to follow Dean's (1999: 27–33) lead in how to analyze regimes of government. He suggests that one should start with "the identification and examination of specific situations in which the activity of governing comes to be called into question, the moments and the situations in which government becomes a problem" (Dean 1999: 27; cf. Foucault [1981] 2007: 141; [1983] 2001: 74). We could follow Foucault and refer to such instances or situations as instances of "problematization"; situations when something becomes articulated as a problem which requires governmental intervention. In modern Western lives, in what we refer to as "domestic" settings (as opposed to international settings), the "activity of government" is very seldom called into question or problematized; the "business of rule" typically persists uninterrupted. In most settings where we would explore inter-governmentality, we would also expect problematizations to be rare. Interaction between different governmental apparatuses is, and has typically been, nonexistent, episodic or continuous. In the case of nonexistent interaction, there are obviously no situations where government becomes a problem. In situations of continuous interaction, government can become a problem at given points, such as declarations of war or peace-negotiations. When interaction is episodic, every encounter has the potential for problematization. Typical situations to look for problematizations would thus be first encounters, episodic interactions and situations where interaction changes.

These situations are not in any way novel to historical scholarship. First encounters, such as between Mongols and those who were in their way and Europeans and inhabitants of the rest of the world, are well known in the literature (Neumann and Wigen 2018; Todorov 1984). And, they typically involved government becoming a problem; more specifically, an acute problem of difference (cf. Inayatullah and Blaney 2004). For how should a governmental apparatus govern itself when facing the unknown? What sort of knowledge would enable what sort of practice?[8] Should the strangers be considered as gods and treated with reverence, as the Aztec governmental apparatus did? Should an established governmental apparatus assume hostility and superiority, as many governmental apparatuses did to their detriment with Mongols on their doorstep?

Episodic interactions were the norm before the rise of resident representation, and in cases of long-distance contact. While often studied for their content in terms of alliance-building and perpetuation of friendship, such episodes also provide ample grounds for studying the perpetuation or modification of regimes of inter-governmentality. Was each encounter treated as a distinct occasion, where knowledge had to be reestablished, or did governmental apparatuses see themselves as engaged in regularized contact with established rituals? Were rituals intended to demonstrate superiority or affirm equality? Scholarship on Medieval Europe suggests that interaction between "princes" was typically seen as regularized as long as both princes were alive. When one of them died, the relationship had to be renegotiated. As to hierarchy, many practices were (perhaps deliberately) ambiguous, allowing both parties to claim at least equality and perhaps also superiority.

Outbreaks of war and their settlements are likewise staple topics of historical analysis, often used as benchmark-dates in international relations. The major peace-conferences are typically treated as system-defining events, even though there is disagreement over which treaties were the most important ones (de Carvalho et al. 2011). In some sense, these disagreements arise from conflicting interpretations of whether and to what extent new knowledge and new ways of governing were laid out in the treaties. Less studied, but potentially equally telling when analyzing how political apparatuses governed themselves according to "their own verity," or tried to challenge that very verity, are the situations where outbreak of war was preceded by war manifestos, detailing how governmental apparatuses understood the world around them, their place in it and the legal ways to act (Hathaway et al. 2018).

As illustrated above, many of the situations when inter-governmentality had the potential to be problematized are not "new" to historical analysis, quite the contrary. Inter-governmentality nevertheless offers new analytics for well-known topics. To take but one example, there has been a long-standing tradition in IR and international law to see the treaties of Westphalia from 1648 as a watershed moment in the establishment of modern states and the modern state system. This view has been thoroughly debunked as empirically unsound. Analytics of inter-governmentality could add to this debunking a conceptual layer, focusing not only on empirical imprecision but also on what sort of regimes of practice existed before and after major peace conferences. Thus, inter-governmentality also opens up for new ways of exploring the government that went on before and after problematizations.

For the more specific analysis of regimes of inter-governmentality, we return to Dean (1999: 29). In his framework for the analysis of government, he suggests analyzing four different but interlocking "regimes of practices," concerning (a) the visibility and spatial dimension of government; (b) the technical dimension of government; (c) the knowledge and practice of government and (d) the identity or identification (subjectification) sought induced through government.

All of these regimes are applicable to pre-modern inter-governmentality. Visibility and spatiality can be of particular importance for approaching relations when there are few or none written sources but are equally important for how they enable later forms of inter-governmentality. Stone reliefs from ancient Egypt depict giraffes being provided as gifts from "Nubia" to Egypt (Laufer 1928), and later monuments and memorials are well-known to show interactions between warring parties (typically ones of triumph) (Neumann 2018). These visualizations have helped establish and perpetuate knowledge of selves and others, as well as the relations between them. Another obviously important way of visualizing and spatializing government is through maps (Branch 2013). They have served different functions across time and space. A typical form of map is the one which places one governmental apparatus at the center, and others along the periphery. Other maps have been more practically oriented towards government, by determining distance and directions. Some maps have defined the boundary between the governable and the ungovernable (typically at sea), while maps associated with treaties, like the one from Tordesillas in 1494, typically have demarcated the authority of different governmental apparatuses. Other forms of visualizing government can be found in the tables of territories, people and cities subordinated to specific governmental apparatuses, much used before modern map-making allowed for clearly defined territories, and in the elaborate family-trees of European noble and royal houses. Other forms of visibility have been less permanent. Ostentatious gifts, such as rare animals, have for instance been used to visualize the status of both gift-giver and gift-recipient, as well as the strength of the ties between them (Leira and Neumann 2017). Engravings, pictures, monuments, maps, tables, family-trees and gifts of splendor are all examples of ways of making inter-governmentality visible.

The technical dimension of governmentality typically concerns the microfoundations of power, where it is applied. For inter-governmentality this will, for instance, imply studying organization. For long periods of time, the most developed organization of inter-governmentality were the armed forces. Technically, one can study how armed forces are organized, and the importance of drill and rituals to their cohesion. One can also study the ways in which envoys were dispatched – if this was patterned or ad hoc, and if there were variations between envoys sent vertically and horizontally.

Knowledge and practice of government are often the hardest to get a grip on in historical research, particularly where there is a dearth of written sources, as one would typically look to treatises and manuals for guidance of how knowledge is turned into practice. In lieu of such sources for inter-governmentality, tables, treaties and correspondence of different kinds might provide important clues. The first contacts discussed above are at a more general level, an example of how knowledge of the world was turned into practice, but also of how practice on the ground in its turn gave rise to new truths. More generally, specialized knowledge of the world beyond one's own governmental apparatus has typically empowered the knowers and enabled their practices of inter-governmentality.

Finally, identification and production of subjectivities can be expressed in a number of ways and brought about through the technologies and knowledges described above. Subjectivities of pre-modern inter-governmentality include, among others, soldiers, envoys, consuls, messengers and traders. For pre-modern inter-governmentality, we should be particularly attuned to identifications at different levels than the one of central authority.

Elaborating a little further on two examples should help make the analytical framework more explicit. They both illustrate how regimes of inter-governmentality can have similar traits across continents and millennia, but at the same time, how seemingly similar regimes contribute to wildly different inter-governmentalities.

The first example concerns kinship. Biological reproduction makes kinship something close to a universal, and ever relevant for international relations (Haugevik and Neumann 2018). In diplomatic interaction, kinship terms and kinship metaphors have been the rule rather than the exception. Even so, kinship has mattered in very different ways across time and space. In the Egyptian New Kingdom (around 1350 BCE), kinship seems to have constituted what we can analyze as an overarching regime of knowledge, making sense of relations between governmental apparatuses (Liverani 2000). In republican Rome, on the other hand, kinship was invoked to establish links to the Hellenized world and as a way of extending favors to allies. Both of these practices are understandable as forms of subjectification – claiming ancestry from Troy and bestowing kinship on others (Battistoni 2009). Yet another variety can be found in renaissance Italy, where kinship among the earliest permanent representatives was quite common. Here, kinship seems to be analyzable along a knowledge-dimension as well as a technical dimension – the established families knew how to perform interaction, and inculcated kin as well as others in these right procedures (Leira 2018: 65–67). Finally, during the 18th century, kinship can be understood as a highly visualized practice of inter-governmentality, with the publication of elaborate genealogical trees and tables. The codification of this visualization took place at the same time as there was a fairly rapid shift in practice, with the inter-governmental regime shifting from vertical relations (cementing ties between liege and lord) to vertical relations (connecting with equals) (Leira 2018: 70–71).

Gift-giving has also been considered as a near-universal feature of human interaction, obviously often connected to kinship. But much as kinship, gift-giving can be analyzed as part of different regimes of government. Here, one single instance might serve. Around 1510, an Indian rhinoceros was gifted from the Sultan of Cambay to Alfonso de Albuquerque, the governor of Portuguese India (Bedini 1997: 125). This can be read as a form of technical practice – establishing patterns of interaction for future trade or cooperation. Albuquerque sent the rhinoceros to Portugal as a gift to King Manuel I, in what we can read as an act of subjection. From there, the rhinoceros was sent as a gift to Pope Leo X. The animal drowned on the way, and only arrived in a taxidermized state. The presentation of this gift can obviously be read as visual practice of inter-governmentality, with the rhino and an elephant, which was gifted the year before, as constant reminders of what the king of Portugal commanded. Indirectly, we can also read this gift-giving not only as an example of splendor, but also as an affirmation of a knowledge-practice; affirming the king of Portugal as the knower of distant lands.

In sum, inter-governmentality has a lot to offer for analyses of historical international relations (Leira and de Carvalho 2015). To the already-mentioned can be added two further benefits. First, as hopefully made clear above, and by being an explicitly analytical concept, inter-governmentality can help make sense of practices which otherwise seem meaningless, and direct attention at overlooked processes. Second, and following from the first point, inter-governmentality can help provide coherence to the relatively sprawling body of literature now referred to as "new diplomatic history."

## Conclusion

Over the preceding pages, I have made the argument that the analytics of inter-governmentality provide a potentially very fruitful approach to historical international relations. Making the argument implied tweaking the original Foucauldian framework, but it proved possible to remain "loyally unfaithful" while doing so. Providing a strictly analytical language for the study of how governmental apparatuses interact has the clear benefit of moving the observer one step away from that which is observed. Ideally, this can provide a sort of *Verfremdungseffekt*, where the past can be approached not simply as prelude. At the same time, through the focus on regimes of inter-governmentality, the analytics can bring out similarities between different times and places.

While the focus here has been on pre-modern history, the proposed framework should also work well for the modern world. The need for analytical distance is generally valid, before the 18th and 19th century conceptual revolution but also for current affairs. The possibility of applying inter-governmentality to vertical relations, which I have hinted at above, should also prove particularly relevant in a day and age with cross-cutting and over-lapping authorities. More specifically, inter-governmentality offers a way of overcoming the methodological nationalism of much IR as well as the statism of a lot of governmentality research. Inter-governmentality, as presented here, suggests a way of studying relations between states and nonstate actors, and between different kinds of nonstate actors operating in the space between and around the states. As such, inter-governmentality provides yet another way of studying what this volume refers to as the globality of governmentality, how government is never only about governing the self (of the state), but also about governing others, or taking part in the totality of government.

## Notes

1 Work on this chapter has been financed by Research Council Norway, under the projects EMPRISE, project number 262657 and CHOIR, project number 288639. Thanks are due to Benjamin de Carvalho for comments on an earlier draft and to the editor for his patience and his incisive comments.
2 It is necessary at once to distinguish the notion of "inter-governmentality" from the Foucauldian take on sovereignty. Whereas the latter is concerned with the free play of sovereign wills the former is intended to capture whatever conduct of conduct we can find in the relations between governmental apparatuses.
3 The mirror of princes was a genre of medieval writing, which primarily consisted of advice to rulers on what to do and what to avoid.
4 Which is also why it has been possible for political realism to claim a writer like Thucydides as a forerunner of a realist tradition. A recent, and very pertinent, example, can be found in the claim, made by Graham Allison (2017), that the US and China are in a "Thucydides trap," where conflict between a rising power and an established power is almost inevitable. For this analogy to work, all historical and contemporary nuance has to be eradicated. The past becomes merely a stage-prop for the present.
5 And, obviously, the very notions of individuals, individuality, and individualism have long genealogies of their own. Our modern conceptions are not likely to have made sense in pre-modern settings.
6 As Bruce Curtis (2002) has argued, "population" in Foucault's accounts is an ambiguous concept covering more than one phenomenon, and possibly wrongly dating the emergence of liberal governmentality. Compare also Mitchell Dean's (1999: 94–95) distinction between pre- and post-Malthusian conceptions of population.
7 The concept of "polity" in principle also allows for studying both anarchical and hierarchical relations, but in practice it is often used as a mere substitute for state-like entities.
8 There is an obvious parallel here to how governmental apparatuses tried (and some-times failed) to govern themselves when facing domestic unknowns after the dis-covery of "population," for example, in the case of nomadic people and indigenous people.

# References

Allison, Graham (2017) *Destined for War: Can America and China Escape Thucydides's Trap* (Boston: Houghton Mifflin Harcourt).

Andersen, Morten Skumsrud (2016) *A Genealogy of the Balance of Power*. PhD thesis (London: The London School of Economics and Political Science).

Bartelson, Jens (1995) *A Genealogy of Sovereignty* (Cambridge: Cambridge University Press).

Bartelson, Jens (2018) *War in International Thought* (Cambridge: Cambridge University Press).

Battistoni, Filippo (2009) 'Rome, Kinship and Dipomacy' in Claude Eilers (ed) *Diplomats and Diplomacy in the Roman World* (Leiden: Brill), 73–97.

Bedini, Silvio A (1997) *The Pope's Elephant* (Manchester: Carcanet).

Berridge, G. R., Keens-Soper, M. and Otte, T. (2001) *Diplomatic Theory from Machiavelli to Kissinger* (Houndmills, Basingstoke: Palgrave Macmillan).

Bigo, Didier (2017) 'Michel Foucault and International Relations: Cannibal Relations' in Philippe Bonditti, Didier Bigo and Frédéric Gros (eds) *Foucault and the Modern International: Silences and Legacies for the Study of World Politics* (New York: Palgrave Macmillan), 33-55.

Branch, Jordan (2013) *The Cartographic State: Maps, Territory, and the Origins of Sovereignty* (Cambridge: Cambridge University Press).

Brubaker, Rogers, and Frederick Cooper (2000) "'Beyond 'Identity'", *Theory and Society* 29:1, 1-47.

Bull, Hedley (1977) *The Anarchical Society: A Study of Order in World Politics* (Houndmills: Macmillan).

Busse, Jan (2018) *Deconstructing the Dynamics of World-Societal Order: The Power of Governmentality in Palestine* (London: Routledge).

Campbell, David (1998) *Writing Security: United States Foreign Policy and Politics of Identity,* 2nd ed (Minneapolis, MN: University of Minnesota Press).

Chatterjee, Indrani (2013) 'Monastic Governmentality, Colonial Misogyny, and Postcolonial Amnesia in South Asia', *History of the Present* 3:1, 57–98.

Chittick, William O. and Annette Freyberg-Inan (2001) ''Chiefly for Fear, Next for Honour, and Lastly for Profit': An Analysis of Foreign Policy Motivation in the Peloponnesian War', *Review of International Studies* 27:1, 69–90.

Cohen, Raymond and Raymond Westbrook (eds) (2000) *Amarna Diplomacy: The Beginnings of International Relations* (Baltimore: Johns Hopkins University Press).

Corbridge, Stuart, Glyn Williams, Manoj Srivastava and Réne Véron (2005) *Seeing the State. Governance and Governmentality in India* (Cambridge: Cambridge University Press).

Curtis, Bruce (2002) 'Foucault on Governmentality and Population: The Impossible Discovery', *Canadian Journal of Sociology* 27:4, 505–533.

de Carvalho, Benjamin (2016) 'The Making of the Political Subject: Subjects and Territory in the Formation of the State', *Theory and Society* 45:1, 57–88.

de Carvalho, Benjamin, Halvard Leira and John Hobson (2011) 'The Big Bangs of IR: The Myths that Your Teachers Still Tell You about 1648 and 1919', *Millennium* 39:3, 735–758.

Der Derian, James (1987) *On Diplomacy: A Genealogy of Western Estrangement* (Oxford: Blackwell).

Dean, Mitchell (1999) *Governmentality. Power and Rule in Modern Society* (London: Sage).

Dean, Mitchell (2017) 'Power as Sumblon: Sovereignty, Governmentality and the International' in Philippe Bonditti, Didier Bigo and Frédéric Gros (eds) *Foucault and the Modern International: Silences and Legacies for the Study of World Politics* (New York: Palgrave Macmillan), 97–114.

Death, Carl (2013) 'Governmentality at the Limits of the International: African Politics and Foucauldian Theory', *Review of International Studies* 39:3, 763–787.

Devetak, Richard (2008) 'Foucault, Discipline and *Raison d'État* in Early Modern Europe', *International Political Sociology* 2:3, 270–272.

Elden, Stuart (2007): "Governmentality, Calculation, Territory." *Environment and Planning D: Society and Space* 25 (3), 562–580.

Ferguson, Yale and Richard Mansbach (1996) *Polities. Authority, Identities, and Change.* (Columbia: University of South Carolina Press).

Foucault, Michel ([1979] 2000) 'Omnes ct Singulatim' in James D Faubion (ed) *Power. Essential Works of Foucault. Vol. 3* (New York: The New Press), 298–325.

Foucault, Michel ([1981] 2007) 'What Our Present Is' in Sylvère Lothringer (ed) *The Politics of Truth* (Los Angeles, CA: Semiotext(e)), 129–143.

Foucault, Michel ([1983] 2001) *Fearless Speech* (ed. Joseph Pearson) (Los Angeles, CA: Semiotext(e)).

Foucault, Michel (2007) *Security, Territory, Population. Lectures at the Collège de France 1977–1978* (Houndmills: Palgrave).

Foucault, Michel (2008) *The Birth of Biopolitics. Lectures at the Collège de France 1978–1979* (Houndmills: Palgrave).

Foucault, Michel (2010) *The Government of Self and Others: Lectures at the Collège de France, 1982-1983* (Houndmills: Palgrave).

Hathaway, Oona A, William S Holste, Scott J Shapiro, Jaqueline Van de Velde and Lisa Wang Lachowicz (2018) 'War Manifestos', *The University of Chicago Law Review* 85:5, 1139-1225.

Haugevik, Kristin and Iver B Neumann (eds) (2018) *Kinship in International Relations* (Milton Park: Routledge).

Hoffmeier, J K (2004) 'Aspects of Egyptian Foreign Policy in the 18th Dynasty in Western Asia and Nubia' in Gary N Knoppers and Antoine Hirsch (eds) *Egypt, Israel, and the Ancient Mediterranean World: Studies in Honor of Donald B. Redford* (Leiden: Brill), 121–141.

Inayatullah, Naeem and David L Blaney (2004) *International Relations and the Problem of Difference* (London: Routledge).

Jobe, Kevin Scott (2015) 'Foucault and Ancient *polizei*: A Genealogy of the Military Pastorate', *Journal of Political Power* 8:1, 21–37.

Jordheim, Helge and Iver B. Neumann (2011) 'Empire, Imperialism and Conceptual History', *Journal of International Relations and Development* 14:2, 153–185.

Joseph, Jonathan (2010) 'The Limits of Governmentality: Social Theory and the International', *European Journal of International Relations* 16:2, 223–246.

Kendall, G. and Wickham G. (1999) 'Lessons from an Old Millennium: Law and Regulation in the Ancient City' in M. Collis, L. Munro, and S. Russell (eds) *Sociology for a New Millennium: Challenges and Prospects* (Melbourne: Monash University Press), 399–406.

Kiersey, Nicholas J. and Doug Stokes (eds) (2011) *Foucault and International Relations. New Crtitical Engagements* (Milton Park: Routledge).

Koselleck, Reinhart (1985) *Futures Past: On the Semantics of Historical Time* (New York: Columbia University Press).

Larner, Wendy and William Walter (eds) (2004) *Global Governmentality: Governing International Spaces* (Milton Park: Routledge).

Laufer, Berthold (1928) *The Giraffe in History and Art* (Chicago: Field Museum of Natural History).

Lee, Chulwoo (2012) 'How Can You Say You're Korean? Law, Governmentality and National Membership in South Korea', *Citizenship Studies* 16:1, 85–102.

Leira, Halvard (2008) 'Justus Lipsius, Neostoicism and the Disciplining of 17th Century Statecraft', *Review of International Studies* 34:4, 669–692.

Leira, Halvard (2009) 'Taking Foucault Beyond Foucault: Inter-State Governmentality in Early Modern Europe', *Global Society* 23:4, 475–495.

Leira, Halvard (2011) *The Emergence of Foreign Policy: Knowledge, Discourse, History.* PhD thesis, (Oslo: University of Oslo).

Leira, Halvard (2016) 'A Conceptual History of Diplomacy', in Costas M. Constantinou, Pauline Kerr and Paul Sharp (eds) *SAGE Handbook of Diplomacy* (London: Sage), 28–38.

Leira, Halvard (2018) 'Kinship Diplomacy, or Diplomats of a Kin' in Kristin Haugevik and Iver B. Neumann (eds) *Kinship in International Relations* (Milton Park: Routledge), 62–80.

Leira, Halvard (2019) 'The Emergence of Foreign Policy', *International Studies Quarterly* 63:1, 187–198.

Leira, Halvard and Benjamin de Carvalho (eds) (2015) *Historical International Relations* (London: Sage).

Leira, Halvard and Iver B. Neumann (2017) 'Beastly Diplomacy', *The Hague Journal of Diplomacy* 12:4, 337–359.

Lipsius, Justus ([1594] 1970) *Six Bookes of Politickes or Civil Doctrine*, done into English by William Jones. (London: R. Field, facsimile reprint) (Amsterdam: Da Capo Press).

Little, Richard (2007) *The Balance of Power in International Relations. Metaphors, Myths and Models* (Cambridge: Cambridge University Press).

Liverani, Mario (2000) 'The Great Power's Club' in Raymond Cohen and Raymond Westbrook (eds) *Amarna Diplomacy: The Beginnings of International Relations* (Baltimore: Johns Hopkins University Press), 15–27.

Neumann, Iver B (2018) 'Halting Time: Monuments to Alterity', *Millennium* 46:3, 331–351.

Neumann, Iver B and Ole Jacob Sending (2010) *Governing the Global Polity: World Politics as Governmentality* (Ann Arbor: University of Michigan Press).

Neumann, Iver B and Einar Wigen (2018) *The Steppe Tradition in International Relations. Russians, Turks and European State Building 4000 BCE–2017 CE.* (Cambridge: Cambridge University Press).

Onuf, Nicholas (2017) 'The Figure of Foucault and the Field of International Relations' in Philippe Bonditti, Didier Bigo and Frédéric Gros (eds) *Foucault and the Modern International: Silences and Legacies for the Study of World Politics* (New York: Palgrave Macmillan), 15–31.

Palonen, Kari (2006) *The Struggle with Time: A Conceptual History of 'Politics' as an Activity.* (Hamburg: LIT Verlag).

Selby, Jan (2007) 'Engaging Foucault: Discourse, Liberal Governance and the Limits of Foucauldian IR', *International Relations* 21:3, 324–345.

Senellart, Michel (2007) 'Course Context' in Michel Foucault, *Security, Territory, Population. Lectures at the Collège de France 1977–1978* (Houndmills: Palgrave), 369–401.

Sheptycki, James (1999) 'European Policing Routes: An Essay on Transnationalization, Policing and the Information Revolution' in H. Bruisma and J.G.A. van der Vijver (eds) *Public Safety in Europe* (Twente: Twente Police Institute), 221–242.

Todorov, Tzvetan (1984) *The Conquest of America: The Question of the Other* (New York: Harper and Row).

Valverde, Mariana (2007) 'Genealogies of European States: Foucauldian Reflections', *Economy and Society* 35:1, 159–178.

Wolpert, Andrew (2001) 'The Genealogy of Diplomacy in Classical Greece', *Diplomacy and Statecraft* 12:1, 71–88.

# 5 Sovereignty and sovereign powers in global governmentality

*Mitchell Dean and Oscar L. Larsson*

## Introduction

The adoption of governmentality as a theoretical and methodological approach in the discipline of International Relations (IR) has been relatively recent and surprisingly narrow in its application (Bonditti 2017). It has been argued that present governmentality analyses of IR often maintains a narrow focus on how security and liberalism cooperate within the international system of sovereign states (De Larrinaga and Doucet 2010). Few scholars have actually addressed global phenomena or globality, with one early and notable exception (Larner and Walters 2004). This current volume seeks to advance a new research agenda by combining globality, or global "oneness," with the analytical framework of governmentality (Busse and Hamilton's introduction to this volume). The volume thus follows Jens Bartelson's conceptualization of globality to "describe a condition characterized by the presence of a single socio-political space on a planetary scale" (Bartelson 2010: 219). Yet, Busse and Hamilton are quick to point out that this also includes multiple, and at times competing visions of globality across time and space, following Van Munster and Sylvest (2016: 3). Globality may therefore be represented in multiple and contested forms, in multiple oneness, "reflected in a range of ideas and practices," (ibid.: 1) including global maps and iconography and the identification of planetary problems related to security, ecology and the continuation of the human race.

Governmentality would seem to be a perfect match to this objective, given that its study is often depicted as "going beyond" sovereignty and the judicial–political approach to politics and power relations within the state. In this way, scholars hope to be able to analyze and explain global governance and global orders in the absence of a single power center, or a global sovereign, a common and enforced legal framework and a manifest monopoly of violence. Governmentality studies could thereby offer a heuristic framework and line of inquiry that combines rationalities, technologies and subjectivities into global regimes and assemblages of power (Zanotti 2013; Walters 2012; Neumann and Sending 2007; Sending and Neumann 2006).

The attractiveness of governmentality as a way to understand global governance and order in the absence of a binding legal framework is understandable but potentially problematic. The governmentality approach was designed to help us understand the presence and functions of various forms of power in relation that fall outside the political–judicial understanding of state-citizens relations (Schiavo 2015; Fournier 2008). Whereas sovereign power often is used as a benchmark to understand alternative ways in which the state and assemblages of actors govern within states, the space outside states and the global scale is often characterized as "anarchical space." Anarchy, or without "arche," can mean without order or rule, but more profoundly without foundations or first principles (Agamben 2011). Yet, in his development of governmentality, Foucault developed a genealogy of governmentality starting from the technologies of the self in Greek and Roman classical civilizations through the history of Christian pastoral guidance. He noticed and discussed a specific rationality of a modern liberal government which is "self-limiting" but nonetheless enables and secures ways of governing society while accepting biological life as both the target and the purpose of governing. Governmentality was developed as an analytical framework to grasp both the presence and the limitations of biopower, understood in terms of securing and governing biological life. It is in relation to biopower in combination with the liberal version of the state, that governmentality becomes both possible and intriguing, as it combines the apparent antinomies of, on the one hand, the imperative to optimize life, and on the other, the liberal anxiety of governing too much. The innovation of neoliberal forms of governmentality will be that they seek to produce and construct human economic activity rather merely secure it.

The displacement of sovereignty is emphasized by Foucault's now canonical definition, "by governmentality I understand the tendency, the line of force, that for a long time, and throughout the West, has constantly led towards the pre-eminence over all other types of power – sovereignty, discipline, and so on [...]" (Foucault 2007: 108). "We [even] live in an era of a governmentality discovered in the eighteenth century" (ibid.: 109). In both liberal and neoliberal governmental approaches, the "conduct of conduct" works through the liberty of subjects. Yet, while Foucault's narrative displaces or substantially downplays sovereignty as new modes of government are said to emerge, all of this takes place in the territorial state in which juridical–political institutions form central parts of the ensemble of governing institutions.

In this chapter, we argue firstly that the analytical and methodological approach of governmentality, especially when transferred and applied to the global scale runs the risk of displacing sovereignty and sovereign powers as merely remnants of the old world order no longer carrying any analytical purchase. Yet, it is precisely at the time when the Leviathan feels threatened that it prepares to fight and the principle of sovereignty reemerges with even more ferocity – as we witness in the responses to the Covid-19 pandemic which began in early 2020. Thus, in response to global challenges and the image of a finite globe, it seems rather to be the case that sovereignty and sovereign powers reemerge from their slumber as states and world leaders seek to take back control as a way to deal with issues in the Anthropocene that have global reach and impact such as globalization, global flows, immigration, development, energy and food policies, terrorism and human rights (Nisancioglu 2019; Latour 2018; Brown 2017), and now, of course, pandemics. As we have witnessed in the face of the Covid-19 pandemic, it is no longer a matter of simply governing populations but of assigning populations to sovereign states and to their health systems.

It is no surprise that governmentality and how to best make use of this approach is a much debated issue in IR. As Laura Zanotti (2013) notes, governmentality has been used in two separate ways in IR scholarship. She distinguishes between governmentality as a "heuristic tool to explore modalities of local and international government and to assess their effects in the contexts where they are deployed [...] [and as] a descriptive tool to theorize the globally oppressive features of international liberalism" (Zanotti 2013: 289). Governmentality as a heuristic tool potentially enables the researcher to perform complex diagnostics of events by including "historically situated explorations and careful differentiations" (Zanotti 2013: 300). It enables "theoretical formulations that conceive the subject in non-substantialist terms and focus on processes of subjectification, on the ambiguity of power discourses, and on hybridization as the terrain for political transformation, open ways for reconsidering political agency [...]" (ibid., 300). This is indeed a promising research agenda but still it is substantially indebted to Foucault's way of conceiving various forms of powers and not least the tendency to essentialize and prioritize new forms of power while treating old forms, such as sovereign powers with only a cursory interest. At the least, researchers need to be open to complex and highly interconnected power relations including the interplay between state and nonstate actors and domestic and international issues (Guerra-Barón 2017), divisions that still owe their logic to the principle of sovereignty, territory and sovereign powers.

But the analytical approach is not the only way governmentality could be understood. It could also be understood as the history of the art of government, or in Foucault's term the "governmentalization of state" (Foucault 2007: 109). The relationship is then reversed and the state itself becomes subject to the tactics of government – a dynamic form and historical stabilization of societal relations (Lemke 2002: 58). We argue secondly, that this narrative of governmentality has fundamental shortcomings.

Initially, Foucault reminded his audience of the importance and continuation of sovereignty as new modes of governmental practices unfold:

> [...] we should not see things as the replacement of a society of discipline by a society, say of government. In fact, we have a triangle: sovereignty,

discipline, and governmental management, which has population as its main target and apparatuses of security as its essential mechanism.

(Foucault 2007: 107f)

This triangularity of powers is however often forgotten. Yet, it is important to remember that the objects of the different modes of power are different. For Foucault, the aim of sovereignty is to hold onto or extend the power of the prince and the territorial space of the state, discipline focuses on the individual body, and governmentality takes aim at the population in general (Lemke 2019: 192). As noted by Fournier (2008) sovereignty must then be seen as a facilitator and historical necessity for ongoing modes of subjection inside the state that forms the basis for new modes of governance but also forms a backdrop for exceptional measures to be enacted when internal liberal order and security are threatened (Fournier 2008; see also Rådestad and Larsson 2018). Considered in this way, "[sovereignty] is at once ontologically prior to power relations because it establishes territorial units in which the latter relations become possible, and is manifest in the disciplinary and securitizing objectives of government" (Fournier 2008: 58). They key point is that sovereignty is not simply one among other forms of power but the condition for those relatively pacified spaces in states within which other forms of power operated.

Foucault's specific understanding of the historical trajectory of the sovereign state has been criticized for leading to a binary and mutually exclusive understanding between sovereign power relations on the one hand, and other relations of power on the other (Valverde 2011). Such a reading may lead to an exaggeration of the pace and influence of nonsovereign relations of power and the displacement of the presence of sovereign powers inside and outside the state. Foucault's approach and ways of theorizing contribute to the establishment of a central antinomy by which sovereignty and law stand on one side and the new forms of powers stand on the other (Dean 2013). The cost of this is that by excluding, rejecting, or abjecting that which is old, archaic and historically outmoded, or claims of transcendence, we tend to essentialize forms of power as *the* new, *the* contemporary, *the* field of immanence etc. Moreover, it is thus not a crisis within sovereignty and ethical problems associated with the transcendent claims to absolutism that leads to the problematizations of sovereignty as an omnipotent and omniscient form of power but the new logic of liberal government. The problem here, as we see it, is one of an indistinction between Foucault's historical narrative and liberalism's self-description as a critique of state reason, which is doubled by his claims to a suspension of normativity. On the one hand, Foucault dissolves the possibilities of democratic–republican and revolutionary eschatology – he would announce the end of the revolution (Dean and Zamora 2021). On the other hand, he renders contemporary neoliberal governmentality as the *telos* of a process of the "becoming immanent" of forms of power so that governmentality will increasingly become concerned with governing through the rationality of the governed themselves and the self-governing capacities of the governed.

This reading stems foremost from a caricature of Thomas Hobbes's image of the Leviathan that indeed places a heart inside the state and thus brings the state to life. Originally, a biblical sea monster contrasted with the land monster, Behemoth, in Hobbes's writing Leviathan appears as monster, machine or as an artificial person with a spring as its heart, where its "artificial" joints are laws, civil harmony is its health, "and the wealth and riches of all the members of the commonwealth are its strength" (Hobbes 1994: 84). Foucault and his followers reject the juridical–political theory of sovereignty precisely because they connect sovereignty to the image of a living monster which serves as an oppressive and dominant form of power stemming from a single center without any checks and balances. "The state has no heart, as we well know, but not just in the sense that it has no feelings, either good or bad, but it has no heart in the sense that it has no interior" (Foucault 2008: 90). The antipathy towards state sovereignty and the decentering of sovereign power have given way to a reductionist and moralizing view of sovereign power that hampers our understanding of the continued transformation of the power constellations present in today's society and where the governmentality analyses are drawn to ward its liberal and neoliberal variants. According to Lemke, the thesis provided by Foucault held that a juridical conception of power was historically tied to feudal-absolutist society and absolute monarchy. However, this does not allow that, during the 19th and 20th centuries, sovereign power was substantially transformed as it was transferred, sometimes due to fierce and swift revolution and sometimes as long reform processes, from monarchs to popular institutions. Monarchs remain in the world today, in some instances as actual rulers but in other instances as figures within a constitutional monarchy. But as the latter example underlines, many modern democracies have not been able to do away with the ceremonies and symbolics of sovereign power. The democratization of sovereign power and popular control is a massively underexplored theme in Foucault's writings and the literature on governmentality.

Obviously, this makes the triangle between sovereignty, discipline and government power all the more intricate to the extent that an emerging security society does not necessarily represent a radical break with previous forms of societies, nor is it simply a matter of adding new technologies of power to the former. Rather:

> modification occurs affecting power mechanisms and their relations to each other. Instead of making them superfluous, the government problematic intensifies questions concerning the conditions of sovereignty and drives discipline forward [...] governing the population demands detailed comprehensive and fundamental leadership; this makes discipline more

necessary than ever, inasmuch as the supposed to function as the counterpart, and completion, of newly won liberties.

(Lemke 2019: 196)

While we generally agree with these formulations, they leave one problem open: the specificity of sovereignty itself as a form of power that claims supremacy within its own domain. It is not simply a matter of rebalancing the books between different forms of power but of recognizing the historical achievement of a kind of power that claims transcendence over all other forms of power and is central to the innovation of the modern territorial state and the state system. In this sense, the geometrical figure of a triangle may be limiting our imagination and analyses in that it assumes an equivalence of different forms of power. It is our contention that sovereign power tends to be viewed in purely negative terms and its full capacity as a power that harbors other forms of power within the power-triangle misrepresented. Thus, as we move our focus from the domestic to the international realm, sovereign power and the institutions and interactions that follow from sovereignty as an organizational principle runs the risk of being misunderstood and diminished in the analysis.

### The attractiveness and dangers of an empty concept

Foucault's concept and analytical model of governmentality enjoys a significant and growing importance in social analysis. For most part, this approach shows substantial analytical advantage if one aims to understand contemporary forms of governance that take place in advanced liberal societies. Governmentality gives us the instruments to understand the presence of multiple forms of power in liberal societies. If we follow Lemke's and Dean's advice to not fixate upon the triangle of power and their technologies, it opens up for a dynamic analysis of moving and transformative concepts and powers (nonreductive analysis of sovereignty), we would be able to build upon the framework of governmentality rather than assume and adopt it as a specific spatiotemporal phenomenon emerging in Europe in the 17th century. Is it then possible to relax the framework of governmentality to also make it applicable to the realm outside the territorial state?

Governmentality could also be used as a methodology or a "heuristic device" (Zanotti 2013) that admits nothing more than a "will to govern" and that this activity is rational to the extent that it is informed by discourses and knowledges. These may be faulty and therefore misguiding but they are still productive as they inform governors on how to craft their instruments and strategies (Bacchi and Goodwin 2016). Accordingly, governmentality as an analytical grid is not limited to any of its liberal versions and does not necessarily oppose sovereignty as a specific form of power. It is an analytical approach to all forms of governance. It follows that governmentality does not necessarily preclude any form or any scale of governance (Walters 2012;

Neumann and Sending 2007). Governmentality simply brings together the practice (and will) of governing and the discourses and knowledge claims as well as normative motivations that render such an activity meaningful and purposeful (Bacchi and Goodwin 2016; Dean 2010). But, it is here we run into problems and mistranslations of governmentality as it is "scaled-up" or applied to the global level (Selby 2007).

When we apply and utilize the framework and insights generated by the governmentality approach, even in its minimalistic and heuristic version, it is important to note the quite different meaning that the various elements will have outside the state. We are certainly not the first to raise concerns on the theoretical shifts that arise as we shift the object of study. Jan Selby argues that the governmentality debate in IR runs the risk of essentializing the notion of anarchy provided by the realist notions of sovereignty and state interests as core elements of the relations between body politics (Selby 2007; see also Bartelson 2014: 59). This contributes to the risk that governmentality, when applied to the international realm is turned into a normative and progressive tradition, promoting a new world order by replacing traditional images of sovereignty with new understandings of global biopolitics and liberal governance acting on independent subjects. According to Selby (2007: 326), there is "an ontological specificity and irreducibility to the international, which poses distinctive analytical problems and demands distinctive theoretical tools." We agree with Selby and add to his criticism by discussing in the following sections the analogies of liberal governing, the presence of population and the wide plethora of nonbiological actors that populates the international space.

As noted in the previous section, Foucault innovatively explored alternatives to a judicial and negative power of restriction and punishment as he found that liberal states substantially engaged in a management and catering of the wellbeing of its populations. The presented "shift," from sovereignty to biopower is a theoretical one based on a problematic reading of the history of European states and a lack of their double standards for coping with the inside/outside of their sovereign status (Dillon and Neal 2011: 2; Hindess 2004). We are therefore torn between understanding governmentality as an emerging analytical and methodological approach to IR and the globe, or as an omitted piece of history that accompanies the temporal–historical analysis of European states and the production of liberal modes of governance. It becomes problematic to adopt a concept in merely "heuristic" fashion if it is to be completely detached from its roots and branches (see Leira in this volume).

Sending and Neumann argue that "studying global governance through the lens of "governmentality" enables us to study how different governmental rationalities are defined by certain rules, practices and techniques and how such rationalities of rule generate specific action-orientations and types of actors" (2006: 668). They rely on a broader conceptualization of governmentality and see it as "a power that works to structure the possible field of action of others" (ibid.: 668). Yet in another article, the authors makes strong connections between governmentality and the liberal rationality of governance, which in fact indicates a shift from governance to governmentality:

> If the international realm is thickening due to the institutionalisation of liberal norms about human rights norms, market economy, democracy and the rule of law, then there seems to be a good case for subjecting the preconditions for the emergence of these norms to a governmental reading.
>
> (Neumann and Sending 2007: 694)

It is, accordingly, "precisely here that the governmental concept of power is useful for an analysis of the international" (ibid.: 694). This however presupposes a governor, or set of governors, the ability to communicate and share specific understandings, but more importantly, to perform a conduct of conduct. The liberal bias may thus create a certain blindness to alternative power relations, not least to the presence of sovereignty and sovereign powers and their transformation and adaptability to liberal norms and liberal discourses (Walker 2010: 11; see also Bartelson 2014; Dean 2013). What governmentality analysis in this form does is to reproduce a liberal imaginary of the current international domain, rather than one that allows us a critical or analytical distance.

However, if we accept this broader application of governmentality, understood as a power that structures the field of others without necessarily being liberal or neoliberal (Walters 2012: 111), it becomes an open and empirical question which images and understandings of the sovereign state shape and condition global governance. A serious disruption of a single global space and thus the emergence of global governmentalities entails "the idioms of territory and sovereignty [that] remain central to our understanding of dilemmas in international affairs, such as human intervention and mass refugee flows" (Lui 2004: 118). Despite globalization and mobility that lend themselves to images of waning states, many scholars call out for attention to geopolitical tendencies, the resurrection of the sovereign state, restricted and controlled mobilities and a geocoded world in which territory plays a decisive role (Latour 2018; Brown 2017; Guzzini 2012; Rose-Redwood 2006). Since the underlying governmental practices ultimately reside on non-sovereign and alternative ways to govern through subtle methods that are not hierarchical, judicial or sovereign while adhering to the notion of free or autonomous subjects, global governmentality seems to enter into a normative indistinction with the working of liberal government. Yet, this analytical bias presupposes liberal norms and values as universalistic and runs the risk of *producing* the foundation for a liberal global governmentality as a result (Selby 2007: 334). Rather, we argue that researchers must be prepared to include the presence of sovereignty and sovereign powers as a constitutive element of the international and global realm, either as a key building block of how things are governed or as the substrate of resistance to any rationality that has omitted it from its calculations (Joseph 2010).

## The co-constitutive inside/outside

According to Hans-Martin Jaeger, the international sphere was pivotal to the emergence of the mid-20th century neoliberal governmentality. Still, Foucault often left out colonial and imperial strategies for dealing with "other" states for which proper market relations could not (yet) be erected. This provides a problematic historical and present understanding of both national and international neoliberal governmentality (Jaeger 2013). Barry Hindess (2004) clearly made the case that liberalism as an art of government has a long history of "double standards" in the international realm. Accordingly, while strong European states cherished the Westphalian Treaty and non-interference in domestic affairs of equal states that was oriented towards liberalism, they simultaneously were involved in imperial projects also devoted to the management and control of populations. Accordingly, "[...] it is hardly possible to understand the way in which liberals have actively participated in the government of both of free peoples and of various subject populations unless we acknowledge the significance they have attached to this latter task" (Hindess 2004: 33). And as Selby points out, the scaling-up and making analogies in Foucault's model of power from the domestic to the international sphere is premised on, but more importantly, productive of, a paradigmatically liberal internationalist understanding of world order (Selby 2007: 334). This becomes further noticeable as we reflect on the conditions for a global biopolitical governance and how to account for the core premises of governmentality that further support liberalism as modus operandi, giving way for a governmentality as the conduct of conduct operating on human beings. However, in the international sphere, it is difficult to account for whom is acting on whom and what the foundation for governing is if one ignores the problematics of sovereignty.

## Population(s) and civil society in the international realm

The genealogy of governmentality including the governmentalization of the state provides an alternative historical account of the governance of the state beyond the monarchies and their business. Rather, it is a history of administration, orchestration, production and reproduction of populations and life that shows that the promotion of life counters the model of sovereign power as the right to kill (Foucault 2004: 247). Governmentality, in this version, includes the notion of population *and* civil society as key building blocks for liberal governance to emerge. The question is to what extent these elements are present in advanced analyses of global governmentality.

Michael Hardt and Antonio Negri (2000) suggest in their book *Empire*, that the modern international order was premised on the presence of sovereign states that enabled an imperialist order of hierarchy between "equals" and the conquest of territory as the sign of utter defeat and submission. This order has now been replaced by a decentralized structure where territory no longer fills a key functionality in global governance – "Empire." Empire should be understood as a "globalized bio-political machine" (Hardt and Negri 2000: 40) in which the "economic production and political constitution tend increasingly to coincide" (ibid.: 41). The authors scale-up the notion of biopolitics to the international arena in which "interventions" emerge as a new practice. Such interventions include unbounded terrain of activities, the singularization and symbolic localization, including the repressive actions taken to secure the biopolitical structure sustaining the new global society (ibid.: 35). Dillon and Reid (2001) also explore the possibilities of biopolitics in the international sphere. Global liberal governance is in fact a form of global biopolitics. Whereas a traditional liberal internationalism worked through contracted relations of sovereigns there is a further development in global liberal governance:

> where liberal internationalism once aspired to some ideal of world government, today global liberal governance pursues the administration of life and the management of populations through the deployment of biopolitical techniques of power.
>
> (Dillon and Reid 2001: 46)

Yet, Dillon and Reid acknowledge that global governance is directed towards a multiple rather than single global population. In fact, they still consider global biopolitical techniques as complements to geopolitics, sovereign states, and the continuation of friend/enemy dichotomies as identified by Carl Schmitt (Dillon and Reid 2001).

Dillon suggests elsewhere that global liberal governance is a Foucauldian system of power/knowledge that depends upon the strategic orchestration of the self-regulating freedoms of populations (Dillon 2003). Again, we see the tendency to place liberal governmentality first, and the rediscovery of sovereign territories and the separation of populations as utterly dependent on the principle and functions of sovereign states. However, on a global scale it is reasonable to assume that the diversity among states and their varying commitment to a liberal world, including human rights and responsibility to protect, would generate quite diverse practices. The European Union may in fact stand out as a "zone" that has experienced not global but transnational governance of the populations of diverse member states (Walters 2004). This latter example further strengthens the idea that liberal governmentality across borders is not equally valid across the globe. Rather, it appears most visible in the European region that helped Foucault develop a specific theoretical but spatiotemporal governmentality. It is indeed possible to discern a substantial Eurocentrism (Amin and Moore 1989) with universalizing tendencies which is ignorant of international liberal double standards, including colonial and postcolonial practices as well as heterogonous power relations that exist in the international sphere and between sovereign entities (Nisancioglu 2019).

Not everything in the international realm can be reduced to the continuation of territory and agency and relations between sovereign states. There are other actors populating the international realm, such as not only international organizations, companies and NGOs, but also individuals who act on the global stage. This is sometimes referred to as a Global Civil Society (GCS) (Lipschutz 2004). The concept and connotations are of course analogous to the concept, its qualities and functions of a space existent within liberal states. The notion of civil society is understood in contemporary liberal discourse as constituting a space for individual and group autonomy that is characterized by freedom from interference and intrusion by the state (Akman 2012: 322). This positive image of civil society as a counterforce to the sovereign state is particularly visible in the writings of Ernest Gellner, who defines civil society as:

> that set of diverse non-governmental institutions which is strong enough to counterbalance the state and, while not preventing the state from fulfilling its role of keeper of the peace and arbitrator between major interests, can nevertheless prevent it from dominating and atomizing the rest of society.
>
> (Gellner 1994: 5)

Foucault viewed civil society as a primary element of liberal governmentality:

> Civil society, is, I believe, a concept of governmental technology, or rather, it is the correlate of a technology of government the rational measure of which must be juridically pegged to an economy understood as the process of production and exchange [...]. *Homo economicus* and civil society are therefore two inseparable elements.
>
> (Foucault 2008: 296)

Proponents of a global civil society provide arguments that such a space does in fact exist and they are willing to treat it as a unitary actor and ontological but emergent entity. Ronnie D. Lipschutz maintains that "emergent forms of global governance constitute a state-like political framework that generates global civil society" (Lipschutz 2004: 246). He finds support for such a view for a global civil society being linked primarily to the market rather than the state, and since the rise of global political economy is prevalent, a global civil society is a function and counterforce to global economic structures. Other scholars make similar functionalistic claims suggesting that new communication technology along with increased globalization "have forced the public sphere to acquire a more complex and transboundary nature" (Feenstra 2017).

However, the idea of a global civil society further encourages governmentality scholars to maintain the analogy between the domestic and international sphere. Thus, questioning the conception and presence of a GCS enables us to identify a more complex image of the international realm without presupposing functionality or functions in neoliberal economic structures or biopolitical governmentality regimes (Higgins and Larner 2017). Indeed, suggesting that assemblages of actors constitute a global civil society further strengthens the tendency to scale-up *liberal* and *neoliberal* governmentality and thus tilts the governmentality towards such forms of regimes (Scholte 2007; Bartelson 2006).

Similarly, Jaeger argues that the presence of nonstate actors in global civil society is devoted to human security and social development and as such tends to depoliticize global governance by engaging in practices devoted to the biology of humans rather than the political aspects of global governance (Jaeger 2007). Global civil society is often used or invoked as a critical counterforce to sovereignty, or rather, faulty sovereign practices, but it is also the foundation for emerging global governance and the assemblages of actors present on the world stage. It may be more accurate to talk of internationally oriented civil society organizations, or the internationalization of politics that follows from globalization. Yet, is this really best grasped by the governmentality framework, either as a descriptive or heuristic analytical device? The application of governmentality to global governance tends to re-produce some of the more problematic aspects previously discussed in relation to how Foucault came to sketch the "governmentalizaton of the state" by emphasizing the replacement and the preeminence of new forms of power over old archaic forms of power – leaving the triangular image of sovereignty, discipline and government power behind.

The notion of an international government of populations and of the utilization of a global civil society both suggest an unproblematic continuity between domestic and international liberal government that restricts the operations of state(s) and state sovereignty. However, as the COVID-19 pandemic has illustrated, under conditions of a health emergency, it became vitally important for states to separate their populations from other populations, both by erecting temporary borders against non-residents, and repatriating their own citizens and permanent residents from across the globe as quickly as possible. This might be read as an atavistic return to a kind of ethno-nationalism, but it might also be read as an attempt to limit the demand on and responsibilities of the state health-care system by ensuring the assignation of populations to sovereign states. In any case, what we witness was not simply a liberal government of populations but a sovereign action to identify populations with their own states. The COVID-19 pandemic became the occasion for extraordinary decrees to regulate the daily lives, movements and activities of a population in a decidedly nonliberal way using the oldest of sovereign measures.

Similarly, global civil society remains a liberal chimera of a space of virtue and energy outside the spheres of states and the market. Against claims that global civil society will deliver solutions to fundamental crisis, the key actors and key capacities in confronting the pandemic remain, as ever, those of the state and system of states. If one looks closely at the frontispiece of Hobbes's *Leviathan*, one finds two figures within the town in the beaked masks of the plague doctor – the only visible figures in the town besides the soldiers guarding the military barracks (Agamben 2015: 37). The town over which the artificial man of the Leviathan rises is commonly thought to be one of the peace and order he brings to it. But, it is possible that what is represented there is the plague town which we are all getting used to. It is under circumstances of global emergency, in which the life of the people is at stake, that we see not the intensification of liberal governmentality but the strongest version of the emergence of the territorial state.

## Globality and Anthropocene and the old ghost

In his book *Down to Earth – politics in the new climatic regime* Bruno Latour (2018) argues that globality, finite space and limited resources became apparent as nations came to agree on the Paris Climate Agreement (COP21). This international agreement, for the first time brought all nations into a common cause to undertake ambitious efforts to combat climate change and adapt to its effects. The Paris agreement acknowledges not only the presence of the Anthropocene but also a human and common responsibility to manage the consequences of human activities on a global scale. As such, it charts a new course in the global climate effort. Since the Paris Agreement also made the case that we no longer can hope for further economic advancement, we need to connect responsible management of the gathered global economic activities and ensure a fair distribution of the finite resources. Bruno Latour then argues that this unique international treaty and the foundation it provides for global responsibility have in fact invoked a counterforce with emerging populism, nationalism and return of geopolitics (Latour 2018: 5).

Globality is intimately connected to the concept of Anthropocene which refers to a geological, and highly political, epoch in which "human activity is seen to have profound and irreparable effects on the environment" (Chandler 2018: 5). The Anthropocene connects humanity to the environment and to the globe. According to the Anthropocene thesis, our activities and interventions have impacted the earth in ways exceeding natural processes. This connects humans to the soil and urges us to consider how historical, social, economic and political processes are intimately connected to globality and the limitations of our globe. Yet, it is not evident that the oneness or singularity underlying globality and Anthropocene produces and lends itself to global governance regimes or a concern for humanity. Rather as was argued by Latour, it was the day when all the signatory countries realized that economic advancement and continued modernization is no longer an option. We stand in need of several planets, more soil and more resources. If there are substantial limitations to our material existence and finite resources we face for the first time, a true crisis of humanity. The climate question is at the heart of all geopolitical issues and it runs the risk of spurring geopolitical and nationalist responses in which sovereignty, territory, soil and strong borders constitute the immediate answer. In this postmodern condition, geopolitics, populism and nationalism sustain new approaches to *Lebensraum* (Latour 2018: 85), a sovereign care for its population that follows a trail which we need no map to know where it leads. It is an open and empirical question what routes and what kind of rationalities lie ahead, and how sovereignty and sovereign powers will be transformed to new conditions and fitted into new constellations that not necessarily are triangular, nor traverse sovereign, discipline and governmental powers, and the latter is by no means limited to its liberal versions.

It is significant that the means by which we have sought to combat climate change in the Anthropocene is not by a new liberal globality but by agreements between states, by a collective exercise of sovereignties. It is the failure of liberal governmentality, with its international correlate of globalization, to provide a systematic understanding of our present that leads today to the attempt to imagine the global in a new and distinctive way. In response to the global destruction of the earth's biosphere, we have no longer the imaginary of a frictionless governance of self-governing individuals and actors beyond states but a new order, or *nomos* that depends vitally on the operation and agreement of states themselves.

## Conclusions

In this chapter, we have argued that the study of global governmentality should not presuppose the absence of sovereignty or sovereign powers but "encourage us to inquire how sovereignty is affected by changing governmental strategies" (Bartelson 2014: 77). In an era of global governance and newfound globality, sovereignty as a principle for organizing political life is by no means in vain. Rather, the Leviathan, a beast as well as a saviour seems to be provoked at the very moment where Anthropocene and globality informs us of the finite resources available for human advancement and wellbeing. In fact, soil and territory becomes increasingly important when human life and wellbeing is being threatened. This provokes a return to sovereignty as a principle, and perpetual war and competition for finite resources becomes a matter of life and death for nations which informs the caretaking of demarcated populations. When the world becomes or is experienced as a hostile and scary place, the principle of state sovereignty seems to make the most sense. Globality becomes intimately connected to geopolitics and sovereignty. Thus, sovereignty as a principle, state as important actors, sovereign powers as state functions, seem to be in transformation rather than eroding in an era of global consciousness.

What we have been arguing throughout this chapter is that while there are attempts of global governmental practices, it does not contradict the presence and importance of sovereign states; rather, it substantially reinscribes the connection between sovereignty and care for distinct populations. The problem associated with sovereignty within the governmentality framework is that it builds on a monarchical absolutist understanding of law. This creates a tendency in the tradition of governmentality studies to overemphasize the pace and presence of alternative governmental techniques while ignoring the presence and interrelation between those techniques, and the substantial transformation of sovereign powers and popular institutions to manage judicial–political power. What might be even more problematic is that attempts to specify a single global governmentality is that it reduces governing complexities to a single rationality and thus downplays conflicts, struggles and double standards. Such an analysis might drive us further away from understanding what sustains sovereignty as a political organization.

There are obvious dangers and mistranslations when the analytical framework and phenomena of governmentality should guide our effort in understanding globality and global governance. As we have argued and shown, there is a tendency to focus on liberal aspects of governmentality as a constellation that aims at conducting the conduct of others. These "others" are however no longer only human biological creatures but a wide set of actors and organizations. Thus, the governmentality framework seems to be stripped from its context and the unique analytical features that have been important for understanding the power constellations and governance within liberal, European states in the 19th century. On the global level and outside the sovereign state, it disrupts the power triangle even further and misrecognizes sovereign power, the disciplining of human bodies and the biological dimensions of governing populations (Dean 2013; Joseph 2009). It remains to be seen how scholars of globality and global governmentality tackle these problems and concerns and to what extent it is useful to apply the governmentality framework as an analytical and methodological framework to grasp the will to govern and subjectivizations on the global level. Is the claim to apply governmentality as a "heuristic" analytical framework (Zanotti 2013), to any scale and any form of governance (Walters 2012) a fruitful way to approach globality and global governance regimes? This book is thus a perfect forum to discuss how such forms of analysis could look and in what ways the authors are able to translate governmentality to a new scale and a new era.

## References

Agamben, Giorgio (2011) *Kingdom and the Glory: For a Theological Genealogy of Economy and Government* (Stanford, California: Stanford University Press).

Agamben, Giorgio (2015) *Stasis: Civil War as Political Paradigm* (Edinburgh: Edinburgh University Press).

Akman, Ayhan (2012) 'Beyond the Objectivist Conception of Civil Society: Social Actors, Civility and Self-Limitation', Political Studies 60:2, 321–340.

Amin, Sami, and Russell Moore (1989) *Eurocentrism* (New York: New York University Press).

Bacchi, Carol, and Susan Goodwin. 2016. *Poststructural Policy Analysis: A Guide to Practice* (New York: Springer Nature).

Bartelson, Jens (2006) 'Making Sense of Global Civil Society', *European Journal of International Relations* 12:3, 371–395.

Bartelson, Jens (2010) 'The Social Construction of Globality', *International Political Sociology* 4:3, 219–235.

Bartelson, Jens (2014) *Sovereignty as Symbolic Form* (London: Routledge).

Bonditti, Philippe (2017) 'Introduction: The International as an Object for Thought' in Philippe Bonditti, Didier Bigo and Frédéric Gros (eds) *Foucault and the Modern International: Silences and Legacies for the Study of World Politics* (New York: Palgrave Macmillan) 1-12.

Brown, Wendy (2017) *Walled States, Waning Sovereignty* (Cambridge: MIT Press).

Chandler, David (2018) *Ontopolitics in the Anthropocene: An Introduction to Mapping, Sensing and Hacking* (London. Routledge).

De Larrinaga, Miguel and Marc G. Doucet (2010) 'Introduction: the global governmentalization of security and the securitization of global govern-ance' in. Miguel De Larrinaga and Marc G. Doucet (eds) *Security and Global Governmentality: Globalization, Governance and the State* (London: Routledge), 1-21.

Dean, Mitchell (2010) *Governmentality: Power and Rule in Modern Society*. 2nd ed (Thousand Oaks: Sage).

Dean, Mitchell (2013) *The Signature of Power: Sovereignty, Governmentality and Biopolitics* (Thousand Oaks: Sage).

Dean, Mitchell and Daniel Zamora (2021) *The Last Man Takes LSD: Foucault and the End of Revolution.* (London: Verso).

Dillon, Michael (2003) 'Global Liberal Governance: Networks, Resistance and War' in Feargal Cochrane, Rosaleen Duffy and Jan Selby (eds) *Global Governance, Conflict and Resistance* (Basingstoke: Palgrave Macmillan), 21–40.

Dillon, Michael, and Andrew Neal (2011) *Foucault on Politics, Security and War* (Basingstoke: Palgrave Macmillan).

Dillon, Michael, and Julian Reid (2001) 'Global Liberal Governance: Biopolitics, Security and War', *Millennium* 30:1, 41–66.

Feenstra, Ramón A (2017) 'Essay: Rethinking Global Civil Society and the Public Sphere in the Age of Pro-Democracy Movements', *Journal of Civil Society* 13:3, 337–348.

Foucault, Michel (2004) *Society Must Be defended: Lectures at the Collège de France, 1975-76.* (London: Penguin).

Foucault, Michel (2007) *Security, Territory, Population: Lectures at the Collège de France, 1977-78* (Basingstoke: Palgrave Macmillan).

Foucault, Michel (2008) *The Birth of Biopolitics: Lectures at the Collége de France, 1978-1979* (Basingstoke: Palgrave Macmillan).

Fournier, Philippe (2008) *Rationalities of Government in Contemporary America: A Foucaultian Study of Domestic and Foreign Policy (1960-2008)* (Doctoral dissertation, United Kingdom: London School of Economics and Political Science).

Gellner, Ernest (1994) *Conditions of Liberty: Civil Society and Its Rivals* (London: Hamish Hamilton).

Guerra-Barón, Angélica (2017), 'Biopower and International Relations', *Oxford Research Encyclopedia of International Studies.*

Guzzini, Stefano (ed) (2012) *The Return of Geopolitics in Europe? Social Mechanisms and Foreign Policy Identity Crises* (Cambridge: Cambridge University Press).

Hardt, Michael and Antonio Negri (2000) *Empire* (Cambridge: Harvard University Press).

Higgins, Vaughan, and Wendy Larner (eds) (2017) *Assembling Neoliberalism: Expertise, Practices, Subjects* (New York: Springer).

Hindess, Barry (2004) 'Liberalism - What's in a Name?' in Wendy Larner and William Walters (eds) *Global Governmentality: Governing International Spaces* (London: Routledge), 23–39.

Hobbes, Thomas (1994) *Leviathan: With Selected Variants from the Latin Edition of 1668* (Indianapolis: Hackett Publishing).

Jaeger, Hans-Martin (2007) "Global Civil Society' and the Political Depoliticization of Global Governance', *International Political Sociology* 1:3, 257–277.

Jaeger, Hans-Martin (2013) 'Governmentality's (Missing) International Dimension and the Promiscuity of German Neoliberalism', *Journal of International Relations and Development* 16:1, 25–54.

Joseph, Jonathan (2009) 'Governmentality of What? Populations, States and International Organisations', *Global Society* 23:4, 413–427.

Joseph, Jonathan (2010) 'The Limits of Governmentality: Social Theory and the International', *European Journal of International Relations* 16:2, 223–246.

Larner, Wendy, and William Walters (2004) 'Introduction: Global Governmentality: Governing International Spaces' in Wendy Larner and William Walters (eds) *Global Governmentality: Governing International Spaces* (London: Routledge), 1–20.

Larsson, Oscar (2018) 'Advancing Post-Structural Institutionalism: Discourses, Subjects, Power Asymmetries, and Institutional Change', *Critical Review* 30:3-4, 325–346.

Latour, Bruno (2018) *Down to Earth: Politics in the New Climatic Regime* (Cambridge: Polity).

Lemke, Thomas (2002) 'Foucault, Governmentality, and Critique', *Rethinking Marxism* 14:3, 49–64.

Lemke, Thomas (2012) *Foucault, Governmentality, and Critique, Cultural Politics & the Promise of Democracy* (London: Paradigm).

Lemke, Thomas (2019) *A Critique of Political Reason: Foucault's Analysis of Modern Governmentality* (London: Verso Books).

Lui, Robyn (2004) 'The International Government of Refugees' in Wendy Larner and William Walters (eds) *Global Governmentality: Governing International Spaces* (London: Routledge), 116–135.

Lipschutz, Ronnie D (2004) 'Global Civil Society and Global Governmentality: Or the Search for Politics and the State in the Midst of the Capillaries of Social Power' in Michael Barnett and Robert Duvall (eds) *Power in Global Governance* (Cambridge: Cambridge University Press), 229–248.

Munster, Rens van and Sylvest, Casper (2016) 'Introduction' in Rens van Munster and Casper Sylvest (eds) *The Politics of Globality Since 1945* (London: Routledge), 1–19.

Neumann, Iver B and Ole Jacob Sending (2007) "'The International" as Governmentality', *Millennium-Journal of International Studies* 35:3, 677–701.

Nisancioglu, Kerem (2019) 'Racial Sovereignty', *European Journal of International Relations* (online first).

Rose-Redwood, Reuben S (2006) 'Governmentality, Geography, and the Geo-Coded World', *Progress in Human Geography* 30:4, 469–486.

Schiavo, Lidia Lo (2015): "Sovereignty, Governmentality, Globalization and the Crisis of the State. Re-Telling the Story Backwards: A Foucauldian Analysis." *Journal of Social Science for Policy Implications* 3 (1), 1-18.

Scholte, Jan Aart (2007) 'Civil Society and Legitimation of Global Governance', *Journal of Civil Society* 3:3, 305–326.

Selby, Jan (2007) 'Engaging Foucault: Discourse, Liberal Governance and the Limits of Foucauldian IR', *International Relations* 21:3, 324–345.

Sending, Ole Jacob, Neumann, Iver B (2006): 'Governance to Governmentality: Analyzing NGOs, States, and Power', *International Studies Quarterly* 50:3, 651–672.

Walker, R B J (2010) *After the Globe, Before the World* (London: Routledge).

Walters, William (2012) *Governmentality: Critical Encounters, Critical Issues in Global Politics* (London: Routledge).

Valverde, Mariana (2011) 'Law Versus History - Foucault's Geneology of Modern Sovereignty' in Michael Dillon and Andrew Neal (eds) *Foucault on Politics, Security and War* (Basingstoke: Palgrave Macmillan), 135–150.

Zanotti, Laura (2013) 'Governmentality, Ontology, Methodology: Re-Thinking Political Agency in the Global World', *Alternatives* 38:4, 288–304.

# 6 Exploring agency and resistance in the context of global entanglements

*Laura Zanotti*

## Introduction

In this chapter, I adopt governmentality in conjunction with complexity and quantum theories to explore practices of government as well as possibilities of counter conduct in the context of global entanglements. This chapter also assesses possible reconceptualization of agency and ethics in a post-Newtonian world. As the introduction of this volume argues:

> if governmentality, globality and the state are all simultaneously co-produced and entangled—rather than existing as a pre-packaged separate scale of concepts to be combined, like puzzle pieces—then new approaches and conceptualizations of politics are required in order to reconsider the globality of conducts and actions.
>
> (Busse and Hamilton, Introduction from this volume, pp. 15–16)

Conceptual tools are politically relevant because they shape the way we see the world as well as the way we see us as exerting agency in it. Carl Death (2010, 2011) has insightfully argued that by focusing on practices rather than actors, a governmentality approach destabilizes binary conceptualizations of power and resistance. In this view, resistance is about opening sites of contestation more than a merely revolutionary form of political change. Foucault defined "governmentality" as the "conduct of conduct" and used this concept as an analytical tool to study the transformations that made modern modalities of government possible. Foucault's focus on processes of subjectification, power and resistance questions the starting point of liberal theories of politics that see humans as endowed with ontological characteristics of unbounded freedom. Foucault's theoretical implant favors instead a non-substantialist view of subjectivity, and invites explorations of *how* freedom is constituted and exerted contextually in relation to practices of government. Governmentality and counter conducts constitute each other in multiple local and global historically shaped and causally complex practices. Differently from scholars who used governmentality as a description of the oppressive and overarchingly powerful features of power (Agamben 1998;

Hardt and Negri 2000), I use governmentality as a heuristic tool to analyze the modalities and ways of functioning of practices of government in the context of a complex and interconnected (or entangled) global world (Zanotti 2013). Both governmentality (as a heuristic concept) and quantum theories, question theoretical constructs that start from assumptions regarding "entities" (or what Foucault calls "universals") as constitutive of (physical and social) reality. By combining governmentality, quantum and complexity theories, this chapter invites to explore the social and the physical world as a series of multifarious temporally oriented human/non-human entangled processes, and to explore specific practices of global governmentality and resistance.

Foucault's understanding and use of governmentality is profoundly nonsubstantialist. Governmentality does not refer to the essence of the power or of the state and its institutions, but to the exploration of specific practices of government.

As Colin Gordon aptly put it:

> State theory attempts the modern activities of government from essential properties and propensities of the state, in particular its supposed propensity to grow and to swallow up or colonize everything outside itself. Foucault holds that the state has no such inherent propensities; more generally, the state has no essence. The nature of the institution of the state is, Foucault thinks, a function of changes in practices of government, rather than the converse. Political theory attends too much to institutions, and too little to practice.
>
> (Gordon 1991: 4)

As a way of conducting conduct, governmentality elicits specific practices of resistance. These practices are co-constituted. Again, according to Colin Gordon:

> As governmental practices have addressed themselves in an increasingly immediate way to "life" [...] individuals have begun to formulate the needs and imperatives of that same life as the basis for political counter-demands. Biopolitics thus provides a prime instance of what Foucault calls [...] "the strategic reversibility" of power relations, or the way in which the terms of governmental practices can be turned around into focuses of resistance. [...] the history of government as the conduct of conduct is interwoven with the history of dissenting counter conduct.
>
> (Gordon 1991: 5)

Karen Barad (2007) relies on quantum physics to offer an ontological imaginary within which agency and counter conduct may be conceived as partially co-constructed human–non-human entanglements. Human intra-actions with other humans and the nonhuman produce morphogenetic and cascade effects within specific material and historical configurations. Barad's notion of intra-agential agency deeply relies on the Foucauldian notion of apparatus. Apparatuses for Foucault are physical constructs that embody processes of knowledge, as well as governmental practices of power. The Panopticon, the architectural artifact through which the constant surveillance of inmates is enabled, disciplinary practices are administered and modern subjects constituted, well exemplifies this concept. Apparatuses are not only observation tools, they are also performative ones. Likewise, for Barad, apparatuses are knowledge-material entanglements that produce specific forms of materialization of matter. In this view, resistance is not the expression of unbounded freedom, but is enmeshed in practices where governmentality and counter conduct are coproduced.

In the pages that follow, I will highlight *how* governmentality is deployed in the context of uncertainty, complexity and global entanglements; what kind of ways of conducting conduct and forms of institutionalization it fosters; as well as what practices of resistance may be possible in this context. I will conclude by arguing that, in spite of Kantian aspirations to ground ethics on the certainty of universal prescriptions regardless of contexts, the nonlinearity of causality and uncertainty are not necessarily obstacles to possibilities of exerting agency and resistance. In fact, if we reimagine the world as complex, interconnected and entangled, we may creatively reimagine the transformative power of micropractices of counter conduct, as well as emphasize the notion of responsibility[1] as the driving concept for ethical and political justification of such practices.

Furthermore, relational ontologies nurture "modest" conceptualizations of political agency and also question the overwhelming stability of "mighty totalities," such as for instance the international liberal order or the state. In this framework, political action has more to do with playing with the cards that are dealt to us in order to produce practical effects in specific contexts than with building idealized "new totalities" where perfect conditions might exist. The political ethics that results from non-substantialist ontological positions is one that privileges "modest" engagements and weighs political choices with regard to the consequences and distributive effects they may produce in the context where they are made rather than based upon their universal normative aspirations. In this framework, ethical decision-making would not be based upon abstract prescriptions but upon assuming responsibility for the contingent and practical effects of political actions.[2]

## Quantum, complexity, resilience: Governmentality in the context of nonlinear causation

The introduction of complexity and quantum theories in political science developed new ways of thinking about the global (Albert 2016; Coole and Frost, 2010; Cudworth and Hobden 2011; Cudworth et al. 2018; Der Derian,

2009; Kavalski 2015; Malette and Stoett 2018; Penttinen 2018; Urry, 2015; Wendt, 2015). Complexity and quantum theories focus on change instead of stability, conceptualize causality in a non-linear manner, and embrace uncertainty as the normal status of human (and nonhuman) existence. A non-linear understanding of causality implies that causes work in clusters, and relations of cause–effect cannot be described, as in Newtonian physics, as mechanical forces representable as a function of momentum and mass. Furthermore, complexity and quantum theories focus on uncertainty rather than on seeking to establish universal laws that explain the past and predict the future. Uncertainty has both an ontological and an epistemological dimension. Epistemologically, uncertainty derives from the impossibility of knowing all causal variables that come to bear on a specific phenomenon. Ontologically, complexity theories maintain that the effect of any causal force applied to a system depends upon the interaction of that force with the status of sensitivity of the system (Cudworth and Hobden, 2011). Complexity theorists, critical materialists and quantum theorists alike, have also emphasized the notion of *emergence*, i.e. the idea that processes occurring within a system and among systems entail nonreversible morphogenetic processes. Time is not a container, and the transformations that occur in complex systems as the results of interactions are nonreversible. Hence, sequencing is important and processes produce ontological effects that change the very "nature" of the system. In this framework, systems cannot be understood in mechanistic ways, as the sum of their parts, but only holistically. This position resonates with Mathias Albert's (2016) who relies on Luhmannian system theory. For Albert the global, or in his own words "world society "is the *"entirety of communications"* (2016: 6, emphasis in original). Albert favors an approach to the social that identifies the historical conditions which make more likely, however not necessary, that certain paths will be taken. While these conditions shape what is, they do not determine it. Feminist quantum physicist Karen Barad (2007) pushed these nonmechanistic ontological understanding of uncertainty a step forward. Barad's account opens the space for consideration of human/nonhuman material entanglements and for social processes beyond language.[3] For Barad, the primary ontological referents are phenomena. Phenomena are relations prior to *relata* and they encompass knowledge as well as material processes. Ontological closure only happens in the context of specific forms of intra-action embodied in apparatuses.[4]

While quantum and complexity theories do not completely overlap, and there are many versions of such positions, they also share views relevant for exploring practices of policy making, agency and resistance. In assessing the relevance of complexity theories for the discipline of International Relations, Cudworth and Hobden argued that "events cannot be controlled through knowledge, as the same actions may result in different consequences as complex adaptive systems change over time. Hence, to see the discipline as one that can make reliable predictions about the future is futile" (2011: 179).

Complexity theories have elicited discussions on how to govern people in condition of uncertainty. In this framework, circulation, adaptation and resilience have become central conceptual tools for devising governmental practices of conduct of conduct. In his recently published book, Jonathan Joseph (2019) argued that resilience is the new version of governmentality in the context of complexity.[5] It focuses on *adaptation* as central goal of policy making. Policy focuses on promoting individuals and communities' resilience, i.e. the capacity of systems to "cope with change," and to be "reborn" or to "rebound" in the aftermath of shocks. While recognizing that there are different ways of conceptualizing resilience as policy tool, Joseph (in relying on Chandler 2014) argued the aim of this form of governmentality, which focuses on population as its target, is no longer the protection of stability, but instead "to encourage change in our ways of organizing and behaving" (Joseph 2019: 16).

Mark Duffield (2007) also argued that resilience is a central tool of liberal governance for promoting security in the context of uncertainty. For Duffield, in the postcolonial era, the Western empire took the form of an assemblage of occupation that centered upon the goal of making what he calls "uninsured" populations "resilient." NGOs have been instrumental in enacting this form of liberal global governmentality and in promoting resilience as a way of taming the circulation of uninsured populations. By enhancing the ability of the poor to cope with shocks such as conflict, natural disasters and economic recessions, without offering a real avenue for development, "resilience" functions as a political strategy for promoting the security of the West by taming the circulation of the rest. In summary, the conceptualization of the international system in terms of risk, uncertainty and the recognition of complexity go hand in hand with the development of forms of governmentality that attempt to "govern at a distance," to borrow Nikolas Rose's (1999) vocabulary, by influencing and regulating the circulation of people and their ability to "cope" with risks. In this framework, the circulation of populations became the direct target of security practices (Zanotti 2011).[6] The pages that follow will illustrate how the problem of governing complexity has been debated and practiced through specific tools for policy making.

## Exploring governmental practices in the context of uncertainty: Manipulating the circulation of ideas or promoting institutionalization?

The policy relevance of complexity theories for devising governmental techniques is testified by the fact that Christopher A. Ford, an Assistant Secretary of State for International Security and Non-Proliferation in the Trump administration, published a reflection on this very technique while exercising those functions. Ford argued that, while complexity theory challenges policy makers' ability to *control* the world, it also offers powerful tools for policy makers to manipulate outcomes by managing the circulation of ideas.

Ford theorizes techniques of government in the time of complexity in a way that is not limited to *adaptation*. Instead, he maintains that *active manipulation of ideas* and their circulation does offer opportunity for policy makers to shape outcomes and to amplify their power. For Ford, complexity theory provides suggestions to policy makers on how to deal with unpredictability in what he calls "perturbation management" and make it possible to salvage "public policy *positive* vision of purposive change" (Ford 2015: 81, emphasis in original). In Ford's words:

> If CT [complexity theory] offers us lessons about the behavior of complex systems, and if it is indeed possible to conceive of human society as a complex adaptive *social* system (CASS), then CT may also have something valuable to teach public policy makers, whose job is not simply to describe the world but in fact also deliberately to *alter* its course in some fashion.
>
> (Ford 2015: 79-80)

In order to achieve these goals, Ford suggests policy makers exploit what he called the "policy-maker paradox," i.e. the complexity theory position that "modest policy inputs *can* indeed bring about transformational change, but such changes are deeply unpredictable" (ibid.). The possibility of shaping political outcomes through the manipulations of ideas is made possible by the fact that, differently from non-human complex systems, human systems respond to *ideational* inputs. Because human systems are sensitive to ideational inputs, ideas become the central target of governmental manipulation. Thus, Ford continues:

> ideational inputs and behavior-structuring of conceptual systems clearly *can* be manipulated [...] by members of the policy making community [...]. [T]he deliberate shaping of *ideas* seems to offer us a chance to affect behavior within complex social systems in ways that are not utterly unpredictable, at least to the extent that such inputs may tend to exert recognizable patterning influences over time.
>
> (ibid.: 96, emphasis in original)

The best way to manipulate behavior through the government of ideas must be targeted at reinforcing what Ford, building upon Dawkins, calls "meme," i.e. "a conceptual unit of culture that shapes decisional behavior in conscious actors and which has a specified information content that can be transferred through mimicry, interaction and teaching" (ibid.: 97).

Ford also informs us, that, in a hyperbolic exacerbation of the convergence of governmentality and security, the manipulation of ideas has become a tool in warfare. In this regard, the U.S. Office of Naval Research contracted a software firm to "build a program to identity and characterize memes as they develop and propagate" (ibid.: 98). Furthermore:

according to officials from the contractor in question, their approach analogizes the "spread of ideas" to the "spread of disease," using computerized natural language analysis of documentary sources to help intelligence analysts identifying brewing social or political ideas as well as specific populations likely to be susceptible to them

(ibid.: 98)

Once purposively manipulated, ideas:

acquire considerable power in shaping actors' behavior and acquiring a sort of cognitive "momentum" of their own. In such dynamics, particular thrusts and themes propagate themselves both laterally ("catching on" among greater number of people) and forward in time, maintain a recognizable "family" resemblance even while changing in response to circumstances.

(ibid.: 101)

In summary, complexity theory and epidemiology combined offer Ford the tools for devising hyperbolic forms of governmentality that also converge with apparatuses of security. Indeed, Ford argues "ideas have a special potency as a means of influencing our fellow man [sic]" (ibid.: 99), and "purposive manipulation of *ideational* inputs may provide a tool with which systemic outcomes may sometimes be influenced in broadly predictable ways" (ibid.: 81). In the context of complexity, Ford argues, "the study, development, and manipulation of the cognitive frameworks that help structure human actions in the social world – e.g. political ideologies – are perforce subjects of surpassing importance for policy makers" (ibid.: 101). As the Assistant Secretary of State for International Security and Non-Proliferation in the Trump administration theorized, ideational manipulation has become a specific target for governmental intervention, and ideology a way of policy. The findings of the ongoing investigation on the Russian meddling with the 2016 US Presidential elections and the increased polarization of the political climate may testify to the frightening effectiveness of this governmental strategy. On a different note and with a different political scope, Andrew Ross (2014) also explored the powerful effects of circulation of ideas and emotions, and warned about the potentially horrific effects it may produce. Ross used epidemiology to explore the way ideas and emotions circulated before and during the genocides in Srebrenica and Rwanda and how this circulation and contagion created the political energy that lead to those outcomes.

Scholars interested in devising normatively driven social change have also assessed the possibilities to tame uncertainty through normatively driven institutionalization in the context of complexity. Mark Olssen (2015), for instance, addressed the compatibility of ethically driven policy making with complexity theoretical frameworks. For Olssen, complexity theories open "possibilities toward a rich new conception of 'complexity based' historical materialism"

(2015: 140) that moves beyond the analytical rigidity and teleological orientation of traditional Marxism and embraces instead "'contextual contingency', 'time irreversibility,' 'non reductionism,' 'self-organization' and 'emergence'" (ibid.: 141). Olssen criticizes simplified versions of complexity theories based on agent-based modeling. He argues that the most productive potential of such theories is not the possibility to construct predictive models based upon mathematical algorithms (which in fact contradict complexity principle of non-additivity). Olssen embraces instead a systemic version of complexity, where systemic factors, and not only individual actors are relevant elements of analysis. For Olssen, this position has important implications for politics. In the context of uncertainty, forms of institutionalization are increasingly important as ways of shaping social outcomes. Thus, "because complexity places emphasis upon each individual's insufficiency in the face of precarious and unpredictable environments, the normative implications for politics in *not* an antipathy to state and global structures, but rather an institutional-regulative approach to politics in general" (ibid.: 157). Thus, institutionalization has causal power in the context of complexity and can be used as a tool for ethically driven policy. As Olssen puts it, "it is through institutions that complexity is managed and by which the present is channeled to the future" (ibid.: 157).

While I am sympathetic to Olssen's overall argument, institutionalization may lead to counterproductive outcomes if embraced as a "one size fits all" solution to social problems that is not supplemented by careful contextual analysis. As I have argued elsewhere (Zanotti 2011), after the end of the Cold War, the United Nations embraced institutionalization as the main tool for peacekeeping and peacebuilding. Under UN Secretary General Kofi Annan, the world organization reimagined security as a complex threat and its role in maintaining security as a task of managing risk. The Report of the Secretary General High-Level Panel on Threats, Challenges and Change (2004) clearly articulates this position. Risk, Ulrich Beck (1992) argued, challenges container theories of society. After the beginning of the New Millennium, The UN adopted a political rationality for international intervention aimed at governing disorder through moral reformation of "rogue" states through institution building. The reduction of risk was to be achieved by reforming governments, in the assumption that such reforms would lead to the transformation of conflict societies. Thus, ethical reconstruction became a central organizing concept for international governmentality (Zanotti 2011: 18). In the post-Cold War era, the UN attempted to tame risks by transforming states that were represented as potential threats to international security into "good citizens" of the international community and "domesticated subjects" that would not escalate global disorder. The performance of these states with regard to democracy and good governance has been increasingly monitored through standardized benchmarks based upon which international rewards and punishments have been measured and administered. However, the UN failed to recognize that institutionalization does not work as a separate sphere of society and does not produce linear effects. For instance, the UN efforts to solve Haiti's problems through reforms of penal institutions failed to take into consideration the multiple entanglements that come to bear in that country. The UN imagined the places it was intervening in through peace-keeping operations as flat and inert instead of complex and entangled. While in Haiti, the UN sponsored police, prison and judiciary reform efforts, UN member states that supported police reform in Haiti did only marginally contribute to sustain its operating budget or the material tools needed by the police to perform its job, for instance cars, fuel, bullets, uniforms and so on.

In the meantime, a more centralized and structured police force increased the backlog in the judiciary and prisons. A modern and effective judiciary requires a strong administrative apparatus, not simply training judges. It requires courts, clerks and extensive technological resources. And prison systems not only require training correction officers. They require means to keep record of inmates, to separate convicted criminals from those awaiting trial, minors from adults, to feed prisoners, etc. In Haiti, computers are scarce, electricity erratic, and even paper and pens are not always a given. Prisons there are places where people are forgotten and die of disease or starvation in overcrowded cells. Thus, while the UN imagined itself to be building the Haitian state along a blueprint formally patterned along the lines of idealized Western models of government, it ended up constructing institutions that were economically and politically unsustainable. The establishment of costly institutions, combined with the lack of international financial support to the Haitian government contributed to the leverage of non-state actors with economic power (such as drug dealers), created trade-offs with alternative uses of resources and stifled instead of promoting a viable local economy and a proliferation of NGOs in the country. The United Nations' assumptions that complex realities can be driven by processes of institutionalization regardless of specific circumstances, together with the UN's member states' lack of commitment to sustaining the institutional apparatus the intervention in Haiti established, ended up setting the stage for failure.

In summary, the United Nations designed international interventions along the lines of abstract rationalities and Newtonian conceptualizations of causality that assume that institutionalization would succeed in directing complex and entangled social realities towards the outcomes desired by peacekeepers. Samuel Barkin (2018) insightfully explored the inadequacy of forms of institutionalization based upon linear planning rationalities for governing complex ecosystems, such as fisheries and the oceans. The Regional Fisheries Management Organizations (RFMO) are regional organizations trying to govern a global fishing industry that exploits highly migratory species. In attempting to govern the industry, RFMO regulate the way fish can be caught and how much can be caught for individual species. In addition, the enforcements of RFMO regulations depend upon nation-states that may be more prone to defend the interests of national fishing industries than protecting the global marine ecosystem. However, these frameworks do not take into account the broad interconnections of different marine species but instead imagine the oceans as a series of separate containers. For Barkin, international fisheries "combine the linear thinking of domestic fisheries regulation with the linear thinking of international regime construction" (2018: 144).

In this section, I have addressed governmental techniques aimed at manipulating the circulation of ideas in order to obtain political goals, or at promoting forms of institutionalization to tame uncertainty and transform the behavior of states in international peacekeeping. Governmentality may be applied through different tools and with different goals for governing a complex and entangled world where linear relations of causality do not necessarily obtain. I will now turn to explore how counter conducts and resistance may be imagined in the context of complexity and uncertainty.

## Micropolitics, circulation, intra-agential ethos: Exploring possibilities for counter conduct and resistance

Complexity theories' focus on adaptation and resilience, Joseph (2019) argues, embraces a "fatalistic social ontology," one that shifts the attention from possibilities of controlling the outside world to a "concern with our own subjectivity, our adaptability, our reflexive understanding, our knowledge acquisition, our life-choices, our risk assessment" (Joseph 2019: 19; see also Joseph in this volume). However, Philippe Bourbeau (2015, 2018a, 2018b) challenged this conceptualization of the notion of resilience as a tool of liberal international governance. Bourbeau and Ryan (2018) insightfully argue that contrasting resistance with resilience treats these concepts as somehow separate entities. Contra these substantialist assumptions, Bourbeau and Ryan propose a relational approach that considers processes of resilience and resistance as enmeshed and entangled. Thus, resilience, as "the process of seeking and maintaining the status quo in the face of shocks" is, in the practice of politics, entangled and intermingled with the process of transforming the status quo through resistance (Bourbeau and Ryan 2018).

Bourbeau and Ryan's anti-substantialist analysis of political processes as co-constituted and entangled is attuned to quantum ontologies and to Karen Barad's (2007) notion of intra-agential agency in particular. By relying on quantum physics, Barad (2007) delineates an onto-epistemological horizon that opens possibilities for reconceptualizing the way we can engage the interdependent world of which we are part. Her position offers an alternative to fatalistic understandings of resistance as well as the conceptual tools for imagining agency beyond resilience and adaptation. For Barad, reality is not an externality, endowed with properties we may discover, but an "externality within." Matter is not inert, but something within which we are entangled by the way of intra-agential activities. In other words, the world is made by *phenomena* that cannot be controlled by humans, but of which humans are part and within which they operate ontological cuts that "close," or bring to realization, a range of possibilities. "What "is" comes into existence as an effect of these ontological cuts. For Barad, the world is characterized by *onto-logical indeterminacy*. Such indeterminacy can only be contingently resolved in the intra-action between the observer and the observed. In relying upon Niels Bohr's physics, Karen Barad argues "things do not have inherently determinate boundaries or properties and words do not have inherently deter-minate meanings" (2007: 138). Objectivity is not predicated upon "distance" from reality, but upon engaging it with *experimental apparatuses* that produce intra-agential ontological cuts in what exists.

Phenomena, Barad argues, "are ontologically pre-existing relations – relations without pre-existing *relata*" (2007: 139). In this framework, "phe-nomena do not only mark the epistemological inseparability of observer and observed, or results of measurements; rather, *phenomena are the ontological inseparability entanglement of intra acting agencies*" (Barad 2007: 139 emphasis in original). Barad points at the difference between intra- and inter-action, i.e. the position that is mostly embraced by com-plexity theorists. While the notion of inter-action presupposes the prior existence of independent entities (i.e. an atomistic ontology), intra-action maintains that "the boundaries and properties of the components of phe-nomena become determinate" (Barad 2007: 139) only in the context of intra-actions. In following Bohr's quantum physics, Barad argues that the property of the components of phenomena emerge differently in different experimental situations. In fact, matter is not passive but it reveals itself to us in these continuously unfolding intra-active processes. Because we are *of* the world not *above* the world, and our acting contributes to defining ontology while the world out there defines our being, epistemology and ontology are deeply entangled and cannot be separated.

Based upon the notion of intra-agential agency, Barad questions both views that maintain the centrality of language and culture and views that reiterate the determinism of matter. She also rejects assumptions that portray matter as "passive, immutable and mute" as well as the "representationalist belief in the power of words to mirror pre-existing phenomena" (Barad 2007: 133). In this way, Barad embraces the notion of performativity of knowledge. Political and theoretical claims are not distinct practices. Instead, theorizing is a prac-tice of *engagement* with the world within which we "have our being" (Barad 2007: 133). A posthumanist position shifts the attention from representa-tion to "mattering practices," thus bringing to the forefront questions about "ontology, materiality and agency" (Barad 2007: 135). The relation between the cultural and the natural (or in other words, the way we are of the world) is for Barad an "exteriority" within, not a "static relationality" that leaves the properties of the terms of the relation unchallenged. The cultural is an "enact-ment of boundaries" (Barad 2007: 135), a practice of operating ontological cuts, that entails "constitutive exclusions" and therefore *requisites questions of accountability*. This kind of onto-epistemology questions a human excep-tionalism that denies nature "any sense of agency and historicity" (Barad

2007: 136) and offers interesting avenues for reframing both ethics and human agency beyond structuralism and determinism. In Barad's words:

> post-humanism eschews both humanist and structuralist accounts of the subject that position the human as either a pure cause or pure effect [...]. posthumanism doesn't presume the separateness of any-"thing," let alone the alleged spatial, ontological, and epistemological distinction that sets humans apart.
>
> (2007: 136)

In this framework, *relata* are not prior to relations: "Matter is produced and productive, generated and generative" (Barad 2007: 136). Difference has generative effects in the production of other differences and causality is not rooted upon ontologically stable properties of entities. Thus, "causal structures" are generated by different patterns of differentiation and processes of materialization that are enacted through practices of knowing and doing.

The notion of apparatus is central for the conceptualization of agency in the context of entanglements. Barad emphasizes that apparatuses are not only observational instruments, but they are "productive (and part of) phenomena" (2007: 142). For Barad, apparatuses are what make possible the determination of boundaries and properties of objects (the intra-agential cuts), as well the embodiment of concepts in the apparatus. "Apparatuses enact agential cuts that produce determinate boundaries and properties of 'entities' within phenomena, where 'phenomena' are the ontological inseparability of agential intra acting components" (Barad 2007: 148). Discursive practices, through which boundaries in the world are enacted, and material phenomena, are ontologically imbricated. Experimental *dispositifs* are not only heuristic but also performative instruments and have a bearing upon resolving ontological indeterminacy. "What is" and the way we know it cannot be conceptualized separately. Nevertheless, phenomena are not the *result* of human agency. Instead "the world is a dynamic process of intra-activity and materialization in the enactment of determinate causal structures which determine boundaries, properties, meaning, and patterns of marks on bodies" (Barad 2007: 140).

Barad's position suggests a radical reconceptualization of our being in the world. In engaging the world as agents, we do not act as monads endowed with *potentia*, but as entangled phenomena that are part of what exists. We do not preordain material dynamics as a result of acts of reason or will. We do instead participate in processes of materialization of which we are part but that we do not control. "All or nothing" political engagements that aim at controlling the world, or at realizing abstract idealistic aspirations may remain caught in complex clusters of causation, open systems and processes of materialization that we as humans may contribute to bringing about but do not determine.

In line with Michel Foucault, Barad embraces the idea that the apparatus or *dispositifs* (i.e. the instruments through which we engage reality in order to know it) are performative and operate ontological cuts. In extending Foucault's radical non-substantialist position to the non-human through Bohr's quantum physics, Barad links a reflection on our being in the world to a reflection on the way we know what we know, and the way we act upon it. For Barad, we are enmeshed in a world of ontological indeterminacy. Such indeterminacy can only be resolved intra-agentially. Humans cannot overdetermine outcomes, but can take part in processes of mattering by operating intra-agential cuts differently. By radically questioning the very notion of separability that underlines notions of individuality, rationality and universal normativity, Barad traces the ontological and methodological horizon for devising an ethics that embraces uncertainty and complexity.[7] Every small action may count for generating cascade effects.

This ontological framework at the same time broadens possibilities for imagining practices of counter conduct and resistance and raises the bar of adjudication of the validity of political action. William Connolly, for instance, outlined the relevance of an ontology of entanglement for grounding his understanding of reflexivity and creativity as political virtues as well as his position on the potential transformative effects of micropolitics. In a non-substantialist framework, options for changing what is, are not limited by causal determinism, or by the possibility to direct the world through planning rationalities. They are found instead in multifarious and contingent struggles of our being in the world (Connolly 2013). Micropolitical action may have amplified ripple effects. These engagements exceed and transform what is out there as well as our being.

Elina Penttinen relies on Karen Barad and on posthumanist philosophy more broadly, to assert a theory of agency that goes beyond paradigms of "human frailty." She argued that "posthumanist understandings that humans are intra-active parts of the continuous flow, becoming and reconfiguration of the world allows us to recognize human subjectivity and agency as a form of pluripotency, as a vitality" (Penttinen 2013: 4). Penttinen regards "uncertainty as a form of potentiality [...] and not something to be feared or something that threatens us" but as part of "aliveness and flow of the world of which we are part. This is [...] an ontology of joy, at the root of our being, the ontology of the world, is indeed uncertainty and change" (Penttinen 2013: 13). The recognition of intra-agential agency and interconnectedness emphasizes the need to focus on "what works" instead of the negative and "what needs to be fixed." While the discipline of IR has focused on broad phenomena, it has overlooked the ability of people to make a difference in specific situations. For Penttinen, resilience is not only a governmental practice of relinquishing the responsibility for caring for people, as for Duffield or the political version of a fatalistic ontology, as for Joseph. Instead, Penttinen shows how women in conflict situations have been able to defy the violence of patriarchy and challenge accounts, also shared by feminist theorists, of women as victims.

Such depictions, for Penttinen do not recognize women's agency and reinforce traditional representations of masculinity and femininity. If we imagine the world as interconnected, personal stories that testify to the ability to "find joy" in horrible situations, may create ripple effects thus ending up changing what exist.

While not embracing Penttinen's optimism, Oded Löwenheim also emphasized the relevance of storytelling not only as an academic endeavor but as a form of political counter conduct. Löwenheim (2010) questioned the militarization and securitization of Israeli identity through the autobiographic account of his time in the Israeli armed forces. Regardless of whether one embraces the optimistic version of storytelling of Penttinen or the less optimistic one of Löwenheim, both of them show that the micro and the particular are politically relevant and that we should consider broadening what counts as valid scholarship as well as a possible form of counter conduct.

The success of the #metoo movement also shows that the power of story-telling combined with technologies that amplify the circulation of such stories offer a space for exerting counter conduct. What started as few women's ini-tiative to break the shame imposed on victims of sexual assault on social media, ended up reversing the shame and producing an amplifying effect that has challenged patriarchy's structural violence. The circulation of personal stories transformed the exposure of personal victimization in public affirm-ation of strength. The conviction of Harvey Weinstein may testify to one of the effects of the #metoo circulation of counter narratives. The #metoo movement has been criticized for being an elite, celebrity-driven movement. While the movement reflects social inequalities among differently positioned women, it has nevertheless shown that circulating personal stories may constitute a powerful tool for counter conduct and not only of hyperbolic governmentality. In summary, autoethnography, story-telling and their cir-culation are not only governmental tools in the hands of powerful politicians who wish to shape politics by controlling the diffusion of ideas. They are also tools for resistance and counter conduct.

These examples show that on the one hand, governmentality and counter conduct are inevitably entangled, and that the same tools through which power exerts control may be adopted for creating movements of resistance. It also shows that counter conduct exerted through micropolitical engagement may create morphogenetic effects and may end up challenging consolidated structures of power. Embracing our being entangled with the world, valuing uncertainty as the horizon for ethical choices, and conceptualizing polit-ical engagements as performative but not omnipotent, paves the way for the affirmation of ethics in methodological terms. Ontologies of entanglement embrace uncertainty not as the *limit*, but as the very *condition of possibility* of ethical action and pave the way for a reconceptualization of political agency that is not rooted upon the possibility to direct linear transformations, but upon responsible engagement with what exists. In a global and entangled world, micropolitical engagements may be better apt than processes of institutionalization for opening possibilities for political change.

The notions of "entanglement," "apparatus" and "intra-agential agency" offered by Karen Barad and Michel Foucault offer the potential for reimaging political agency and resistance in the context of uncertainty in a way that is not only reactive but deeply engaged and proactive. If reality is entangled and the apparatuses through which we engage the world have morphogenetic effects, then situational assessment and responsibility for the outcomes of our actions are the grounds for adjudicating strategies of resistance. In this view, asking *how* questions is not only a matter of academic methodology, but it is an ethical and political virtue. Furthermore, because in an entangled world, our actions produce morphogenetic effects, the assumption of responsibility for outcomes we contribute to bring about needs to be at the center of the reconceptualization of agency and ethics in International Relations. Intra-agential agency is a powerful way for reimaging possibilities of resistance and counter conduct in a global and entangled world. It points at the importance and causal power of what we do, yet not in an idealistic way that conceptualizes reality as malleable to action and presupposes linear relations of causality between planning rationalities and their effects. In fact, positions that embrace this view deeply resonate with the naive IR idealism that E.H. Carr criticized as being, together with realist determinism, at the root both of policy failures, and poor imagination regarding political agency engrained in the discipline of IR. Quantum ontologies conceptualize our being in the world in a way that supports Derrida's vision of ethics as a decision that exceeds rules and is rooted upon radical assumptions of responsibility. In this framework, ethics is a virtue to be exercised more than a behavior warranted by the apodictic recognition of universal truths.

## Conclusions

In this chapter, I have explored how complexity and quantum theories reframe possibilities for governmentality as well as counter conduct in an entangled world. However, intra-agency points not only at the importance of looking at causal relations among multiple variables, as complexity theories. It also points at the fact that agency and the apparatuses we adopt to engage with what "is" have morphogenetic properties. It thus broadens possibilities for counter conduct beyond "adaptation" or "resilience." As I have shown above, imagining the world as entangled, points at the political relevance of how we inhabit the world and at the (yet nonlinear) causal power of micropolitical processes. Alexander Wendt argued that in contrast with atomism's tendency to promote individualism and competition, an ontology of entanglement may favor cooperation. In a quantum ontology while there is no guarantee that "individuals will put their agency to progressive causes, at least [...] they have the option" (Wendt 2015: 282). This view questions deterministic understandings of power and conceptualizations that see it in a binary opposition to resistance. In addition, the very notion of entanglement points at the ethical relevance of practices. Thus, it raises the bar for adjudication of ethical action. In this way, it opens the way for imagining an ethos based upon situational analysis and radical assumption of responsibility for the morphogenetic processes we enable. In this ontological horizon micropolitical interventions while not revolutionizing the status quo, may be relevant to trigger desirable, and maybe unexpected changes.

## Notes

1  I regard responsibility not only as the result of governmental practices of risk-management (Löwenheim 2007) but as an ethical position that embraces mindfulness and care as central attitudes for the exertion of political agency.
2  For a more in depth elaboration on this concept, see Zanotti (2019).
3  See also my elaboration of the differences between Barad and Wendt (Zanotti 2019: 48–64).
4  For a more in-depth illustration of these concepts see below.
5  See also Joseph's contribution to this volume.
6  For a discussion of the connections between security and circulation for Foucault see also Claudia Aradau and Tobias Blanke (2010).
7  Scott Hamilton (2017) argued that "ethical and moral responsibility [...] derive not from (quantum) science nor from entanglement, but from a social world within which humans possess the agency to mediate and judge how to act through such concepts" (Hamilton 2017: 579). Barad's position is radically ad odds with such conceptualization of ethics that requires an ontologically substantialist starting point in order to justify agency.

## References

Agamben, Giorgio (1998) *Homo Sacer: Sovereign Power and Bare Life* (Stanford: Stanford University Press).

Albert, Mathias (2016) *A Theory of World Politics* (Cambridge: Cambridge University Press).

Aradau, Claudia and Tobias Blanke (2010) 'Governing Circulation: A Critique of the Biopolitics of Security' in Miguel de Larrinaga and March Doucet (eds) *Security and Global Govenmentality. Globalization, Governance and the State* (London: Routledge), 44–58.

Barkin, Samuel J (2018) 'Fish and International Relations', in Erika Cudworth, Stephen Hobden and Emilian Kavalski (eds) *Posthuman Dialogues in International Relations* (New York: Routledge), 143–158.

Barad, Karen (2007) *Meeting the Universe Halfway: Quantum Physics and the Entanglement of Matter and Meaning* (Durham: Duke University Press).

Beck, Ulrich (1992) *Risk Society: Towards a New Modernity* (London: Sage).

Bourbeau, Philippe (2015) 'Resilience and International Politics: Premises, Debates, Agenda', *International Studies Review* 17:3, 374–395.

Bourbeau, Philippe (2018a) *On Resilience: Genealogy, Logics, and World Politics* (Cambridge: Cambridge University Press).

Bourbeau, Philippe (2018b) 'A Genealogy of Resilience', *International Political Sociology* 12:1, 19–35.

Bourbeau, Philippe, and Caitlin Ryan (2018) 'Resilience, Resistance, Infrapolitics and Enmeshment', *European Journal of International Relations* 24:1, 221–239.

Carr, Edward H (1946) *The Twenty Years' Crisis, 1919-1939: An Introduction to the Study of International Relations* (London: Macmillan).

Chandler, David (2014) *Resilience: The Governance of Complexity* (Abingdon: Routledge).

Coole, Diana, and Samantha Frost (2010) *New Materialisms: Ontology, Agency, and Politics*. (Durham: Duke University Press).

Connolly, William (2013) *The Fragility of Things: Self-Organizing Processes, Neoliberal Fantasies, and Democratic Activism* (Durham: Duke University Press).

Cudworth, Erica and Stephen Hobden (2011) *Posthuman International Relations. Complexity, Ecologism, and Global Politics* (London and New York: Zed Books).

Curdworth, Ecrica, Stephen Hobden and Emilian Kavalski (eds) (2018): *Posthuman Dialogues in International Relations* (London: Routledge).

Der Derian, James (2009) *Critical Practices in International Theory: Selected Essays* (New York: Routledge).

Death, Carl (2010) 'Counter Conducts: A Foucauldian Analytics of Protest', *Social Movement Studies* 9:3, 235–251.

Death, Carl (2011) 'Counter Conducts in South Africa: Power, Government and Dissent at the World Summit', *Globalizations* 8:4, 425–438.

Duffield, Marc (2007) *Development, Security and Unending War. Governing the World of Peoples* (Cambridge: Polity).

Ford, Christopher A (2015) 'Musings on Complexity, Policy and Ideology' in Emilian Kavalski (ed) *World Politics at the Edge of Chaos. Reflections on Complexity and Global Life* (Albany: SUNY Press), 79–110.

Gordon, Colin (1991) 'Governmental Rationality: An Introduction' in Graham Burchell, Colin Gordon and Peter Miller (eds) *The Foucault Effect: Studies in Governmentality* (Chicago: University of Chicago Press), 1–51.

Hamilton, Scott (2017) 'Securing Ourselves *from* Ourselves? The Paradox of 'Entanglement' in the Anthropocene' *Crime, Law and Social Change* 68:5, 579–595.

Hardt, Michael and Antonio Negri (2000) *Empire* (Cambridge: Harvard University Press).

Joseph, Jonathan (2019) *Varieties of Resilience: Studies in Governmentality* (Cambridge: Cambridge University Press).

Kavalski, Emilian (2015) 'Introduction: Inside/Outside and Around: Observing the Complexity of Global Life' in Emilian Kavalski (ed) *World Politics at the Edge of Chaos. Reflections on Complexity and Global Life* (Albany, SUNY Press), 1–27.

Löwenheim, Oded (2007) 'The Responsibility to Responsibilize: Foreign Offices and the Issuing of Travel Warnings', *International Political Sociology* 1:3, 203–221.

Löwenheim, Oded (2010) 'The "I" in IR: An Autoethnographic Account', *Review of International Studies*: 36:4, 1023–1045.

Malette, Sebastian and Peter Stoett (2018) 'Post Humanist International Relations and Ecopolitics' in Erika Cudworth, Stephen Hobden and Emilian Kavalski (eds) *Posthuman Dialogues in International Relations* (New York: Routledge), 109–127.

Olssen, Marc (2015) 'Ascertaining the Normative Implications of Complexity Thinking for Politics: Beyond Agent-Based Modeling' in Emilian Kavalski (ed)

*World Politics at the Edge of Chaos. Reflections on Complexity and Global Life* (Albany: SUNY Press), 139–166.

Penttinen, Elina (2013) *Joy and International Relations: A New Methodology* (London: Routledge).

Ross, Andrew (2014) *Mixed Emotions. Beyond Fear and Hatred in International Conflict* (Chicago: The University of Chicago Press).

Rose, Nikolas (1999) *Powers of Freedom: Reframing Political Thought* (Cambridge: Cambridge University Press).

United Nations (2004) *The Report of the Secretary General High Level Panel on Threats, Challenges and Change. A More Secure World, our Shared Responsibility.* Available at www.un.org/ruleoflaw/blog/document/the-secretary-generals-high-level-panel-report-on-threats-challenges-and-change-a-more-secure-world-our-shared-responsibility/

Urry, John (2015) 'The Complexities of the Global', *Theory, Culture & Society* 22:5, 235–254.

Wendt, Alexander (2015) *Quantum Mind and Social science: Unifying Physical and Social Ontology* (Cambridge: Cambridge University Press).

Zanotti, Laura (2011) *Governing Disorder: UN Peace Operations, International Security, and Democraziation in the Post-Cold War Era* (University Park: PSU Press).

Zanotti, Laura (2013) 'Governmentality, Ontology, Methodology: Re-Thinking Political Agency in the Global World', *Alternatives: Global, Local, Political* 38:4, 288–304.

Zanotti, Laura (2019) *Ontological Entanglements, Agency and Ethics in International Relations. Exploring the Crossroads* (London: Routledge).

# Part II

# Governing practice

# 7 Governmentality, authoritarianism, or capitalist realism?

## Explaining austerity with Foucauldian political economy

*Nicholas Kiersey*

## Introduction

In the years following the 2008 financial crisis, it was not controversial to suggest that the choice by many European governments to pursue austerity was one *caused* by neoliberal economic theory. Surveying the pages of *The Economist* (2009), *The New York Times* (Krugman 2012), the volumes of any number of publicly acclaimed economists (Soros 2009; Stiglitz 2016), or even a joint-signed public letter by a number of high-profile commentators to German chancellor Angela Merkel (Piketty et al. 2015), it was clear that neoliberal thought had become a somewhat mainstream object of critique. Within academia, too, constructivist scholars of International Political Economy (IPE) like Mark Blyth (2013) described at length how neoliberal theory had become a powerful mechanism of cultural normalization, instilling in political elites a confidence that the path to recovery was one not of re-regulation or systemic change, but one rather where the system should be rescued through the nationalization of large amounts of banking debt, with the costs to be passed on to the general public in the form of cuts to government services.

Yet, as plausible as it may seem that an economic theory might have been the primary factor guiding the mindsets of policymakers and practitioners during the crisis, the constructivist position is a contested one. In this chapter, we will examine a lively and ongoing debate over the role of neoliberal ideas, as a force driving austerity. We will approach this debate obliquely, however, focusing on a secondary debate taking place within the first. Namely, the debate over whether or not we should use the work of Michel Foucault to guide our understanding of what neoliberalism is, and how it functions (for an engagement with neoliberalism in the context of BRICS see Jaeger in this volume). It makes sense to take this oblique approach, we will argue, not only because Foucault was among the very first scholars to intuit the nature and scope of neoliberalism (see Read 2009; Mirowski 2013) but also because, despite the significant volume of commentary about Foucault emanating from both sides of this debate, it not clear that either has an especially helpful stance on his applicability to explaining the politics of austerity. Indeed, we will argue, it is possible that Foucault is a more useful ally in this task than either side will admit!

Critically, in contrast with the constructivist position described above, many Foucauldian scholars contend that neoliberalism is actually much more than just an economic theory. In fact, they contend, detailed examination of neoliberal discourse reveals it to be something more like a form of global governmentality or, that is, a "political project" (Mirowski 2013) with world-spanning ambitions, focused on the transformation of everyday life by means of an explicit "set of political strategies" (Davies and Mills 2014). From this perspective then, austerity is seen less as an irrational choice driven by a purely economic theory, and more as a logical consequence of neoliberalism's wider political vision. Conversely, however, as we will see, Foucauldians are keen to emphasize that this vision is one solely of a discursive nature; we are not supposed to infer any connection to questions of capitalism, or other "Marxist concepts" (Mirowski 2013).

Marxist scholars, for their part, find a general agreement with Foucauldians, that the decision to pursue austerity was more than merely an intellectual accident (see Tansel 2016a). However, critically, while their approach does place some explanatory burden on the role of discourse, it does this only insofar as it understands discourse to be tied functionally to the need to secure the prerogatives of capitalism. Indeed, with austerity having proven itself immensely unpopular amongst European populations in recent years, a good deal of Marxist analysis has lately begun to move away from legitimacy-based explanations of austerity's persistence altogether, preferring instead to explain it in terms of a rising global tide of neoliberal *authoritarianism* (see Bruff 2014; Tansel 2016b). That is, an emerging mode of global neoliberal capitalism premised on a suspension of the rules of the "normal" democratic order, in favor of a more disciplinary articulation that requires a good deal less popular legitimacy in order to prevail.

As elaborated in the introduction to this volume, Marxists in IPE and International Relations (IR) have long been critical of the supposition of "globality" in much of Foucauldian research (see Kiersey 2009; Reid 2004; Selby 2007;). As Joseph (2009) puts it, while the governmental techniques of power that so preoccupied Foucault may be claimed to have achieved a certain "scale" among highly individualized populations of western societies, it makes little sense to apply them in contexts such as those of the developing world, where relations of a more disciplinary nature prevail. Crucially, the authoritarian neoliberalism (AN) hypothesis marks an evolution of this critique, suggesting that the passage to austerity has revealed what was always already true even in the supposedly developed context of the western world. Namely, as the Marxist sociologist Nicos Poulantzas once put it in a critique of Foucault, that the most fundamental measure of capitalist order is the state's capacity to discipline and repress those who would seek to resist it (cited in Tansel 2016b: 4). Overemphasizing the constitutive ambitions of neoliberalism's anthropological imagination then, say the AN critics,

Foucauldian scholarship loses sight of the necessary internal connections between ideology and capitalism's continuous need to extract surplus value from labor. Lacking this framework, they claim, such scholarship becomes invariably "lost in the game of discursivity and the play of contingency," and reduces the hard reality of capitalism's expropriative logic to an indeterminate theory of "fetishized self/other differences" (Bieler and Morton 2018: 66).

Taking these two positions at face value then, it would appear we are confronted with a fundamentally irreconcilable difference in opinion not only about the forces motivating the decision to pursue austerity, but about the utility of Foucauldian theory in explaining those forces. This in mind, the main task of this chapter is to argue that the Foucault presented in this debate is actually something of a mirage, reflecting a deep and profound shared misunderstanding of his project. To be clear, a scholar unfamiliar with the work of Foucault, and coming to him for the first time through the lens of this debate over austerity, would be justifiably forgiven for drawing two erroneous conclusions about Foucault's thought. First, that Foucault was content to limit the analytical stakes of neoliberalism to questions merely of its fragmentary discursive genealogy. Secondly, that Foucault in his lifetime had no truck with the Marxist critique of capitalism. As we will develop below, however, not only are these two conclusions wrong but they squander the possibility for a more efficacious and transformative understanding of the dynamics of Europe's financial collapse at precisely the time when the region's shockingly cruel and seemingly interminable austerity programs appear to be driving those who would resist them to seek solace in culture war dynamics and performativity. For this reason, we will conclude, the task of articulating a Foucauldian Political Economy has become urgently necessary.

This chapter is divided into five sections, including the present one. The next section develops the argument that critics of austerity who restrict themselves solely to Foucault's observations on neoliberal discourse, and its anthropological imaginary, present a *lopsided* version of governmentality. Critically, as outlined in the introduction of this book, Foucault used the notion of governmentality in at least three different, yet complementary, ways. In this chapter, however, we will be preoccupied primarily with the first sense of the word. That is, the version described by Gordon as "wide" governmentality (1991: 2). Used this way, governmentality is simply a heuristic for thinking about the kind of power involved in the development of any regime featuring a modicum of self-government. For Foucault, even unbeknownst to their subject populations, distributed social beliefs, and practices can aggregate to produce governing effects. The basic methodological insight behind the idea of governmentality is thus one of immanence; "we need to understand specific effects of power, to analyze how power actually works, at the level of its 'strategies'" (Kelly 2014). Focusing especially, but not exclusively, on modern societies, Foucault held that self-governing societies that were those organized primarily on the basis of an "immanent tie," or confessional loop, between widely shared organizing *rationalities* and a range of socially distributed confessional *practices* which lead subjects ever to return to these rationalities, as they seek guidance on how to assess the quality of their performance (2007: 105, 185).

What is interesting, however, despite the obvious importance Foucault attributed to confessional practice, is the apparent incongruence of the way some governmentality scholars take up this question in relation to European austerity. As we will see in the second section, focusing specifically on the work of Mirowski (2013), while this approach situates austerity policies within a wider political project inspired by neoliberalism's anthropological imagination, it refuses the idea that this project has any necessary internal connection to the practical dynamics of capitalist political economy. It is thus understandable, as I will develop in the third section, that AN scholars might reject the strict discursive focus of such approaches as nothing more than bourgeois obfuscation of the objective class interests at stake in the implementation of austerity. For them, austerity is self-evidently something more like a "shock doctrine" logic (Klein 2008). That is, an intentional class strategy of leveraging the trauma of economic crisis as an opportunity to wield the powers of the state, and to further expropriate and subjugate workers and other marginal peoples.

The third section will show how the same neoliberal discourses that governmentality scholars present as merely *political* beliefs are presented by AN scholars as the expression of an internally tied logic of specifically *capitalist* discourse and practice, an ensemble of power that functions primarily to legitimizing the narrow interests of capitalist elites (see, for example, Bieler and Morton 2018: 68–71). However, notwithstanding the fact that AN scholars identify the stakes of austerity as being of specifically capitalist provenance, we should note the tautological manner of their approach to the question of austerity's continued popular legitimacy. As suggested above, AN scholars believe that neoliberalism is experiencing a legitimacy crisis. With traditional democratic institutions of power breaking down, neoliberal elites are unable to respond to democratic demands (Bruff 2014). Against this background, claim the AN theorists, social movements have begun to bypass traditional institutions, and seek now instead to leverage their capacity to cause disruption at key sites of local, everyday life (Bailey et al. 2016). Elites, for their part, are cracking down. We are thus witnessing the emergence of a global order that might more appropriately be referred to as "neo-illiberalism" (Hendrikse 2020), where the analysis of political legitimacy has become effectively redundant.

Now, while it cannot be gainsaid that numerous authoritarian trends can be observed at work throughout the world today, there is ample reason to think that contemporary capitalism still depends to a great extent upon voluntary servitude for its everyday reproduction. Fortunately, however, the great contribution of Foucault's theory of governmentality was to equip us intellectually to engage with precisely this question, posing the subject's *confessional* practice as a critical factor sustaining the legitimacy of capitalism. Advancing this claim in the fourth and fifth sections, we will invoke an alternative reading of

Foucault, based on the idea of a confessional capitalism. Indeed, borrowing not only from Foucault but also from the likes of Martijn Konings (2015), and Spinozist Marxists like Mark Fisher (2009), Frederic Lordon (2014), and Hardt and Negri (2019), we will assert this theory as a way of identifying the left's current fixation with everyday forms of resistance as itself a symptom of capitalist voluntary servitude.

## Austerity as neoliberal governmentality?

As noted at the outset, one of the most popular explanations of the choice to pursue austerity after 2008 was the idea that politicians and policymakers had been seduced by neoliberal theory. Indeed, one figurative example of the popularity of this explanation occurred late in 2010, when a video by the constructivist International Political Economy scholar Mark Blyth went viral on YouTube.[1] In the video, Blyth explained that the recovery strategies being pursued by world leaders in the aftermath of the events of 2008 were being driven by what he termed, a "balance-sheet" perspective. This perspective, he contended, had led them to perceive a need to control sovereign debt and caused them, therefore, to commit a "fallacy of composition." That is, to accept the fundamentally mistaken belief that what is good for any one economic actor in a given situation is necessarily good for the whole. In the wake of the 2008 financial crisis, this fallacy led to the implementation of austerity: a counterproductive mass-cutting of spending on important government services, in the midst of a collapse in global demand.

Breaking with this constructivist perspective, however, much of the Foucault-inspired work on the crisis has been focused less on the narrow, technical prescriptions of key elites and intellectuals and more on the complex philosophical genealogies of neoliberalism, especially insofar as these might reveal clues as to austerity's political function. Taking its cue from Foucault's (2008) *Birth of Biopolitics* lectures, wherein he explored the origins of liberal political economy, this literature recognizes Foucault as possibly the first theorist to grasp the full breadth of neoliberalism's anthropological ambition. The first, that is, to grasp neoliberalism's commitment to using markets and governance to completely recast, as Mirowski puts it, "the totality of human existence into a novel modality, to be disciplined and punished by structures of power/knowledge" (2013: 94).

Building on this insight, Mirowski observes that a core enabling tenet of neoliberalism is the belief that the market is "an information processor more powerful and encompassing than any human being or organization of humans" (2013: 98). With its great and unbeaten capacity to anticipate change in complex relations of exchange, the market is seen as the superlative tool of social governance. First, and most obviously, because it is capable of optimizing the efficient allocation of resources throughout society. But secondly, and more interestingly, because it is the essential mechanism by which it becomes possible to achieve neoliberalism's anthropological vision. For the subject of neoliberal governance is, as Foucault hinted, a creature that bears a certain ethical responsibility. In Wendy Brown's terms: "As human capital, the subject is at once in charge of itself, responsible for itself, yet an instrumentalizable and potentially dispensable element of the whole" (2015: 38). This "political" aspect of neoliberalism is perhaps best captured by Margaret Thatcher's famous axiom, "Economics are the method but the object is to change the soul" (quoted in Hilgers 2012: 82). Neoliberal theory thus expresses both the fantasy ideal of an order spontaneously self-organizing around the principles of the market, while also evoking the possibility of a pedagogical mechanism by which that fantasy might be realized.

Critically, this idea of neoliberalism as a "political project" is ubiquitous in research on neoliberal governmentality (Larner 2003; Davies and Mills 2014), and it clarifies the approach's methodological contrast with constructivism. In Mirowski's terms, neoliberalism cannot be explained by the mere "consilience of [neoliberal] doctrine and function" (2013: 89). Rather, through governmental processes, neoliberalism has become "integrated directly into the makeup of modern agency," and "fills up the pores of our most unremarkable day" (2013: 94). And, it is in precisely this sense then that the research agenda of what we might call neoliberal governmentality studies addresses, per Jessop's definition, the problem of "a political project that is justified on philosophical grounds and seeks to extend competitive market forces, consolidate a market-friendly constitution and promote individual freedom" (Jessop 2013: 70). Addressing discourses that target everyday life and practice, in other words, neoliberal governmentality distinguishes itself from constructivism by taking neoliberalism seriously as a vision of government.

Yet, it is unclear to what extent this vision is understood as one of capitalist provenance or, indeed, whether it has any relationship to capitalism at all. Reviewing the historically and spatially fragmented genealogy of neoliberalism, governmentality scholars appear to want to disaggregate neoliberalism, in space and time. Scrutinizing the historical record of its immense internal diversity on key issues, including the relative merits of regulating corporate monopolies (Gane 2013), they ask questions such as, "at what point in history do the specifically neoliberal technologies of power and accompanying rationalities kick in, as it were?" (Birch 2015). Similarly, in terms of space, following the framework laid out in the Introduction to this volume, governmentality scholars are curious to problematize neoliberalism's "globality." Can neoliberalism be described as a monolithic project with world-spanning ambitions? Or should it, per Larner (2003), be grasped as a collection of locally emergent discourses, alloyed with other specific local knowledges that share only the most tenuous of affinities?

Prioritizing such questions, the governmentality approach thus focuses on problematizing neoliberalism's genealogical specificity, in space and time. Notice, however, the constitutive significance of *discourse* as a variable in the framing of these questions. Economic practices, like those associated with capitalism, are not seen as relevant. In this sense, it cannot be gainsaid that a political effect of this research has been to discourage the possibility that economic practices might themselves be an explanatory variable in the development of neoliberal ideology, or its relation to the global. Indeed, governmentality scholars can frequently be found arguing that such contentions are economically reductionist, a trait which Larner, for example, attributes to problematic and suspicious theoretical traditions, like "Marxis(m) or Neo-Marxis(m)" (2003: 511). Hamilton, similarly, in a review of Joseph's *The Social in the Global* (2012), contends that Foucauldian and Marxist concepts are "at their foundation antithetical" (Hamilton 2014: 130). Mirowski, finally, is unequivocal in his view that "Marxist concepts of exploitation and surplus value" can have no place in a Foucauldian political economy (2013: 100).

Now, critically, one can certainly debate in good faith the merits of various perspectives on scale in global governmentality (see Kiersey 2009). For the arguments of this chapter, however, the more important issue is the expectation that neoliberal ideas operate autonomously from economic practices and forces. In this sense, the normative agenda of the governmentality approach bears more than a family resemblance to that of constructivism. Crucially, what these Foucauldians appear to forget is that an account of the *governmentality* of European austerity would require equally some reckoning with the immanent practices to which these ideas are tied. Ignoring this question, governmentality studies risk advocating what is effectively no more than a simple or naïve Polanyism. That is, as Konings (2018) puts it, a belief that austerity policies bespeak no more than a temporary, exceptional capture of the political by the (ir)rationality of the market. An accidentally mistaken form of thought, in other words, which will be corrected when political leaders finally awaken, as they inevitably must, from their theoretical slumbers.

As plausible an account of the impulse to implement austerity as they may seem to offer then, the governmentality approach offers little by way of consideration as to whether or how austerity might be *more* than an innocent mistake. Mirowski (2013), for example, explicitly criticizes the naïveté of those on the left and right who believed in the post-2008 conjecture that the financial crisis itself would force a realignment in economic thought. Even as he does this, however, he himself explains the absence of such a realignment by means of reference to something he calls the "Neoliberal Thought Collective." That is, an informal network of economic scholars, first crystalized in 1947, with the gathering of foundational neoliberal figures like Friedrich Hayek, Ludwig von Mises, Lionel Robbins, and Milton Friedman, at the Mont Pèlerin Institute in Switzerland, and which has continued since to exert enormous influence over the thinking of the world's most powerful policymakers. Determined not to "let a good crisis go to waste," the success of this network of intellectual partisans for neoliberalism is, for Mirowski, largely attributable to the group's capacity to act as a metaphorical "Russian doll," prosecuting by means of combined esoteric and exoteric discourses a meticulous strategy of popular legitimation (2013: 44). Mirowski thus effectively offers us a theory of the success of neoliberal theory predicated on the idea that its most major historical figures have advanced their intellectual agenda through a strategic and premeditated program of deceit.

Now, our problem with Mirowski's argument is not so much his dependence on the idea that neoliberal theorists are liars. Indeed, as Foucault himself insisted, political discourses should never be read at face value: "power is tolerable only on condition that it masks a substantial part of itself" (Foucault 1990: 86). No, our problem with Mirowski is that he never broaches the possibility that the will to engage in such calculated deceit might have been driven by anything other than the neoliberal political imaginary itself. On this score, Foucault was himself equally clear: notwithstanding neoliberalism's celebration of the universal entrepreneurialism of *homo economicus*, a central if unstated stake of the advent of biopolitics was the "indispensable" role it was to play in the development of capitalist "valorization" (1990: 140–141).

To make this observation is by no means to gainsay the core contributions of neoliberal governmentality scholarship, or to suggest that henceforth, we must all now read Foucault as some sort of class reductionist. After all, not once did Foucault stint from his core claim about the complexity of modern power relations, insisting that it is never clear "that those who exercise power […] have a vested interest in its execution; nor is it always possible for those with vested interests to exercise power" (Foucault and Deleuze 2006). Yet, as we will see, it is questionable whether Foucault himself afforded neoliberal discourse anything like the degree of analytic autonomy from capitalism afforded to it by Mirowski.

To be sure, as Ryan (2018) observes, a key reason we may want to talk about neoliberalism as a problem is not, as governmentality theorists would seem to believe, so that we can then justify the claim that ideas are somehow in the final instance determinative. Rather, it is to make what is potentially a much more powerful point: we need to go beyond ideas if we are to understand, as Konings (2015) demands of us, how it is that certain ideas can seem so intuitive to us, in the first place. Indeed, on this score, it is not implausible that Konings has Mirowski in mind when he notes that the fundamental question of capitalism is how it "gets into our heads, becomes part of our identity, disposition, and desires, our basic sense of self" (2015: 28). To wit, we will need to address an aspect of Foucault's work that is all-too-frequently ignored by scholars of governmentality, and one most certainly ignored by Mirowski. That is, the category of confessional desire. We will return to this question below, when we examine how governmentality studies should engage this question of the hidden capitalist stake of neoliberalism. Before we do so, however, we should pause and review the arguments of those who repudiate Foucault from a Marxist perspective.

## Austerity as authoritarian neoliberalism?

If, as we have just seen, scholarship on neoliberal governmentality tends to posit economic discourse in a position of more or less absolute externality to capitalism then, conversely, AN scholarship appears to argue that the causal variables driving austerity are necessarily "internally tied" to the prerogatives of capital (see Bieler and Morton 2018; Tansel 2016b). Thus, those discourses popular in the public sphere that support austerity should be read as the expression of capitalist elite self-interest or, at the very least, the selectively empowering effects of the proximity of procapitalist "organic intellectuals" to powerful capitalist elites who can amplify their voices (Bieler and Morton 2018: 68–71).

The concept of authoritarian neoliberalism, as Bruff notes, has its roots in debates about the role of capitalist power in pushing authoritarian tendencies within the apparatus of the British state, in the late 1970s (Bruff 2014: 115). Crudely summarized, there were optimistic and pessimistic strands in these debates. The arguments of the optimists varied in nature, but one thing that they all appeared to have in common was a certain faith in the political potential of collective human action, and the possibilities of a universal program of democratized decision-making over an increasingly technologically advanced means of production. Aside from their technological optimism, advocates of this position tended also to be intellectually informed by the debates of the Second International, and a commitment to a politics of overcoming capitalism at least partially by means of a *parliamentary* strategy (Barrow 2008).

This optimistic position was perhaps most famously represented by the sociologist Ralph Miliband. Writing of the "desubordination" of vast swathes of the population of Western capitalist countries by the post-War economic compact, Miliband believed that the capitalist state was becoming the focus of new social demands, and that the political power of the dominant classes was beginning to fracture. These fractures, he contended, could be exploited by progressive movements by means of a relatively integrated and "resolute" mass-movement politics, with the achievement of a parliamentary majority at the center of its focus (Panitch 2019).

Crucially, the AN hypothesis reflects thinking from the more pessimistic strands of those debates. Here, insofar as it advocates government through the application of market-based principles to an everexpanding domain of everyday life, neoliberalism is understood as the principle ideological condition of possibility for a number of disastrous crises which have, together, contrived to undermine the reputation of the postwar compact (Bruff 2014). Neoliberalism may have enjoyed several decades of relative popularity in the West, and was seen by many as the natural model for equitable and democratic government. However, with the 2008 financial crisis, the project seems to have suffered a precipitous loss of prestige, and elites are now struggling to reestablish its legitimacy. For AN scholars, the electoral successes around the world of anti-democratic leaders, from Trump to Erdoğan, and from Duterte to Bolsonaro, suggest that capitalist elites may now be giving up on the idea refloating the reputation of neoliberalism at all (Streeck 2020; Tansel 2016b). Indeed, these elites appear now to be turning to nonideological solutions to ensure their purchase on political power.

This pessimistic strain of Marxist thought thus worries that the opportunities for electoral strategy are narrowing. A diversity of states around the world have become relays for austerity, "internalizing the interests of transnational capital at the expense of labor" (Bieler and Morton 2018: 239). Addressing the European context, for example, Bieler and Morton discuss a number of legal mechanisms introduced since the outbreak of the crisis, empowering institutions of the European Union (EU) to impose fines on countries that do not live up to the standards of the EU's Stability and Growth Pact. Policies such as these are, of course, ratified by national parliaments, ostensibly by democratic means. Once in place, however, they trade-off significant amounts of economic and political sovereignty. The upshot, Bieler and Morton aver, has been a certain generalization of austerity as a crisis recovery model and, thusly, a general "depoliticization" of economic governance. To wit, echoing Bruff, they suggest that we can now observe a degree of such disempowerment among European labor movements that they are no longer capable of leveraging the state in pursuit of their demands; institutions of economic decision-making have been relocated to the supranational level and are, thus, effectively "insulated" from "social and political dissent" (Bieler and Morton 2018: 241).

It is worth noting at this point the rather different emphasis on the role of ideas in the AN hypothesis, compared to that discussed in the preceding section. In Bieler and Morton's framing, for example, while ideas are said to "establish the wider framework" within which political outcomes are generated, we are encouraged to remember that they are also part of the material world, and so cannot be abstracted "from the prevailing social order" (2018: 72). Ideas thus become hegemonic only when they can connect with the organized social forces operating on the terrain of already-ongoing social production. A key figure here is the organic intellectual. Unlike traditional intellectuals (ascetic philosophers, "ivory tower" intellectuals, and the like), organic intellectuals play a direct, instrumental role in social production, insofar as they are engaged in the world and seek, via argument and persuasion, to "organize the hegemony of social class forces" (2018: 71).

For Bieler and Morton then, the material structure of ideology must be understood as the unfolding of a historically enduring ensemble of "class conflict and struggles over hegemony" (2018: 73). Critically, they are conscious that such an account might be read as economically reductionist. By way of a preemptory response to this accusation, however, they suggest that their arguments be construed not as an attempt to defend an economistic perspective, but rather to posit a theory that is open to contingency. For them, political outcomes should never be read as the unilinear determinations of the logic of capital. To the contrary, as they put it, "integration into forms of transnational capital does not imply the absence of conflicts or contradictions"

(2018: 175). The upshot, they say, is that while state geopolitics and capital are internally related, there is need for specificity in understanding the struggle among the intra-class fractions who wield state power.

Thus, in a manner consistent with this approach, their analysis of the European financial crisis starts with the premise that the imposition of austerity should be read as but a chapter in an ongoing history of class struggle, and a mark of the success of European capital in its ongoing strategy of "dispossessive" accumulation (2018: 218). Paraphrasing Ellen Wood, however, and in tension with the trajectory of desubordination laid out by Miliband above, they caution us to consider the fact that the state itself retains a considerable autonomous capacity to manage problems for capitalism, and is thus capable of "offsetting crisis conditions in the accumulation of capital by providing a temporary spatial fix for surplus value extraction" (2018: 122). The point, for Bieler and Morton, is not to insist that the spatial scale of the interstate system is somehow obdurate in the face of forces of globalized capital but, rather, to sidestep what they believe to be a tired debate, and focus instead on "the manner in which capital operates through nodal rather than dominant points" (2018: 119).

These tenets inform Bieler and Morton's approach to the study of austerity in interesting and provocative ways. For example, they contend that an appropriate periodization of the crisis cannot begin simply with the introduction of the Euro currency in 1999. Rather, it should begin with the accession to the EU in the 1970s, of less-developed, peripheral countries, like Ireland, Greece, and Portugal. Now, economic asymmetry is by no means solely a Marxist concept, and a number of Keynesian scholars, like Lapavitsas (2013) and Patomäki (2013) are also sensitive to the role of the Stability and Growth Pact. Introduced in the late 1990s, the Pact restricted the latitude of states to pursue competitiveness to tight wages and restrictive labor conditions, thus contributing to the generation of indebtedness on the periphery. Yet, for Bieler and Morton, what these scholars tend to miss is the "geopolitical dynamic" of the uneven development of capitalism, which was a pillar of the EU from its very foundation, with the Customs Union of 1968, and entrenched subsequently with the introduction in the 1980s of the Internal Market (2018: 224–227). Thus, given capitalism's intrinsic tendency towards crisis, one should not be surprised to see the unevenness of the EU reproduced, as indeed it must be, in the shift towards austerity.

All considered, Bieler and Morton go some lengths to identify the hidden stakes of what we might term, with Cahill (2014) and Ryan (2018), "actually existing neoliberalism." Yet, as we will explore in the next section, a question remains. That is, despite the margin that they claim exists within their theory for emergence of debate and fractionated interests among the capitalist class, they do not specify the mechanism by which those interests remain nevertheless *capitalist*, in their nature. All they mention, as we noted, is the role of organic intellectuals. But this is a problem because, to borrow from Beggs (2013), while capitalism is surely predicated on the extraction of surplus value from commodified labor, it does not necessarily follow that the ideas in the heads of capitalist elites and planners represent a perfect roadmap of "the preconceived needs of the economic system," or that those ideas should be so intuitively popular among ordinary people.

## Austerity as confessional capitalism?

It cannot be gainsaid that AN theorists hold Foucault in a dim light. Reviewing the claims of Mirowski and others, we have seen already how governmentality scholars dismiss the applicability of Marxist concepts in Foucauldian research. But what is interesting is how Marxists tend to mirror this idea suggesting, as do Bieler and Morton, that Foucault was a theorist solely of "fetishized self/other differences," with no specified internality to capitalism (2018: 66). Equally, Bruff argues that while Foucauldians often justify their research agenda on the grounds of an appeal to "epistemological honesty," and the desire to avoid deterministic accounts of state power, they tend to externalize discourse from material forces and, in so doing, reduce society to the status of a mere relay of power; because "power relations" are always in the final instance "the singular source of all human practice," concludes Bruff, the Foucauldian ontology is ultimately a totalizing one (2009: 341).

Interestingly then, Marxists and Foucauldians appear to agree that Foucault was agnostic at best on the question of capitalism. No wonder then, that some Marxists (Zamora 2014) go so far as to impute that Foucault was himself a neoliberal![2] Yet, as Hansen details, not only is there no actual evidence for this latter claim, those making the argument all seem to do so on the basis of a methodological conviction that if we would only just read between lines of Foucault's work, the truth of his "hidden" neoliberal agenda would be plain for all to see (2015: 292). Beyond this debate, it is strange that so many insist on this idea of a fundamental clash between Marx and Foucault when there is by now such a significant body of research identifying multiple points of overlap between them (see Macdonald 2002; Read 2003; Springer 2012). And this overlap is no mere one-way affair, either. On the one hand, as Dardot and Laval demonstrate, it is clear that capitalism for Marx was not just "a system of economic production," but was in fact also a system of "anthropological 'production'" (2014: 25). On the other, it hardly seems like Foucault was prevaricating when he linked the birth of biopolitics to the inauguration of a "permanent economic tribunal," and suggested that the transformative goal of neoliberalism was a societywide implementation of the "enterprise form" as the hegemonic "model of social relations and of existence itself" (Foucault 2008: 94).

If this is true, then we find in Marx and Foucault two theorists whose thoughts about capitalism bear affinities to each other. Affinities which, moreover, open up interesting possibilities for our debate, especially insofar as they help us specify at least two mistakes made consistently by scholars in both camps. The first mistake concerns the nature of governmental power which, for Foucault, operates locally, but which is always articulated through bodily desire. Or, more specifically, through the experience of joy, or pleasure (Foucault 2001: 120). For Foucault, the confessional technologies of the Christian pastoral are the first real historical application of the model of "wide" governmentality (2007: 183). The development of these technologies is significant, as Konings (2015) further develops, insofar as they augur a key historical passage, from idolatrous religion to generative faith. One key strand in the story of this passage, suggests Konings, concerns the role of the icon; a self-evident, short-hand signal that "the autonomous regions of the brain" can recognize quickly, and which is therefore capable of guiding our preconscious, instinctual behaviors as we go through our daily lives (Konings 2015: 57). Citing Judith Butler, Konings states the political upshot of the icon: we should not presume that the confessional subject operates via the "linear internalization of norms" (2015: 23). Rather, whether it is the religious confessional subject or the "iconoclastic" subject of capitalist money, the subject of government is an adaptively reflexive one, drawing on autonomically held memories to *feel out* its response to changing conditions in his or her social milieu (2015).

But if governmentality scholars and Marxists both overlook the role of desire in Foucault's theory of power, we must state how this missing element can help us shed light on the hidden stake of austerity, and the question of globality. This is the question that leads us to identify the second mistake common to both camps. Namely, the presumption that capitalism is a "cold logic," intrinsically resistant to biopolitical affect. Governmentality scholars may claim, on the one hand, that their whole point is to go beyond mere discourse, and to address actual practices of social reproduction. Yet, in their hands, the actual mechanisms by which the legitimacy of austerity remains secure remain unexplained. Focusing on technocratic neoliberal discourse the way Mirowski does, for example, their account is a paradoxically economistic one; it is a scheme within which neoliberal discourse can gain or lose power, yet the point of application of that power continues to be something called "the economy." Thus, as Konings (2015: 4) observes, it amounts to little more than a reproduction of Polanyi's characterization of autonomous money as a cold, instrumentalizing abstraction: a "fiction that exists only by virtue of all-too-human irrationality."

The same problem can be observed among Marxists, too. Admittedly, some Marxists in IR are bit more charitable on Foucault's theory of power. Joseph, for example, following Reid (2009), contends that "biopower" is a useful concept, insofar as it can be understood as "referring to how the basic biological features of human beings are objects of a general strategy of power" (Joseph 2012: 29). However, he insists, there is "something underlying" (ibid.: 14) the liberal rationalities and technocratic practices that circulate and subtend our global order: capitalism. Thus, on the one hand, so long as we can accept that it finds its scalar limits necessarily in the cold logic of global capitalism, governmentality can be a useful cipher for understanding various facets of life in the western world. On the other hand, states Joseph, to evoke a notion of *global* governmentality is to neuter the Marxist critique of uneven development, as the profound, inner truth of capitalist globalization. Shorn of this critical insight, says Joseph, global governmentality effectively reproduces the illusion of globalization's inevitability, a myth closely associated with the triumphalist discourses of a whole array of Western-dominated international organizations (2012: 106). What governmentality theory cannot do, he concludes, is help us explain the scalar disjunction between liberal rationalities and deeper sociological pressures, like "hegemony, state strategy, and capital accumulation" (2012: 15).

Joseph is, of course, correct to emphasize the ontological pressure exerted by these significant capitalistic formations. Yet, by insisting that the deployment of liberal technologies of government is by necessity tied internally to the cold logic of "capital," he effectively brackets the possibility of a role for biopolitics at the point of capitalism's constitution. In other words, he is dismissing the possibility that capital might itself be a *confessional* phenomenon. Konings (2015) already articulates the basic intellectual coordinates of this theoretical possibility, to some extent, differentiating as he does between the "conscious" ideological expressions of neoliberal values that show up in reality television programs and the like, which encourage us to equate iconophilia with maturity, and the deeper, preconscious role of the icon of capitalist money itself, which fuels neoliberalism's logic of wounded attachments. Critically, for Konings, to speak of such a logic is not to suggest that we are all somehow the victims of capitalist brainwashing. Rather, it is to suggest that survival in our social context gives us little choice except to habituate ourselves in the use of money. In capitalism, because money is the primary symbol by which the adequacy of our critical self-awareness is assessed, the market is the confessional apparatus to which we *must* continuously return if we are to orient our lives. For Konings then, it is this precise dynamic that defines capitalism's perverse "alchemy of trauma and faith" (2015: 117).

The stakes of money in this sense are perhaps nowhere more forcefully demonstrated than in the emergence of austerity capitalism, and its so-called "gig" economy. One key example here is that of the Uber driver, the pseudoemployee of the well-known social network-based taxi platform (Srnicek 2017). Here, on the one hand, we have drivers who ostensibly work for themselves, compensating for the effects of austerity by using the platform as a "side gig" to earn a "piece-wage" supplement to a minimum-wage job. On the other hand, however, we have a company that practically disappears in the production process, operating on an algorithmic basis, with radically outsourced overheads, and drawing its profit solely from a "rent" charged to the driver for the use of its network. As if this wasn't cynical enough, however, the driver must fulfill tasks far surpassing those of the traditional taxi driver. The worker's attractiveness to customers on the platform is based on "performance" ratings, given by previous customers. Subsumed within this "gamified" feedback system then, as Mason (2018) contends, the driver is forced to engage in additional value-creation for the firm by engaging in continuous affective labor, relationship-building, self-directed criticism, etc., if he or she is to is to succeed.

Thus, if we invoke here the concept of voluntary servitude, we do not mean it in the sense of some kind of simplistic false consciousness. To the contrary, and in line with the argument we have been developing in this section, it might be better to explain it in terms of what the Spinozist Marxist Lordon (2014) calls "passionate servitude." The premise here is that our now more or less global regime of so-called Late Capitalist production appears particularly shot through with such confessional mechanisms, as it makes evergreater emotional demands of its workers under conditions of austerity. "Epithumogenesis," as Lordon puts it, or the task of aligning the worker's desire with those of the firm, has become a paramount concern for managers, who must now deploy "managerial methods of enlistment" to solicit the total emotional investment of the worker in his or her job (2014: 52). Again, however, as in Konings's (2015) argument earlier, the worker of confessional capitalism is not some tragic brainwashed figure. To the contrary, the proletarian reason of this worker is painfully clear. He desires to live, and to feel joy, but to live and feel joy he knows he must first desire money, and therefore he must also desire employment and, equally, desire the love of the manager. In Lordon's poignant terms, the best explanatory metaphor for understanding this choiceless form of confessional expropriation is thus that of "the girl-friend experience" (2014: 84).

## Conclusion

To summarize, the concept of governmentality allows us to think about neo-liberalism as something more than a mere discourse. For Foucault, as Read puts it, neoliberalism is an assemblage of word and deed, generated not just by the state, or by a dominant class, but "from the quotidian experience of buying and selling commodities from the market" (2009: 26). Of course, if they are drawing their reading of Foucault largely from the work of governmentality scholars, then it is perhaps understandable that Marxists might seem so unaware of this reading of Foucault. For, as we saw above, while scholars of governmentality fully understand Foucault's dematerialization of the structural in subjectivity, they overlook his materialization of discourse in the productivity of the body (see Kiersey 2014). Mirowski's (2013) prevarications notwithstanding then, we could see in the last section clear linkages between Marxist readings of capitalist expropriation and Foucauldian understandings of confessional power.

What might this mean in terms of our appraisal of the *political* stakes of global austerity? If the debates rehearsed above are any metric, then the idea of a global governmentality is a dubious one. But this is not to yield to the equally strange idea that we should think of the world solely in terms of the rise of a global archipelago of authoritarianism. If we are seeking to apply Foucauldian concepts to our contemporary moment in global political economy, it may be that we should instead be taking our cues from the alternative Marxist scholarship we have attempted to outline, in this chapter. It is through the use of concepts like confessional production that we can begin to perceive the complexity and contradictions of contemporary global order. Hardt and Negri, for example, thus seem to be on the right track when they speak of contemporary globalization as taking place within two nested, yet "increasingly out of sync," spheres. On the one hand, the "inner" sphere of "planetary networks of social production and reproduction." On the other, the exterior sphere, composed of "intertwined political and legal systems," encompassing "national governments, international legal agreements, supranational institutions, corporate networks, special economic zones and more" (Hardt and Negri 2019: 68–69).

As noted in the third section, even a cursory review of recent political developments upon the exterior sphere shows immediately that AN theorists are correct to worry about the fundamental political problems exacerbated by the authoritarian neoliberal turn. Nevertheless, in their reductive focus on the power of the authoritarian state, the AN hypothesis may have lost sight of the extent to which the reproduction of contemporary order remains predicated upon trends playing out within the internal sphere, of Late Capitalist production. Focusing solely on authoritarian dynamics taking place upon the external sphere, it seems AN scholars spare little thought for the *political* implications of shifting trends in global production. On the one hand, they warn us, because the all-powerful elites of capitalism are surrounding themselves with the fortress walls of the police state, the prospects for a democratic entering of that state must be seen as improbable, if not fantastical. On the other hand, they say, this shift in elite strategy is a reaction to the increasingly efficacious and sophisticated demands of the movements, from below.

Yet, there is a paradox here. In a move indicating their libertarian political commitments, AN theorists do not attempt to justify the adequacy of this or that expression of resistance to the task that confronts them. Bruff and Tansel (2018), for example, say the onus is instead on the scholar to take into account a "broader range of resistances," from the struggles of indigenous peoples, to those who seek refuge from gender or citizenship-based discrimination, to those who seek to defend "black lives" from militarized policing (2018: 242). Bieler and Morton, for their part, celebrate what they see as a globally emerging "multitude and diversity of class struggles existing today" which, they contend, operates experimentally, without "blueprint" (2018: 274) or telos. They pose briefly the question of whether we might also need to enter the capitalist state, only to dismiss it as an afterthought and "beyond the constraints" of their project (2018: 272).

Such optimism is surely appreciated. Yet, with no metrics offered to assess whether this or that expression of resistance is good, or worth pursuing, it is understandable that symptomatic appraisals of these readings of everyday resistance have begun to surface. Some suggest, for example, that these readings are "folk political," fetishizing what are in fact narcissistic and defeatist movements, with little to show by way of capacity to generate transformative victories (Srnicek and Williams 2015). Others still read this defeatism as symptomatic of a kind of confessional trauma, the result of decades of successful neoliberal individualization, and a slow but steady defeat of organized labor. Taking up this argument, for example, the Spinozist Marxist Mark Fisher (2009) suggests that the problem is not so much the rising tide of authoritarianism as the grip of Late Capitalism's gaslighting logic of production, where we are urged increasingly to find the solutions to our problems within ourselves: to smile, to "practice gratitude," to "lean in," to "find our bliss," to "become resilient," and to have "difficult conversations" about our daily struggles, all while simultaneously having the basic conditions of our existence pulled out from under us.

The upshot, says Fisher, is a phenomenon called "hedonic depression" (2009: 36). We seek joys, as all humans must (according to Spinoza), by means of the channels available to us. But such channels today are limited, and increasingly permit only individualistic behaviors. Thus, for example, we might seek to engage in politics by posting on social media platforms, like Twitter. We might even become addicted to the hormonal surge of the "likes" we receive from such activity. But, as Fisher notes, the depressive aspect of this practice cannot be ignored. We know fully well, even as we seek this kind of recognition, that what are experiencing is "sad passion." That is, we know that, through collective power, the possibilities do exist for other, genuine and truly collective kinds of joy. Yet, for lack of concrete institutions like organized labor to express our collective power, we return over and over to the well. Indeed, Fisher laments, it is precisely this inability to perceive the defeat of its own strategic imagination that explains a lot of the "call out" culture and "witch-hunting moralism" of the online left today, as it engages in what he terms the politics of "the vampire castle" (2013).

The point of this chapter has not been to argue that there are no authoritarian aspects to the way contemporary capitalism reproduces itself. To the contrary, as Fisher himself contends, the fundamental point of his theory of Capitalist Realism is to explain the harmonious coexistence of "internment camps and franchise coffee bars" (2009: 2). What we have tried to suggest, however, is that the intrinsically performative prescriptions of the AN approach suggest that it may be based on a somewhat symptomatic diagnosis of our situation. Dismissing the need for further investigation of the political significance of trends in Late Capitalism, AN theory invites a kind of Manicheanism, where libertarian politics are presumed virtuous and unproblematic, while any suggestion of entering the state is automatically deemed to be a form of complicity. Yet, this extreme fetishization of the performative leaves the AN hypothesis vulnerable to political marginalization, as so-called "normies" (see Nagle 2017), or working-class voters without the benefit of middle-class college educations, struggle to see how it can deliver on their demands.

In one of his greatest moments, Foucault (1984) recognized the potential strategic value of the institutions of the Enlightenment, and warned us against succumbing to the "blackmail" logic of thinking we have to be for or against them. Today, if any Enlightenment institution can be said to present a potential strategic value for anti-capitalist movements, it is that of the state (Frase 2014). To be sure, the multitude approach possesses a tried and trusted capacity for tactical, network-based auto-generation that more traditional hegemonic models lack (Arditi 2014). Read symptomatically, however, and as the argument here hopefully attests, the goals of the movements are likely to remain frustrated until they can transcend their hedonic depression, and acknowledge the need to accumulate more meaningful forms of power, and to battle for the conditions of their own long-term strategic survival, upon the uneven surfaces of the external sphere of globalization.

## Notes

1   http://youtu.be/FmsjGys-VqA and http://youtu.be/go2bVGi0ReE.
2   Conversely, it is worth noting that some liberal scholars are quite suspicious of the claim that Foucault was a neoliberal. Prozorov (2014), for example, believes that he was a closeted Stalinist.

## References

Arditi Benjamin (2014) 'Post-Hegemony: Politics Outside the Usual Post-Marxist Paradigm,' in Alexandros Kioupkiolis and Giorgos Katsambekis (eds) *Radical Democracy and Collective Movements Today: The Biopolitics of the Multitude versus the Hegemony of the People* (Abingdon, Oxon: Routledge), 17–44.

Bailey, David, Monica Clua-Losada, Nikolai Huke, et al. (2016) Challenging the Age of Austerity: Disruptive Agency After the Global Economic Crisis. *Comparative European Politics* 16:1, 9–31.

Barrow Clyde W (2008) 'Ralph Miliband and the Instrumentalist Theory of the State: The (Mis)Construction of an Analytic Concept', in Paul Wetherly, Clyde W Barrow, Peter Burnham (eds) *Class, Power and the State in Capitalist Society* (London: Palgrave Macmillan), 84-108.

Beggs, Mike (2013) 'Dollar Diplomacy', *Jacobin*, 16 July, https://jacobinmag.com/2013/07/dollar-diplomacy, accessed 19 January, 2018.

Bieler, Andreas and Adam Morton (2018) *Global Capitalism, Global War, Global Crisis* (Cambridge: Cambridge University Press).

Birch, Kean (2015) *We Have Never Been Neoliberal* (Winchester: Zero Books).

Blyth, Mark (2013) *Austerity: The History of a Dangerous Idea* (Oxford: Oxford University Press).

Brown, Wendy (2015) *Undoing the Demos: Neoliberalism's Stealth Revolution* (Brooklyn: Zone Books).

Bruff, Ian (2009) 'The Totalisation of Human Social Practice: Open Marxists and Capitalist Social Relations, Foucauldians and Power Relations', *British Journal of Politics & International Relations*, 11:2, 332–351.

Bruff, Ian (2014) 'The Rise of Authoritarian Neoliberalism', *Rethinking Marxism*, 26:1, 113–129.

Bruff, Ian and Cemal Burak Tansel (2018) Authoritarian Neoliberalism: Trajectories of Knowledge Production and Praxis, *Globalizations* 16:3, 233–244.

Cahill, Damien (2014) *The End of Laissez-Faire?* (Cheltenham: Edward Elgar).

Chitty Christopher (2012) 'Towards a Socialist Art of Government: Michel Foucault's "The Mesh of Power"', 12 September, https://viewpointmag.com/2012/09/12/towards-a-socialist-art-of-government-michel-foucaults-the-mesh-of-power/, accessed 13 July 2020.

Dardot, Pierre and Christian Laval (2014) *The New Way of the World* (London: Verso Books).

Davies, William (2014) *The Limits of Neoliberalism: Authority, Sovereignty and the Logic of Competition* (London: Sage).

Davies, William & Tom Mills (2014) 'Neoliberalism and the End of Politics', *New Left Project*. 22 August www.newleftproject.org/index.php/site/article_comments/neoliberalism_and_the_end_of_politics, accessed 16 November 2016.

Economist (2009) 'What Went Wrong with Economics', 16 July, www.economist.com/node/14031376/print?story_id=14031376, accessed 13 July 2020.

Fisher, Mark (2009) *Capitalist Realism* (Winchester: Zero Books).

Fisher, Mark (2013) *Exiting the Vampire Castle*. 24 November, www.opendemocracy.net/en/opendemocracyuk/exiting-vampire-castle/, accessed 14 July 2020.

Foucault Michel (1984) 'What is Enlightenment?' in Paul Rabinow (ed.) *The Foucault Reader*. (New York: Pantheon), 32–50.

Foucault, Michel (1990) *The History of Sexuality: An Introduction, Volume I* (London: Vintage).

Foucault, Michel (2001) 'Truth and Power' in J.D. Faubion (ed) *Power* (New York: The New Press), 111–133.

Foucault, Michel (2007) *Security, Territory, Population; Lectures at the Collège de France, 1977-1978* (Basingstoke: Palgrave Macmillan).

Foucault, Michel (2008) *The Birth of Biopolitics; Lectures at the Collège de France, 1978-1979* (Basingstoke: Palgrave Macmillan).

Foucault, Michel (2012) 'The Mesh of Power', *Viewpoint Magazine*, www.viewpointmag.com/2012/09/12/the-mesh-of-power/, accessed 1 January, 2019.

Foucault Michel and Gilles Deleuze (2006) 'Intellectuals and power: A conversation between Michel Foucault and Gilles Deleuze', https://libcom.org/library/intellectuals-power-a-conversation-between-michel-foucault-and-gilles-deleuze, accessed 14 July 2020.

Frase, Peter (2014) 'Beyond the Welfare State', *Jacobin*, http://jacobinmag.com/2014/12/beyond-the-welfare-state/, accessed 30 June 30, 2015.

Gane, Nicholas (2013) 'The Emergence of Neoliberalism: Thinking Through and Beyond Michel Foucault's Lectures on Biopolitics', *Theory, Culture & Society* 31:4, 3–27.

Gordon, Colin (1991) 'Governmental Rationality: An Introduction' in Graham Burchell, Colin Gordon and Peter Miller (eds) *The Foucault Effect; Studies in Governmentality* (Chicago: University of Chicago Press), 1-52.

Hamilton, Scott (2014) 'Review: Add Foucault and Stir? The Perils and Promise of Governmentality and the Global', *European Review of International Studies* 1:2, 1–13.

Hansen, Magnus Paulsen (2015) 'Foucault's Flirt? Neoliberalism, the Left and the Welfare State; a Commentary on *La dernière leçon de Michel Foucault* and *Critiquer Foucault*', *Foucault Studies* 20, 291–306.

Hardt, Michael and Antonio Negri (2019) 'Empire, Twenty Years On', *New Left Review* 120, 67–92.

Hendrikse, Reijer (2020) Neoliberalism Is Over – Welcome to the Era of Neo-Illiberalism. Available at: www.opendemocracy.net/en/oureconomy/neoliberalism-is-over-welcome-to-the-era-of-neo-illiberalism/, accessed 13 July 2020.

Hilgers, Mathieu (2012) 'The Historicity of the Neoliberal State', *Social Anthropology* 20:1, 80–94.

Jessop, Bob (2013) 'Putting Neoliberalism in Its Time and Place: A Response to the Debate', *Social Anthropology*, 21:1, 65–74.

Joseph, Jonathan (2009) 'Governmentality of What? Populations, States and International Organisations', *Global Society*, 23:4, 413–427.

Joseph, Jonathan (2012). *The Social in the Global* (Cambridge: Cambridge University Press).

Kelly, Mark G E (2014) 'Foucault and Neoliberalism Today', *Contrivers Review*, www.contrivers.org/articles/12/, accessed 30 June 2015.

Kiersey, Nicholas (2009) 'Neoliberal Political Economy and the Subjectivity of Crisis: Why Governmentality is Not Hollow', *Global Society* 23:4, 363–386.

Kiersey Nicholas (2014) ' "Retail Therapy in the Dragon's Den:" Neoliberalism and Affective Labour in the Popular Culture of Ireland's Financial Crisis.' *Global Society* 28:3, 356–374.

Konings, Martijn (2015) *The Emotional Logic of Capitalism* (Stanford: Stanford University Press).

Konings, Martijn (2018) 'Against Exceptionalism: The Legitimacy of the Neoliberal Age', *Globalizations*, 15:7, 1007–1019.

Klein Naomi (2008) *The Shock Doctrine: The Rise of Disaster Capitalism* (New York: Picador).

Krugman Paul (2012) *Those Revolting Europeans*. Available at: www.nytimes.com/2012/05/07/opinion/krugman-those-revolting-europeans.html?_r=2&hpw&pagewanted=print (accessed 13 July 2020).

Lapavitsas, Costas (2013) *Profiting Without Producing* (London: Verso Books).

Larner, Wendy (2003) 'Neoliberalism?', *Environment and Planning D: Society and Space* 21:5, 509–512.

Lordon, Frédéric (2014) *Willing Slaves of Capital* (London: Verso).

Mair, Peter (2009) *Ruling the Void* (London: Verso).

Macdonald, Brad J. (2002) 'Marx, Foucault, Genealogy,' *Polity* 34:3. 259–284.

Mason Sarah (2018) 'High Score, Low Pay: Why the Gig Economy Loves Gamification.' 20 November, www.theguardian.com/business/2018/nov/20/high-score-low-pay-gamification-lyft-uber-drivers-ride-hailing-gig-economy, accessed 14 July 2020.

Mirowski, Philip (2013) *Never Let a Serious Crisis Go to Waste: How Neoliberalism Survived the Financial Meltdown* (London: Verso).

Nagle, Angela (2017) *Kill All Normies* (Winchester: Zero Books).

Panitch Leo (2019) '*Miliband's Masterpiece*', 6 August, https://tribunemag.co.uk/2019/06/milibands-masterpiece, accessed 13 July 2020.

Patomäki, Heikki (2013) *The Great Eurozone Disaster* (London: Zed Books).

Piketty, Thomas, Jeffrey Sachs, Heiner Flassbeck, et al. (2015) 'Austerity Has Failed: An Open Letter From Thomas Piketty to Angela Merkel', *The Nation*, 7 July, www.thenation.com/article/archive/austerity-has-failed-an-open-letter-from-thomas-piketty-to-angela-merkel/, accessed 13 July 2020.

Prozorov, Sergei (2014) 'Foucault and Soviet Biopolitics', *History of the Human Sciences* 27:5, 6–25.

Read, Jason (2003) *The Micro-Politics of Capital* (Albany: SUNY Press).

Read, Jason (2009) 'A Genealogy of Homo-Economicus: Neoliberalism and the Production of Subjectivity', *Foucault Studies* 6 25–36.

Reid, Julian (2004) 'War, Liberalism, and Modernity: The Biopolitical Provocations of 'Empire'', *Cambridge Review of International Affairs* 17:1 63–79.

Reid, Julian (2009) *The Biopolitics of the War on Terror* (Manchester: Manchester University Press).

Ryan, Matthew D. J. (2018) 'Interrogating 'Authoritarian Neoliberalism': The Problem of Periodization', *Competition & Change* 23:2, 116–137.

Selby Jan (2007) 'Engaging Foucault: Discourse, Liberal Governance and the Limits of Foucauldian IR', *International Relations* 21:3, 324–345.

Soros, George (2009) *The Crash of 2008 and What It Means* (New York: PublicAffairs).

Stiglitz, Joseph E. (2016). *The Euro: How a Common Currency Threatens the Future of Europe.* (New York: W. W. Norton & Company).

Springer, Simon (2012) 'Neoliberalism as Discourse: Between Foucauldian Political Economy and Marxian Poststructuralism', *Critical Discourse Studies* 9:2, 133–147.

Srnicek Nick (2017) *Platform Capitalism* (Cambridge: Polity).

Srnicek, Nick and Alex Williams (2015) *Inventing the Future* (London: Verso).

Streeck Wolfgang (2020) 'Engels's Second Theory', *New Left Review* 123, 75–88.

Tansel, Cemal Burak, ed, (2016a) *States of Discipline* (London: Rowman & Littlefield).

Tansel, Cemal Burak (2016b) 'Authoritarian Neoliberalism: Towards a New Research Agenda' in Cemal Burak Tansel (ed) *States of Discipline* (London: Rowman & Littlefield), 1-28.

Zamora, Daniel (2014) 'Foucault's Responsibility', *Jacobin.* 15 December, www. jacobinmag.com/2014/12/michel-foucault-responsibility-socialist/?setAuth=822ec d1f989ac753726f872a1378fd34, accessed 30 June, 2015.

# 8 Gender, global governance, and the limits of expertise on women

## A feminist critique of postconflict statebuilding[1]

*Audrey Reeves*

## Introduction

This chapter considers the enabling effects of the construction of gender expertise as expertise on women in global governance processes. Global governance has been described as "an ongoing process of competition for the authority to define what is governed, how, and why" (Sending 2015: 4). This authority is typically conferred to expert knowledge, the generation and circulation of which enables the government of populations, including on a global scale (Larner and Walters 2004). Although gender expertise has been defined in various ways, I understand it as the recognized expert knowledge that informs what counts as gender inequality and how to overcome it through targeted interventions. Since these two points are contested, including within the diversity of feminist movements, gender expertise is "intrinsically political" (Kunz et al. 2019: 23). The struggle over the definition of who counts as the expert on gender, and what counts as reliable knowledge, is an attempt to establish power (Harrington 2013).

Over the past two centuries, and as efforts to govern populations increasingly articulated themselves around notions of globality (see Busse's and Hamilton's introduction to this volume), transnational women's movements gained power through the production and circulation of knowledge about women (Harrington 2013: 47). Their distinct knowledge became increasingly recognized as a form of expertise within global knowledge networks. Simultaneously, they successfully established women as a transnational category of person worthy of dedicated attention on the part of national and international agencies invested in global governance. The construction of women's knowledges as valuable and trustworthy is undoubtedly a feminist success, as is the widespread commitment to gender equality within a wide range of agencies involved in governing social relations on a global scale (Harrington 2013). The ostensible pursuit of women's empowerment, and a related need for what is now called gender expertise, has become a frequent feature of foreign aid, development, and security policy globally. According to the most optimistic observers, this has come along with the emergence of feminist governance, or the multiplication of places where "feminism is running things" through legal projects, institutional policies, and activism (Halley 2008: 21).

The rise of gender as an object of government nonetheless came along with the cooptation of feminist knowledge in service of international institutions' other agendas. For instance, in the 1980s, demographers and economists became interested in gender as a set of social relations "through which women's reproductive and productive labor could be reorganized, manipulated and rendered more efficient" (Repo 2015: 106). This came with limited concrete gains for women and girls on the ground (True 2003: 379). Although gender experts have "achieved small victories against considerable odds" (Kunz and Prügl 2019: 5), the pragmatic need to compromise often strips gender of its critical potential, and turns it into a new management strategy in international bureaucracies (Whitworth 2004: 17; Squires 2005: 374; Reeves 2012).

I want to suggest that the apparent contradiction between the rising profile of gender expertise and the lack of improvement in the condition of a vast majority of women and girls globally can be better understood by paying attention to tacit understandings of gender expertise in global governance networks. More specifically, this chapter argues that, while enabling important feminist victories, the establishment of expertise on women as the primary form of gender expertise still recognized by globally oriented agencies has not been accompanied by the recognition of feminist critiques of androcentric concepts and practices. I illustrate this argument with reference to statebuilding initiatives targeting conflict-affected states in the Global South in the years 2000–2010. From the 1990s onward, statebuilding initiatives have been launched ostensibly to bring peace, development, and gender equality to conflict-affected countries where state institutions were perceived to be deficient. In devising statebuilding, policymakers integrated forms of gender expertise, defined narrowly as expertise on individual women's rights. While such expertise is certainly important, I argue that its impact is limited without a consideration of feminist critiques of the liberal state. The latter reveals that, in its very structure and values, statebuilding promotes the globalization of an unequal gender order (Shepherd 2017: 37–65). Considering this important limitation helps explain why statebuilding programs struggle to realize their declared gender equality goals. Indeed, the masculinized design of the project itself cannot be resolved by mere attempts to include more individual women in plans for implementation.

My analysis progresses in the following way. First, I provide a working definition of gender and an overview of the rising importance of expertise on women in global knowledge networks. Second, I show how, in the context of international statebuilding, gender expertise was reduced to an emphasis on the political rights of individual women. Third, I turn to feminist knowledges not normally invoked in the context of statebuilding policy, namely feminist critiques of the liberal state (e.g., Pateman 1988). I conclude that treating concept-focused feminist critiques as important forms of gender expertise opens new possibilities for a critical reevaluation of key governance projects such as statebuilding as vehicles for progressive gender relations on a global scale.

My approach builds on insights from governmentality-inspired feminist research on global governance. I understand governmentality in its most general sense – as a way of governing that shapes human conduct "by working through our desires, aspirations, interests and beliefs" (Dean 2010: 11). It entails the regulation of social relations through suggestion and encouraged self-discipline, as well as more coercive forms of control (Lipschutz 2005: 15). Although Foucault himself "never specifically examines the subordination of women," his work is useful to investigate the power exercised over women's lives through subtle and diffused channels (Hekman 2004: 200, 205). Governmentality scholars see attempts to govern as coming from multiple actors and agencies organized in fluid networks that overlap with but exceed nation-states (Lipschutz 2005: 14; Dean 2010: 228–229). They share with most feminists a conceptualization of politics as reaching beyond the formal sphere of legislatures, ministries, diplomatic meetings, and other male-dominated parts of the state apparatus, and into social spaces and everyday locales (McLaren 2002: 167; Hekman 2004: 200), such as tourist resorts or art museums (Enloe 2000; Sylvester 2006). A diffused understanding of power undermines the gendered hierarchies of public/private and global/local, the naturalization of which invisibilizes women's oppression (Hekman 2004: 204).

Moreover, a governmentality lens helpfully supports a feminist project that goes beyond a liberal stance for respecting women's choices, however important these may be. A more ambitious feminism pays attention to how social environments orient individual practices. This includes the availability of "woman" as a political subjectivity one can perform (Butler 1999). Drawing on Foucault, Judith Butler famously theorized that the category of sex is a social construct, and more precisely "a regulatory ideal" that produces the bodies it governs through organized, repetitive practices (Butler 2011: 2). As this argument suggests, many feminists also take interest in how gendered practices shape the social world, including when these may inadvertently entrench gender inequalities (Bartky 1990). Women (and people of any gender) nonetheless also express resistance to sexism (McNay 1992: 49; McLaren 2002: 60), and occupy shifting forms of agencies wherever gender discrimination intersects with race, sexuality, ability, age, citizenship, and other identity markers (McNay 1992: 64–65). Governmentality frameworks are able to account for this diversity of individual experiences and responses because they cast the modern subject as creatively navigating different subject positions. They recognize that attempts at managing populations around the globe are not totalizing but clash "with the messiness of actually existing places, with localized power structures, accumulated historical legacies, and pluralities of peoples and identities" (O Thuatail and Dahlman 2004: 138).

## Governing gender on a global scale: The rise of feminist knowledge

A growing body of literature draws on the affinities between governmentality studies and feminist thought to analyze the global governance of gender. By gender, I refer first of all to the social conventions and norms that inform the classification of bodies as male or female, and the regulatory practices that assign different "labor, responsibilities, moral attributes, and emotional styles" to different individuals on the basis of their biological sex (Halberstam 2014: 117). Gender is also "a primary mode of oppression" (Halberstam 2014: 117), in that the characteristics assigned to men and women are typically attributed unequal value. In many social contexts, women are expected to be vulnerable, passive, and emotional, and men to be comparatively strong, active, and rational. The latter characteristics are deemed superior to the former, and provide the basis for the male entitlement to manage all things historically conceived as nature, including "women's sexuality, bodies, and labour" (Peterson 1999: 40). These binary characteristics also provide an example of how gender operates as a marker of difference and a social relation not only between bodies (Halberstam 2014: 117), but also between concepts or attributes (e.g., when we think of a line of work as feminine or masculine). These gender hierarchies sustain material power imbalances between men and women, and between masculine and feminine fields of activity.

Gender and understandings of "the global" are co-constituted through overlapping regulatory practices targeted at global populations and phenomena, such as the "regulatory edifice of the global economy" (Prügl 1999: 4). As mentioned in the volume's introduction, Foucault theorized that governmentality emerged in the 18th century in combination with new forms of calculation and planning that encompassed the entire globe as a frame of reference. The production of gender as a social norm is embedded in this co-constitutive exchange between modes of governing at a distance and understandings of globality. For instance, the global governance of economic remittances as a strategy for the alleviation of poverty relies on and reproduces stereotypical gendered subjectivities (Kunz 2013). In the Mexican context, men are expected to work abroad and send remittances to female relatives, who are expected to stay at home. In other contexts, notably in South-East Asia, a transnational network of actors attempts to discipline the bodies of women who work as domestic migrant workers so that they conform to a docile and productive ideal of feminine working class subjectivity (Elias 2018). As these examples related to the global governance of migration suggest, gender "pervades world politics" while also being "a global construct" (Prügl 1999: 3–4).

The importance of gender as a structuring principle of global forms of governmentality emerged first through the violence of colonial conquest. In the mid-18th century, when Europe first understood itself as needing "the world for its unlimited market" (Foucault 2008: 55), colonial enterprises initiated attempts at imposing European gender codes in the colonies. This was notably the case during the colonization of Yorubaland in Nigeria by the

British in the 19th and early 20th century (Oyewùmí 1997, ix). Prior to colonization, the Yoruba people cultivated social stratifications organized around age and kinship – not gender. Individuals of any sex indiscriminately occupied leadership roles. This changed under British rule. In the colonial era, boys and girls were educated unequally; men received better employment opportunities; colonial judges adjudicated customary law in favor of men; and British authorities did not recognize female leaders. In most colonies, similar gender regulations prevailed, so that if the male colonized population was treated as subaltern vis-à-vis the colonisers, their female counterparts were left "more deeply in shadow" (Spivak 2010: 41).

From the 19th century onward, transnational networks of women's organizations intervened to reverse some of these trends, and successfully established women as "a transnational category with shared problems in need of international resolution" (Harrington 2013). Prior to this, European authorities had regulated women's lives on a national level through attempts at governing the family unit (Foucault 1991: 100; Rose 1999: 74). Women's organizations headquartered primarily in Europe and North America, such as the International Council of Women, established in 1888, assembled statistics on women in various parts of the world in order to advocate women's suffrage, international labor legislation, and the prevention of prostitution and human trafficking (Berkovitch 1999: 21; Harrington 2006: 350). This helped construct women as a globally relevant category of personhood in their own right, while also establishing the knowledge of women's organizations as valuable (Harrington 2013: 55). After World War II, the newly established UN would give an increasingly global dimension to this trend in the context of its Commission on the Status of Women (Harrington 2013: 54) and, from 1976 onward, its International Research and Training Institute for the Advancement of Women and the UN Development Fund for Women (Berkovitch 1999: 146).

Women of color, who had been minority elements in earlier arenas of transnational women's activism, were the majority of participants at the Third World Conference on Women in Nairobi in 1985 (Davis 1990: 110). From this moment, women of color were better positioned to diversify the feminist knowledges accepted as expertise on a global scale. Up to this point, these knowledges were mostly informed by white and middle-class perspectives (Harrington 2013: 53), and often aimed to incorporate women into global development initiatives that took Europe as its point of reference (Berkovitch 1999: 16). In 1995, during the Fourth World Conference on Women in Beijing, women from the Global South and particularly Africa reoriented the global governance of gender beyond development, to better account for problems of war and insecurity (Hawkesworth 2006; Tripp 2006: 68). The Beijing Platform for Action committed to integrate women's concerns in matters of "armed and other conflicts" (art. 141). Soon after, the UN International Criminal Tribunals and the International Criminal Court reinterpreted the laws of war to better recognize rape, sexual slavery, forced pregnancy, forced sterilization, trafficking, and gender-based persecution as war crimes and crimes against humanity (Kinsella 2005: 252; Hawkesworth 2006: 97–98). In 2000, the relentless advocacy of women's organizations led the UN Security Council to adopt the first resolution on Women, Peace, and Security. This event firmly initiated the mainstreaming of gender perspectives in the armed conflict and security-side of the UN (Cohn 2008: 185). Although these efforts are often tainted by colonial undertones, women across the globe have been mobilizing to influence and reclaim the resolution to promote their interests (Holvikivi and Reeves 2020).

## From women's knowledge to gender expertise

As bureaucratic activities and bodies dedicated to the government of women's affairs proliferated, knowledge on the condition of women globally became increasingly professionalized. By the 1990s, designated women-focused components and positions had appeared within various international organs and the vast majority of national governments around the world (Berkovitch 1999: 163). In the 1990s, the UN increasingly positioned gender equality, and not simply women's rights, as an important aspect of a healthy global order (Prügl 2010; Repo 2015). This led to a new interest in knowledge known as "gender expertise" and to the proliferation of gender expert positions (Kunz and Prügl 2019: 4). Indeed, as Foucault theorized, forms of expertise rise in prominence when they are seen as necessary to achieve "the welfare of the population, the improvement of its condition, the increase of its wealth, longevity, health, etc." (Foucault, 1991, pp. 93–100). In 1985, upon her return from the Nairobi World Conference on Women, the feminist scholar and activist Angela Davis noted that this was the "first assembly to take place at a time when world public opinion is finally acknowledging the legitimacy of women's quest for equality" (Davis 1990: 110). A few years later, this new global consciousness had created a need for expertise on how to establish gender equality. Thus, in 2002, the UN Secretary-General Report on women, peace, and security stated that "gender expertise at both [UN] Headquarters and [in-country] mission levels is necessary to support top management in carrying out their responsibility for gender mainstreaming" (UN Secretary-General 2002).

While gender expertise is varied and complex (Kunz and Prügl 2019: 3), the vastly influential UN definition of gender mainstreaming circumscribes its meaning in global governance contexts. In 1997, the momentum that gathered around the Beijing conference led the UN to endorse gender mainstreaming as a program of government relevant to all other global governance policies and projects. The UN defined gender mainstreaming as "the process of assessing the implications *for women and men* of any planned action [...] so that [...] inequality is not perpetuated" (ECOSOC, 1997, my emphasis). The definition of gender mainstreaming as the assessment of implications of policy for "women and for men," in a context of global governance where most policy was gender-blind, pursued the important goal of turning "critical attention from men to women" (Halberstam 2014: 117), or to differences between women and men. However, gender remained understood overwhelmingly as having to do with relations between *individuals*, rather than as a hierarchical norm that also structures political concepts and subjectivities. For instance, the World Bank interpreted gender mainstreaming as the promotion of new models of coupledom in which individual women join the job market and individual men learn to be caring spouses (Bedford 2009). It did not, however, interrogate the gendered hierarchies that allow international agencies to present themselves as the masculinized protectors of feminized local populations (Shepherd 2017: 59–61). In other words, by focusing on individual women (and men), gender mainstreaming as it is most commonly defined does not require an investigation of the "conceptual schemes" that structure global governance institutions (Harding 1995: 297).

This second form of gender analysis involves the exposition of "a seemingly neutral analysis as male oriented" (Halberstam 2014: 117), an alternative form of feminist knowledge. I will refer to it as feminist critique. Feminist critique is not typically recognized under the label gender expertise, which remains widely interpreted as expertise on women. While men, boys, and nonbinary subjects are sometimes included within the scope of gender expertise, women typically remain the focus on the grounds that despite being the larger part of the global population, they remain an afterthought in most global governance initiatives. Without feminist critique, expertise on women (and other gendered individuals) often risks reducing gender mainstreaming to what Sandra Harding famously referred to as "add women and stir" (1995) – attempts to make individual women fit into projects designed by and for men. Such projects reproduce, consciously or not, inequalities between femininity and masculinity, with material and practical implications for men and women. Policymakers and political analysts may not be consciously aware of the gender biases in the language they use (Cohn 1987). These conceptual biases nonetheless structure global governance initiatives and contribute to reproducing unequal gender orders despite formal commitments to include women. Expertise on women alone cannot problematize these gender biases; feminist critique is therefore its essential complement.

## Gender and statebuilding: "Building states that work for women"?

I now turn to substantiate my claim through an exemplary illustration: postconflict statebuilding. As a major global development aid and security project, its influence as a global governance paradigm is considerable. In the late 1990s and early 2000s, statebuilding established itself among international organizations and donor states of the Global North as the primary paradigm for intervention in conflict-affected countries (see for instance World Bank 1997: 3). Among these agencies, the Organisation for Economic Cooperation and Development (OECD) acted as a "primary coordination body" (Paducel and Salahub 2011: 2). It defined statebuilding as the process of "building the relationship between state and society" through international engagement aimed at increasing, first of all, the accountability and legitimacy of the state; and second of all, its capacity to fulfil "core functions," defined primarily around the provision of security (OECD-DAC 2007). This definition became cited by the UN and the World Bank (2011: 6–7) as well as by NGOs and think tanks (see for instance Castillejo 2011: 1) who adopted statebuilding as a paradigm (Chandler 2008: 6). In the UN as elsewhere, statebuilding became tightly tied to the notion of "good governance" (Chandler 2008: 6), and increasingly became synonymous with peacebuilding (Shepherd 2017: 37).

From a governmentality perspective, statebuilding entails patterned efforts, on the part of the globe's major donor states and international organizations, at producing "responsible" state institutions in the Global South, in the hope that these states can eventually self-govern without international intervention (Baaz and Stern 2017: 213). Such regulatory attempts have historical precedents. Many colonial enterprises sought the reorganization of colonial social spaces into modern state institutions. This is what gave the Western idea of a modern state "a global significance" in the contemporary world (Mitchell 2000, viii). Following decolonization, similar attempts remained part of the policies of imperial powers, as in the case of the American effort at nationbuilding in Vietnam (Latham 2006). In the 1990s and 2000s, UN peacekeeping operations engaged in creating "orderly, predictable, disciplinary and disciplined administrations," or more generally states that would be "legible and manageable" from the perspective of the UN and its principal funders (Zanotti 2006: 152). Considering this history, governmentality scholars correctly observe that statebuilding is the latest iteration of "various and sometimes cross-cutting projects of disciplinary, regulatory and liberal rule and values beyond 'the West'" (Gabay and Death 2014: 2).

Political support and funding for statebuilding originate overwhelmingly in the Global North. Headquartered in the stately Château de la Muette in Paris, France, the OECD, and its influential Development Assistance Committee (DAC) presided over early discussions of statebuilding among large funders of foreign aid. The OECD understands itself as "the venue and voice of the world's major bilateral donors" (OECD 2006: 3), most of whom are from the political West. Therefore, it should not be surprising that the construction of statebuilding as a concept was heavily influenced by Western understandings of the liberal state. Others have rightly argued that the critical reception of these policies in the South should be understood with attention to "experiences of racism and memories of colonialism" (Baaz and Stern 2017: 208). With similar attention to global histories of conquest, I suggest here that formulations of statebuilding by donor states should be read in relation to the state's development as a form of political organization *in Europe*.

This historical and philosophical heritage came with gendered implications. An important set of feminist critiques applies to the liberal state as it developed in Europe and its settler colonies (MacKinnon 1989: chap. 8; Connell 1987: 129–130, in Kantola 2006: 125). Carole Pateman developed a version of this critique in her canonical book *The Sexual Contract* (1988), which examines theories of the state developed by Thomas Hobbes and John Locke in England, and Jean-Jacques Rousseau in the city-state of Geneva. She exposes how these influential authors imagined the social contract as one between men that excluded women from political affairs (Pateman 1988: 1, 5). They posited that men's presumed superior capacity for reasoning allowed them, and not or less so women, to enter the contract by which they agreed for the state to regulate interactions in the public sphere. These theories informed law and custom in Europe and the colonies, thus leading to the prolonged exclusion of women from formal politics in these contexts. Prevalent understandings of the state continue to privilege a masculinized construction of the political subject as independent, competitive, profit maximizing, and self-interested, as opposed to cooperative, caring, connected, and shaped by family relations (Di Stefano 1990: 77; Carver 1996: 678). Men remain more likely to successfully perform forms of personhood coded as masculine and therefore remain more numerous in decision-making positions in the public sphere.

In contrast to such a historically situated account of the liberal state, most commitments to mainstreaming gender in statebuilding are ahistorical and future-oriented. The OECD does recognize that statebuilding "intervention in fragile states should consistently promote gender equity" (OECD-DAC, 2007, para. 6). In articulating this, the OECD draws on expertise on women. Statebuilding initiatives should "ensure the protection and participation of women" (OECD 2008b: 19; see also OECD/DAC 2008: 32). First, with respect to protection, the OECD committed to greater attentiveness to women's security needs. It discussed women as a vulnerable group who are more susceptible to human rights violations, particularly those of a sexual nature, and therefore in need of special protection (OECD-DAC 2007: para. 6; OECD, 2008a: para. 2, 2010a: 7, 2010b: 25). Such commitments led to the deployment of disciplinary techniques such as military justice trials, vetting for human rights abuses, and training workshops that would instruct armed forces personnel on "gender awareness and the ills of sexual violence" in contexts like the Democratic Republic of the Congo (Baaz and Stern 2017: 214). Second, with regard to participation, the OECD identifies women in fragile states as needing increased inclusion in public life and greater access to state power (OECD 2008a, sec. 2). It notably recommends "measures to promote the voices and participation of women" (OECD-DAC 2007, para. 6). The OECD's position in support of women's political rights was echoed in the statebuilding policy of important donor states and other globally oriented development agencies. For instance, the UK Department for Foreign Development committed to statebuilding initiatives that would increase women's access to key state functions in order to compensate for their existing "political, social and economic exclusion" in contexts of state fragility

(UKAID, DFID 2010: 42). The emphasis that national and international aid agencies have put on women's participation in state legislatures in postconflict environments was so important that it may partly explain women's remarkably high presence in legislative bodies in countries recovering from civil war, such as Rwanda (Hughes 2009: 189).

Influential think tanks intervened in the development of such policy through the deployment of expertise on women. In a representative document, the North-South Institute explained that in contexts of state failure women suffer from "weak legal protections" and discriminatory state policies (Baranyi and Powell 2005: 2). Offering remedies to such problems, the Foundation for International Relations and Foreign Dialogue (FRIDE) and the United States Institute of Peace (USIP) encouraged donor agencies to facilitate women's participation in the negotiation of political settlements at the end of a conflict, in political parties and elected positions, in the executive branch of the government and in legal, justice, and security structures (Ali 2011; Castillejo 2011). Similarly, the Netherlands Institute for International Relations Clingendael advocated security sector reforms in postconflict states that would address "obstacles to female participation" in security forces, and "the gender-specific needs of intended beneficiaries," such as women's greater risk of experiencing rape and sexual assault (Schoofs and Smits 2010: 2).

These interventions almost uniformly emphasized the protection and participation of individual women, and thus primarily provided expertise on women as opposed to feminist critique of statebuilding itself. Their advocacy draws on the important liberal insight that women have a right to be protected from violations of their bodily integrity and deserve equal access to participation in public affairs and government. These think tanks, and the policies that came out of their recommendations, certainly filled a significant gap in mainstream approaches to postconflict reconstruction and peacebuilding. The latter have long neglected problems of human trafficking and rape in both wartime and ostensibly postconflict contexts (Cockburn 2004: 43; Giles and Hyndman 2004). Similarly, mainstream efforts most often excluded women from peace processes and negotiations (de Alwis et al. 2013: 169). Gender experts in the aforementioned think tanks eloquently argued for the protection and inclusion of women as participants and stakeholders in statebuilding processes. Thanks to their advocacy, statebuilding policy repositioned women's gendered vulnerability to physical violence and exclusion from formal political processes as social ills to address through statebuilding programs.

The gender champions in the aid and development policy community who informed these changes adopted a pragmatic approach, accepting statebuilding as the best available policy vehicle for fighting gender inequality in postconflict contexts. USIP argued that "with political will, resources, and a clear gendered strategy, the process of state building can open up opportunities for stronger support of women's human rights and gender equality in the long run" (Ali 2011). Among a number of gender experts, statebuilding became "widely regarded as an opportunity for securing greater gender equity and equality" in fragile states, provided that stated commitments translate into well-resourced activities on the ground (O'Connell 2011: 455; see also Tryggestad 2010: 169). These stated beliefs suggest an attachment to an image of the liberal state as gender-neutral; as "the location that settles [gender] differences, rather than the form that gives rise to them" (Stevens 1999: 4). On this question, the pragmatic gender champions diverge from feminist critics of the liberal state such as Anne Phillips, who argued that "no feminist in her right mind would have thought liberal democracy could deliver the goods" of gender equality (Phillips 1991: 61; see also Pateman 2011 [1983]). It therefore seems that in the development of statebuilding policy, such feminist critiques were not recognized as a relevant form of gender expertise. The next section shows why they should be.

## A feminist critique of postconflict statebuilding

While expertise on women matters, the example of statebuilding suggests that it is insufficient to deliver substantive equality. Feminist critique exposes statebuilding as an *already gendered* program of government structured by androcentric principles. Taking feminist critique seriously would entail redefining statebuilding's definition and priorities in a way that embraces both masculine and feminine activities and subjectivities, and not simply men and women. The notion of the political subject inherent to the statebuilding project is a masculinized subjectivity inherited from European social contract theory. Indeed, the social contract, as the World Bank and the UN recognize, "is central to the discourse on statebuilding" (Ingram 2010: 6). As previously mentioned, social contract theory constructed the realm of the state as a space where men interact with other men (Phillips 1991: 3; Carver 2004: 154). In so doing, contract theory naturalized what we take for granted today as the public–private divide. The domestic sphere, contract theorists argued, should remain beyond the scrutiny of the state apparatus. As a result, liberal democracies emerged as systems where individuals are granted their primary rights in the public sphere, *not* in the realm of reproductive labor, where women's labor and primary identity have historically been anchored (Brown 1995: 182; Carver 1996: 676). Relatedly, women's demands for bodily autonomy within one's home, for control over when and with whom one has sex and children, for a secure livelihood while parenting, for accessible childcare or for fair compensation especially in female-dominated sectors, have historically been harder to establish as worthy of political attention.

Concerns relating to marriage, parenting, sexuality, and fair remuneration similarly remain imperfectly addressed in statebuilding policy, in at least two ways. First, statebuilding policy inherits from social contract theory a greater concern for violence in the public sphere and a relative neglect of violence in the private sphere. In classic social contract theory, a man could set and enforce his own rules and use violence in his private household (Phillips

1991: 30; Moller Okin 1998). This made sexual and domestic violence not only possible, but relatively unquestioned at least until the 1960s and 1970s. Statebuilding policy did recognize women in fragile state as affected by "early marriage, domestic violence, obstacles to educational opportunities and discriminatory family laws" (OECD/DAC 2008: 8). However, these problems are seen as evidence of state failure, and not in relation to their historical and structural causes, including colonial history and exploitative structures in the global economy. Nor are they a focus of policy implementation. Early statebuilding policy addressed problems of gender-based violence "in an ad-hoc and superficial manner (if at all)" (Schoofs and Smits 2010: 1). The momentum surrounding the adoption of UN Security Council Resolution 1820 did succeed at making sexual violence in postconflict contexts a major area of postconflict intervention and international attention (Dersnah 2019). However, policy responses focused on creating law enforcement institutions that can better protect women's physical integrity and bodily autonomy in the public sphere, for instance by tackling assaults perpetrated by security forces. Typical interventions have focused on the creation of responsible police and armed forces (see for instance, Baaz and Stern 2017). Such initiatives leave unaddressed problems of violence *inside the home*, reproducing historically liberal democratic states' failure to effectively address such violence by insisting on marking a boundary between the public and private spheres. They also treat gender-based violence as a problem of discipline on the part of the state, and moral failure on the part of individuals, rather than a phenomenon fed by structural problems of economic inequality and disempowerment (True 2010; Baaz and Stern 2017).

In failing to address these limitations, the discourse of statebuilding as a remedy to gender-based violence in postconflict zones cultivates a form of Othering that legitimizes foreign intervention in postconflict contexts without providing effective solutions. This is the case in a range of globally oriented foreign aid, development, and peacebuilding policies that commit to support women's empowerment. These initiatives often recode former imperialist efforts to "save brown women from brown men" into projects targeted at "women in development" (Spivak 2010: 52), and often rely on simplified representations of "third world women" as lacking in comparison to women from the "first world" – poorer, less educated, and more oppressed by patriarchal traditions (Mohanty 2003). An examination of the feminist critique of the liberal state and its complicity with the perpetuation of gender-based violence in the Global North would allow for a more cautious and critical relationship to statebuilding as a vehicle of women's empowerment.

Second, statebuilding imagines the construction of liberal states as geared towards the consolidation of aspects of the state linked to security (typically understood in the narrow sense of armed and police forces), electoral processes, and law enforcement, all of which are coded as masculine. Conversely, statebuilding initiatives systematically neglect the consolidation of health, education and social services, coded as feminine (Ryan and Basini

2017; Shepherd 2017: 46). For instance, OECD policy on statebuilding lists the core functions of the state as, in this order of priority, security and justice, tax raising, basic service delivery, economic performance, and employment generation (OECD-DAC 2007). Although statebuilding policy sometimes gestures towards better service delivery in the fields of health care and primary education (OECD/DAC 2008), this has not evolved as a key priority. The UN and the World Bank also treat security sector and law enforcement as "essential capabilities" of the state, while placing the feminized sectors of "service delivery" and "livelihood security" as secondary concerns (see for instance, Ingram 2010: 6–7). In line with such definitions, statebuilding has been said to rely on "the centrality of security through military force" (McMahon and Western 2017: 6). The scholarly literature on statebuilding similarly centers on military, police, and judiciary institutions as sectors that international actors should target "if they are intent on strengthening a targeted country's state" (McMahon and Western 2017: 6). The emphasis on statebuilding as primarily security sector reform locates statebuilding within the most masculinized domains of state power (Shepherd 2017: 49). As such, it relegates social programs of health, education, and welfare – the feminized realm of reproductive labor and care work – beyond the scope of its priority sphere of intervention.

The identification of security as the most essential public service reproduces a hierarchy, whereby masculine activities and values prevail over feminine ones. This has important political repercussions. Social programs and economic redistribution help ensure that responsibilities for care work are more equally distributed and better valued and remunerated. Gender experts at the North-South Institute pointed out that statebuilding could redress situations where women disproportionately suffer from "weak social services" (Baranyi and Powell 2005: 2). However, statebuilding as a program of government remained de facto committed, in continuation of the social contract, to an idea of the state as first of all an instrument of pacification between men. It remains blind to the "gendered power relations" that structure this ideal and enable the domination of women by men (Shepherd 2017: 63). This entrenches a hierarchical binary between supposedly essential masculine activities (law and order) and less essential feminine ones (social services that guarantee what is sometimes framed as a fuller form of human security). Without collective arrangements and investments in education, childcare, and health care, women are often expected to provide these on an individual, and therefore unequal and precarious, basis. By locating care services as secondary rather than essential to a functioning polity, statebuilding is entrenching the notion that this labor is less valuable and can be left to the care of private entities.

A feminist critique therefore helps explain the extent to which statebuilding has repeated, rather than resolved, the democratic deficit of the "good governance" agenda that emerged as a dominant approach to global development and security in the 1990s. Efforts to support "good governance" in what was then called the developing world have previously been critiqued as a way through which "the North maintains and legitimizes its continued power and hegemony in the South" (Abrahamsen 2000, ix). As noted by Abrahamsen, a key problem of the good governance agenda is that democratization efforts rarely progress beyond the electoral stage, as social reforms to reduce inequalities are often ruled out from the outset (Abrahamsen 2000, xiv). As previously noted, statebuilding developed in the 2000s as an extension of the good governance agenda (Chandler 2008). Statebuilding consolidates and entrenches, among Northern donors, a reliance on masculinized state logics as an imagined resource for the solving of global security and development problems. Investments in security institutions can be presented as an effective approach to managing undisciplined states in the global periphery – because the myth of the social contract posits that this is how "functioning" states emerged in Europe. Meanwhile, the feminization of global health and social programs contributes to make it seem legitimate to ignore them.

The implicit naturalization of women as the informal and unpaid providers of health, education, and other forms of care is supported by a tendency in statebuilding policy to cultivate expectations around women's supposedly natural ability to provide care with selflessness and docility. These expectations apply to women's interventions in the public sphere. In the Global North, arguments in favor of including women in political parties, elections, and government often state that "women would bring to politics a different set of values, experiences and expertise" (Phillips 1991: 63). Similarly, the OECD stated that women "can do much to reduce fragility and strengthen social cohesion by maintaining services, supporting social cohesion and negotiating a safe space between communities in conflict" (OECD/DAC 2008: 32). References to "social cohesion," "services," and "safe space," all borrow from a vision of women as involved in activities of care, comfort, peace, and nurturance. Women in postconflict states are also expected to bring distinctly feminine qualities to the formal capitalist economy (Griffin 2010: 97). The OECD expects them to "perform effectively as service providers, even when they have been excluded from education and community decision making in the past" (OECD/DAC 2008: 32). The characterization of women as placid and service-oriented troublingly echoes Jean-Jacques Rousseau's depiction of the obedient wife, who is docile and supportive, and who recognizes "the voice of the [male] head of the house" (Pateman 1988: 98). Like Rousseau's contract theory, statebuilding policy naturalizes women as subservient service providers – but without noting that economic sectors and roles dominated by women are often underfunded, less paid, and insecure.

Simultaneously, the statebuilding discourse falls short of recommending structural changes that would facilitate women's participation in the public sphere. Statebuilding draws generously on neoliberal frameworks that, in various contexts, cast women (and people in general) as "seemingly free of [unpaid] care and household work" (Woehl 2008: 70). Such framings lead to an occlusion of public initiatives that would help women *as a group,* including laws to bridge gender pay gaps, social measures for family planning, collectively organized and accessible childcare, and parental leave policies. Instead, "women's empowerment" is a code word for perfunctory measures focused on small groups of women that favor individualized understandings of economic responsibility (Keating et al. 2010: 165). These include the dissemination of grants to encourage women to start up small businesses or vocational courses (see for instance, Ali 2011: 6). One of the most popular options, microcredit programs, lead women to contract debts without addressing broader economic inequalities (Keating et al. 2010). Measures to integrate individual women into masculinized institutions, such as police forces, parliaments, and entrepreneurship initiatives will remain of limited impact as long as these measures are not accompanied by an equally strong commitment to value and collectively fund health systems, childcare, and measures to ensure that women are equally paid and have resources that better account for the impacts of family life on a woman's public persona.

## Conclusion: On agency, voice, and resistance

I started this chapter by pointing out that global governmentality approaches are in many ways compatible with, and supportive of, feminist concerns with the capillary circulation of power, and a study of domination that draws attention to agency and resistance. I discussed the rise of some (primarily white, primarily Western) feminist knowledges to the status of gender expertise in agencies invested with global governance mandates. I have argued that the definition of gender mainstreaming as the consideration of individual women and men's needs and perspectives has favored the definition of gender expertise as expertise on women. I illustrated this claim with reference to postconflict statebuilding. Feminist critiques of governmental projects, I suggest, productively expose some of the implicit androcentric assumptions that underlie programs of government. However, these critiques have been relatively ignored as a form of gender expertise in global governance contexts. Thus, statebuilding policy and gender experts who influenced it unanimously expressed the conviction that statebuilding *can* deliver gender equality (see for instance, Ingram 2010: 6), without addressing the concerns that feminist critiques of the liberal state have raised. I conclude that expertise on women delivers an important but incomplete integration of feminist knowledge into transnational programs of government, one that on its own has so far failed to deliver substantive equality.

I want to end by returning to questions of agency, voice, and resistance (also see Laura Zanotti's contribution to this volume). One of the weaknesses of many studies anchored in global governmentality approaches is that they often continue to obscure the voices and bodies of marginalized women. I am thinking of women who are often the intended beneficiaries of governmental projects, the women-in-development (Mohanty 2003), the women-in-conflict (Cook 2016), the subaltern women who are kept on the wrong side of the global division of labor (Spivak 2010). Statebuilding policy presumes women of fragile states to helpfully put their energy, time, and labor at the service of a statebuilding project designed by Western elites. Rarely is there space to consider how women may actively critique or resist statebuilding projects, coopt it to pursue other ends, or strategically ignore it. Feminist methods, whether based on interviews, participant-observation, or participatory methods, provide useful strategies to complement text-based analysis, as they help assure that findings remain informed by the experiences of those on the receiving end of programs of government (Kunz 2013; Baaz and Stern 2017). I am hoping that future research on gender and global governmentalities may help translate and value conflict-affected women's alternative visions of how the world might be governed.

## Note

1  I would like to express my gratitude to those who reviewed earlier versions of this chapter, Terrell Carver, Jutta Weldes, Marysia Zalewski, Joanna Tidy, Aiko Holvikivi and Scott Hamilton, as well as two fantastic research assistants, Molly Todd and Jessica Herling. I am also very grateful to Jan Busse for inviting me to contribute this volume and for his indefatigable and patient support.

## References

Abrahamsen, Rita (2000) *Disciplining Democracy: Development Discourse and Good Governance in Africa* (London: Zed Books).

Ali, Nada Mustafa (2011) *Gender and Statebuilding in South Sudan* (Washington, DC: United States Institute for Peace).

Baaz, Maria Eriksson and Stern, Maria (2017) 'Being Reformed: Subjectification and Security Sector Reform in the Congolese Armed Forces', *Journal of Intervention and Statebuilding* 11:2, 207–224.

Baranyi, Stephen and Powell, Kristiana (2005) *Fragile States, Gender Equality and Aid Effectiveness: A Review of Donor Perspectives* (Ottawa: The North-South Institute).

Bartky, Sandra Lee (1990) *Femininity and Domination* (New York: Routledge).

Bedford, Kate (2009) *Developing Partnerships Gender, Sexuality, and the Reformed World Bank* (Minneapolis: University of Minnesota Press).

Berkovitch, Nitza (1999) *From Motherhood to Citizenship: Women's Rights and International Organizations* (Baltimore: Johns Hopkins University Press).

Brown, Wendy (1995) *States of Injury: Power and Freedom in Late Modernity* (Princeton: Princeton University Press).

Butler, Judith (1999) *Gender Trouble: Feminism and the Subversion of Identity* (New York: Routledge).

Butler, Judith (2011) *Bodies that Matter: On the Discursive Limits of 'Sex'* (Abingdon: Routledge).

Carver, Terrell (1996) "Public Man' and the Critique of Masculinities', *Political Theory* 24:4, 673–686.

Carver, Terrell (2004) *Men in Political Theory* (Manchester: Manchester University Press).

Castillejo, Clare (2011) *Building a State that Works for Women: Integrating Gender into Post-Conflict Peacebuilding* (Madrid: FRIDE).

Chandler, David (2008) *International Statebuilding* (London: Routledge).

Cockburn, Cynthia (2004) 'The Continuum of Violence: A Gender Perspective on War and Peace' in Wenona Giles and Jennifer Hyndman (eds) *Sites of Violence: Gender and Conflict Zones* (Berkeley: University of California Press), 24–44.

Cohn, Carol (1987) 'Sex and Death in the Rational World of Defense Intellectuals', *Signs* 12:4, 687–718.

Cohn, Carol (2008) 'Mainstreaming Gender in UN Security Policy: A Path to Political Transformation?' in S.M. Rai and G. Waylen (eds) *Global Governance: Feminist Perspectives* (Basingstoke, Hampshire: Palgrave Macmillan), 185–206.

Cook, Sam (2016) 'The 'Woman-in-Conflict' at the UN Security Council: A Subject of Practice', *International Affairs* 92:2, 353–372.

Davis, Angela Y (1990) *Women, Culture & Politics* (New York: Vintage Books).

de Alwis, Malathi, Mertus, Julie and Sajjad, Tazreena (2013) 'Women and Peace Processes' in: Carol Cohn (ed) *Women & Wars* (Cambridge, UK: Polity Press).

Dean, Mitchell (2010) *Governmentality: Power and Rule in Modern Society*. 2nd ed. (London: Sage).

Dersnah, Megan Alexandra (2019) 'United Nations Gender Experts and the Push to Focus on Conflict-Related Sexual Violence', *European Journal of Politics and Gender* 2:1, 41–56.

Di Stefano, Christine (1990) 'Dilemmas of Difference: Feminism, Modernity, and Postmodernism' in L J Nicholson (ed) *Feminism/Postmodernism* (London: Routledge), 63–82.

ECOSOC (1997) *Report of the Economic and Social Council for 1997* (New York: United Nations General Assembly). Available at www.un.org/documents/ga/docs/52/plenary/a52-3.htm [28 February 2010].

Elias, Juanita (2018) 'Governing Domestic Worker Migration in Southeast Asia: Public–Private Partnerships, Regulatory Grey Zones and the Household', *Journal of Contemporary Asia* 48:2, 278–300.

Enloe, Cynthia (2000) *Bananas, Beaches and Bases: Making Feminist Sense of International Politics* (Berkeley: University of California Press).

Foucault, Michel (1991) 'Governmentality' in G. Burchell, C. Gordon and P. Miller (eds) *The Foucault Effect: Studies in Governmentality* (Chicago: The University of Chicago Press), 87–104.

Foucault, Michel (2008) *The Birth of Biopolitics: Lectures at the Collège de France, 1978-79* (New York: Palgrave Macmillan).

Gabay, Clive and Death, Carl (eds) (2014) *Critical Perspectives on African Politics: Liberal Interventions, State-Building and Civil Society* (London: Routledge).

Giles, Wenona Mary and Hyndman, Jennifer (2004) *Sites of Violence: Gender and Conflict Zones* (Berkeley: University of California Press).

Griffin, Penny (2010) 'Gender, Governance and the Global Political Economy', *Australian Journal of International Affairs* 64:1, 86–104.

Halberstam, Jack (2014) 'Gender' in B Burgett and G Hendler (eds.) *Keywords for American Cultural Studies* (New York: New York University Press), 116–118.

Halley, Janet (2008) *Split Decisions: How and Why to Take a Break from Feminism* (Princeton: Princeton University Press).

Harding, Sandra (1995) 'Just Add Women and Stir?' in Gender Working Group of the United Nations Commission on Science and Technology for Development (ed) *Missing Links: Gender Equity in Science and Technology for Development* (London: International Development Research Centre), 295-307.

Harrington, Carol (2006) 'Governing Peacekeeping: The Role of Authority and Expertise in the Case of Sexual Violence and Trauma', *Economy and Society* 35:3, 346–380.

Harrington, Carol (2013) 'Governmentality and the Power of Transnational Women's Movements', *Studies in Social Justice* 7:1, 47–63.

Hawkesworth, Mary E (2006) 'Outsiders, Insiders, and Outsiders Within: Feminist Strategies for Global Transformation' in *Globalization and Feminist Activism* (Lanham: Rowman & Littlefield), 67–110.

Hekman, Susan (2004) 'Feminist Identity Politics: Transforming the Political' in D Taylor and K Vintges (eds) *Feminism and the Final Foucault* (Chicago: University of Illinois Press), 197–213.

Holvikivi, Aiko and Reeves, Audrey (2020) 'Women, Peace and Security After Europe's "Refugee Crisis"' *European Journal of International Security* 5:2, 135–154.

Hughes, Melanie M (2009) 'Armed Conflict, International Linkages, and Women's Parliamentary Representation in Developing Nations', *Social Problems* 56:1, 174–204.

Ingram, Sue (2010) *State-Building: Key Concepts and Operational Implications in Two Fragile States. The Cases of Sierra Leone and Liberia* (Washington: World Bank and United Nations Development Programme).

Kantola, Johanna (2006) 'Feminism' in C Hay, M Lister and D Marsh (eds) *The State: Theories and Issues* (New York: Palgrave Macmillan).

Keating, Christine, Rasmussen, Claire and Rishi, Pooja (2010) 'The Rationality of Empowerment: Microcredit, Accumulation by Dispossession, and the Gendered Economy', *Signs: Journal of Women in Culture and Society* 36:1, 153–176.

Kinsella, Helen M (2005) 'Securing the Civilian: Sex and Gender in the Laws of War' in M Barnett and R Duvall (eds) *Power in Global Governance* (Cambridge: Cambridge University Press), 249–272.

Kunz, Rahel (2013) *The Political Economy of Global Remittances* (London: Routledge).

Kunz, Rahel and Prügl, Elisabeth (2019) 'Introduction: Gender Experts and Gender Expertise', *European Journal of Politics and Gender* 2:1, 3–21.

Kunz, Rahel, Prügl, Elisabeth and Thompson, Hayley (2019) 'Gender Expertise in Global Governance: Contesting the Boundaries of a Field', *European Journal of Politics and Gender* 2:1, 23–40.

Larner, Wendy and Walters, William (2004) 'Globalization as Governmentality', *Alternatives: Global, Local, Political* 29:5, 495–514.

Latham, Michael E (2006) 'Redirecting the Revolution? The USA and the Failure of Nation-Building in South Vietnam', *Third World Quarterly* 27:1, 27–41.

Lipschutz, Ronnie (2005) *Globalization, Governmentality and Global Politics* (Abingdon: Routledge).

MacKinnon, Catharine A (1989) *Toward a Feminist Theory of the State* (Cambridge: Harvard University Press).

McLaren, Margaret A (2002) *Feminism, Foucault, and Embodied Subjectivity* (Albany: State University of New York Press).

McMahon, Patrice C and Western, Jon (2017) *The International Community and Statebuilding* (Abingdon: Routledge).

McNay, Lois (1992) *Foucault and Feminism: Power, Gender and the Self* (Cambridge: Polity Press).

Mitchell, Timothy (2000) 'Preface' in T Mitchell (ed) *Questions of Modernity.* (Minneapolis: University of Minnesota Press), vii–x.

Mohanty, Chandra Talpade (2003) *Feminism Without Border: Decolonizing Theory, Practicing Solidarity* (Durham: Duke University Press).

Moller Okin, Susan (1998) 'Gender, the Public, and the Private' in Anne Phillips (ed) *Feminism and Politics* (Oxford: Oxford University Press), 116–41.

O Thuatail, Gearoid and Dahlman, Carl (2004) 'The Clash of Governmentalities: Displacement and Return in Bosnia-Herzegovina' in W Larner and W Walters (eds) *Global Governmentality: Governing international spaces* (New York: Routledge), 136–154.

O'Connell, Helen (2011) 'What Are the Opportunities to Promote Gender Equity and Equality in Conflict-Affected and Fragile States? Insights from a Review of Evidence', *Gender & Development* 19:3, 455–466.

OECD (2006) *DAC in Dates: The History of OECD's Development Assistance Committee* ( Paris: OECD). Available at www.oecd.org/dac/1896808.pdf.

OECD (2008a) *State Building in Situations of Fragility*. Organisation for Economic Co-operation and Development (Paris: OECD). Available at https://www.oecd.org/dac/conflict-fragility-resilience/docs/41212290.pdf

OECD (2008b) *Accra Agenda for Action* ( Paris: OECD). Available at www.oecd.org/dataoecd/11/41/34428351.pdf

OECD (2010a) *Peacebuilding and Statebuilding: Priorities and Challenges. A Synthesis of Findings from Seven Multi-Stakeholder Consultations* (Paris: OECD). Organisation for Economic Co-operation and Development. Available at www.oecd.org/site/dacpbsbdialogue/documentupload/45454619.pdf

OECD (2010b) *The State's Legitimacy in Fragile Situations: Unpacking Complexity.* (Paris: OECD). Available at http://dx.doi.org/10.1787/9789264083882-en [5 November 2012].

OECD-DAC (2007) *Principles for Good International Engagement in Fragile States and Situations* (Paris: OECD). Organisation for Economic Co-operation and Development. Available at www.oecd.org/dac/conflict-fragility-resilience/docs/38368714.pdf.

OECD/DAC (2008) *Service Delivery in Fragile Situations: Key Concepts, Findings and Lessons* ( Paris: OECD). Available at: www.oecd.org/dac/conflict-fragility-resilience/docs/40886707.pdf.

Oyewùmí, Oyèrónke (1997) *The Invention of Women: Making an African Sense of Western Gender Discourses* (Minneapolis: University of Minnesota Press).

Paducel, Anca Hermina and Salahub, Jennifer Erin (2011) *Gender Equality and Fragile States Policies and Programming: A Comparative Study of the OECD/DAC and Six OECD Donors.* (Ottawa: The North-South Institute). Available at www.nsi-ins.ca/wp-content/uploads/2012/10/2011-Gender-Equality-and-Fragile-States-Policies-and-Programming.pdf

Pateman, Carole (1988) *The Sexual Contract* (Cambridge: Polity Press).

Pateman, Carole (2011) *Democracy, Feminism, Welfare* (Abingdon: Routledge).

Peterson, V. Spike (1999) 'Political Identities/Nationalism as Heterosexism', *International Feminist Journal of Politics* 1:1, 34–65.

Phillips, Anne (1991) *Engendering Democracy* (Cambridge: Polity Press).

Prügl, Elisabeth (1999) *The Global Construction of Gender: Home-Based Work in the Political Economy of the 20th Century* (New York: Columbia University Press).

Prügl, Elisabeth (2010) Expertise, Empowerment and Domination: Antinomies of Feminist Struggle. Paper presented at the International Studies Association Convention in New Orleans.

Reeves, Audrey (2012) 'Feminist Knowledge and Emerging Governmentality in UN Peacekeeping', *International Feminist Journal of Politics* 14:3, 348–369.

Repo, Jemima (2015) *The Biopolitics of Gender* (Oxford: Oxford University Press).

Rose, Nikolas (1999) *Powers of Freedom: Reframing Political Thought* (Cambridge: Cambridge University Press).

Ryan, Caitlin and Basini, Helen (2017) 'UNSC Resolution 1325 National Action Plans in Liberia and Sierra Leone: An Analysis of Gendered Power Relations in Hybrid Peacebuilding', *Journal of Intervention and Statebuilding* 11:2, 186–206.

Schoofs, Steven and Smits, Rosan (2010) *Aiming High, Reaching Low: Four Fundamentals for Gender-Responsive State-Building* (The Hague: The Netherlands Institute of International Relations 'Clingendael').

Sending, Ole Jacob (2015) *The Politics of Expertise: Competing for Authority in Global Governance* (Ann Arbor: University of Michigan Press).

Shepherd, Laura J (2017) *Gender, UN Peacebuilding, and the Politics of Space: Locating Legitimacy* (Oxford: Oxford University Press).

Spivak, Gayatri (2010) 'Can the Subaltern Speak?' in R Morris (ed) *Can the Subaltern Speak? Reflections on the History of an Idea* (New York: Columbia University Press), 21–80.

Squires, Judith (2005) 'Is Mainstreaming Transformative? Theorizing Mainstreaming in the Context of Diversity and Deliberation', *Social Politics* 12:3, 366–388.

Stevens, Jacqueline (1999) *Reproducing the State* (Princeton: Princeton University Press).

Sylvester, Christine (2006) 'Bringing Art/Museums to Feminist International Relations' in B A Ackerly, M Stern and Jacqui True (eds) *Feminist Methodologies for International Relations* (Cambridge: Cambridge University Press), 201–220.

Tripp, Aili Mari (2006) 'The Evolution of Transnational Feminisms: Consensus, Conflict, and New Dynamics' in M Marx Feree A M and Tripp (eds) *Global Feminism: Transnational Women's Activism, Organizaing, and Human Rights.* (New York: New York University Press), 51–75.

True, Jacqui (2003) 'Mainstreaming Gender in Global Public Policy', *International Feminist Journal of Politics* 5:3, 368–396.

True, Jacqui (2010) 'The Political Economy of Violence Against Women: A Feminist International Relations Perspective', *Australian Feminist Law Journal* 32:1, 39–59.

Tryggestad, Torunn L (2010) 'The UN Peacebuilding Commission and Gender: A Case of Norm Reinforcement', *International Peacekeeping* 17:2, 159–171.

UKAID, DFID (2010) *Building Peaceful States and Societies: A DFID Practice Paper* (London; Glasgow: UK Department for International Development, UKAID). Available at www.dfid.gov.uk/Documents/publications1/governance/Building-peaceful-states-and-societies.pdf

UN Secretary-General (2002) *Report of the Secretary-General on Women, Peace and Security (2002)* (New York: United Nations).

United Nations (2011) The PBF and Gender Equality. *United Nations Peacebuilding Fund.* Available at www.unpbf.org/news/pbf-gender-promotion-initiative/ [14 October 2012].

United Nations Economic and Social Committee (1997) *Report of the Economic and Social Council for 1997.* (New York: United Nations General Assembly). Available at www.un.org/documents/ga/docs/52/plenary/a52-3.htm [28 February 2010].

Väyrynen, Tarja (2004) 'Gender and UN Peace Operations: The Confines of Modernity', *International Peacekeeping* 11:1, 125–142.

Whitworth, Sandra (2004) *Men, Militarism & UN Peacekeeping: A Gendered Analysis* (Boulder: Lynne Rienner).

Woehl, Stefanie (2008) 'Global Governance as Neoliberal Governmentality: Gender Mainstreaming in the European Employment Strategy' in S M Rai and G Waylen, (eds) *Global Governance: Feminist Perspectives* (Basingstoke: Palgrave MacMillan), 64–83.

World Bank (1997) *World Development Report 1997: The State in a Changing World* (Oxford: Oxford University Press).

World Bank (2005) *Afghanistan - State Building, Sustaining Growth, and Reducing Poverty* (Washington DC: World Bank).

World Bank (2011) *Conflict, Security, and Development* (Washington DC: World Bank).

Zanotti, Laura (2006) 'Taming Chaos: A Foucauldian View of UN Peacekeeping, Democracy and Normalization', *International Peacekeeping* 13:2, 150–167.

# 9 Crisis, post-neoliberal global governmentality and BRICS' deconstructive signature of power

*Hans-Martin Jaeger*

## Introduction

The birth of BRICS resulted from the fusion of a new investment category with geopolitical ambition. Conceived in 2001 by Goldman Sachs chief economist Jim O'Neill to name a promising investment vehicle for their clients, the acronym developed a life of its own when subsequently appropriated by Brazilian, Russian, Indian, and Chinese policymakers[1] to register their countries' world-political aspirations in the face of the early 21st-century twin crisis of US hegemony and neoliberal governmentality ("bookended" by the bursting of the Twin Towers in 2001 and of the US housing bubble in 2008; Dean 2010: 264). The global financial and economic crisis of 2008–2009 (see the chapter by Kiersey on this topic) in particular looms large in accounts of the rise of BRICS, although it is usually considered a contextual rather than constitutive factor for the group's political birth. More importantly, the dual descent of BRICS from Western economic–financial and post-Western geopolitical calculations is often reduced to a single trajectory.

Following along the economic–financial line of descent, for instance, BRICS is explained in terms of a "[capitalist] heartland-contender cleavage" in global governance (Stephen 2014), transnational class and state formation (Robinson 2015) or "passive revolution" (Taylor 2016), long-term economic decline (from the early 19th to the mid-twentieth century) and rise (since the 1980s) (Nayyar 2016), "sub-imperialism" (Bond and Garcia 2015, chs. 1–3), or "escaping the middle-income trap" (Elsenhans and Babones 2017). Along the post-Western geopolitical line, BRICS is either dismissed as a global-governance nonstarter (Castañeda 2010; Patrick 2010; Pant 2013) or investigated in terms of its influence on liberal–hegemonic world order (Roberts 2010; Laïdi 2012; Xing and Agustín 2014), a power shift from the West to the rest (Armijo and Roberts 2014), the "pursuit of multipolarity" (Papa 2014) or "coexistence" (De Coning et al. 2015), as a "coalition of the Global South" (Thakur 2012) or "flexible multilateralism" (Abdenour et al. 2014).[2]

This chapter examines BRICS as a project of post-neoliberal global governmentality instigated by crisis. As such, it foregrounds the liberal and neoliberal articulations of governmentality while keeping in perspective their historical precursors (as well as governmentality's sovereign antagonist).[3] Connecting the historically specific (liberal) and transhistorically variable articulations I argue, are recurring diagnoses of crises of governmentality. BRICS' post-neoliberal global governmentality not merely refers to an "international order [...] in crisis," but deploys "the concept of *crisis* [...] to order the international" (Jordheim and Wigen 2018: 425) along both economic and geopolitical trajectories.[4] On the one hand, BRICS problematizes "crisis" (initially, the global financial and food crises of 2007–2009) to advance quasiordoliberal reforms of international financial institutions (and perhaps the G-20) and biopolitical strategies. On the other hand, crisis simultaneously motivates state-capitalist economic development and demands of multipolar world order. BRICS' global governance approach exemplifies "the introduction of economy into [geo-]political practice" (Foucault 2007: 95) as much as a "geopoliticization" of economy. It thereby constructs globality, or so this chapter will argue, through an interplay of governmental-economic and sovereign-multipolar political rationalities and practices.

Governmentality may appear as an unlikely analytic to interpolate geopolitics into economic management and biopolitical regulation,[5] which Foucault sometimes sharply set off against a putatively more archaic domain of sovereign power (Foucault 1990: 135–145; 2003: 239–254). However, a recent sovereigntist–statist turn in governmentality studies (Lemke 2007; Jessop 2011; Biebricher 2013; Vasilache 2014) has sought to balance this picture (see also the chapter by Dean and Larsson in this volume). Specifically drawing on Dean's (2013) notion of the "signature of power," the following analysis interprets BRICS as a global governance arrangement and construction of globality interweaving governmental-economic and sovereign-multipolar modes of power, though with a "deconstructive" twist: BRICS' efforts to regulate and manage the global economy are often conducted through conventional diplomatic procedures, existing international institutions and state apparatuses; conversely, its propagation of multipolar international order issues from acclamations by "civil society" (think tanks, journalists, academics, etc.) as much as from traditional symbology of sovereignty. This dialogical and deconstructive reading of BRICS' signature of power adds analytical texture to the "mono-logical" state-centric, institutional, structural, and class-based accounts mentioned above.

BRICS' post-neoliberal signature of power may have challenged the neoliberal global governance approach reigning until recently (and persisting in "zombified" form in the EU and some other Western quarters, international financial institutions, and parts of the UN system). This could have led to a "clash of global governmentalities" (see Lipschutz 2002). However, in the current world-political conjuncture BRICS' post-neoliberalism may well be in secret complicity with another post-neoliberal – and arguably equally "deconstructive" – signature of power emerging under US auspices and marked by the concurrence and entwinement of state- and corporate-regulated neoliberal economic management and an anti-elitist or "populist" rediscovery of glorified "greatness" and sovereignty. One difference of emphasis (though not necessarily of effect) here could be that BRICS embrace multilateralism along with multipolarity, while the "people-powered" return to sovereign "greatness" (at least rhetorically) rejects the former without embracing the latter. One might say that BRICS' post-neoliberalism constructs a "political" globality of agonistic cooperation (see Jaeger 2014), whereas the US variant appears to veer between a "schizoid" globality of splendid isolation and a "narcissistic" one of presumed hegemony.

The first section of the chapter highlights the largely overlooked significance of the notion of crisis to the development of Foucault's account of governmentality and argues that it provides an immanent point of entry for both the Agambenian economic theology of government and the Schmittian political theology of sovereignty instantiating Dean's "signature of power." The second section of the chapter illustrates the constitutive significance of "crisis" for BRICS' biopolitical and ordoliberal governmentalities as well as their sovereign-multipolar geopolitical comportment.[6] However, rather than recycling conventional neoliberalism and traditional sovereignty, I argue, practices and technologies of state-capitalism and traditional diplomacy on the one hand, and transgovernmentalism and "civil society"-driven glorification of multipolarity on the other deconstruct BRICS' signature of power.

## Crisis and the signature of power

Crisis is the midwife of governmentality. While this is rarely noted,[7] Foucault points to recurrent crises of governmentality as critical junctures for the birth of new forms of governmentality. This section briefly outlines the catalytic role of crisis in Foucault's genealogy of governmentality and traces some of its ramifications. The following one will make the case that the diagnosis of crisis – specifically, the twin crisis of neoliberal global governance and US hegemony – was also pivotal for the gestation of BRICS' distinctive brand of post-neoliberal global governmentality and signature of power.

In his course summary of *Security, Territory, Population* Foucault refers to "[a] general crisis of the [Christian-medieval] pastorate in the fifteenth and sixteenth centuries;" "a general questioning of [...] governing and governing oneself" which "accompanies the birth of new forms of economic and social relations and [...] new political structures," and specifically the involvement of "the conduct of [...] individuals [...] in the exercise of sovereign power" with the emergence of *raison d'État* (Foucault 2007: 364). "[T]he crisis of the pastorate [...] assumed the dimension of governmentality" through the development of various counter-conducts (asceticism, communities, mysticism, etc.) (Foucault 2007: 193; see also 202ff) which stimulated new forms of governing suited to addressing the "economic crises" of the late Middle Ages (urban and peasant revolts, feudal–bourgeois conflicts) (Foucault 2007: 215; see also

231). It is thus the interaction of religious and economic crises which gives rise to the proto-governmentality of *raison d'État*.[8]

Fast forward to "the great crisis of the 1930s" (Foucault 2008: 194–195) and the birth of neoliberal governmentality. If the crisis of the pastorate instantiated a mode of governing centered on the state as its primary instrument and object of intervention, in the 20th century a "state-phobia" rather indiscriminately directed against communism, socialism, National Socialism, fascism, the New Deal, and Keynesianism crystalizes "a crisis of liberalism" which instigates the ostensibly anti-statist art of government now known as neoliberalism.[9] The crisis of liberalism that neoliberalism sought to overcome was that state interventions intended to produce freedom risked producing the opposite (Foucault 2008: 68–70, 76). Hence, neoliberalism's initial ordoliberal formulation[10] would attempt to unshackle freedom by reconfiguring the state as a legal-institutional "framework" or "economic constitution" securing competition in the market along with the promotion of entrepreneurial and responsible conduct (Foucault 2008, ch. 7). When the German neoliberal model travels to France and the US in the 1970s and 1980s, this too takes place through the discursive mobilization of economic or political crisis (Foucault 2008: 192–197). Ironically however, and we will see below that this irony recurs with BRICS, the diffusion of the German neoliberal model in France occurs "on the basis of a strongly state-centered, interventionist, and administrative governmentality" (Foucault 2008: 192).

Crisis then has historically served to call forth both forms of governmentality oriented towards the state (*raison d'État*) and others (liberalism, neoliberalism) foregrounding the self-regulatory capacities of markets, populations, and individuals. To appreciate governmentality's discursive mobilization by "crisis," it is instructive to consider a broader set of resonances incidentally also echoed in Dean's "signature of power" and BRICS' approach to global governance. Koselleck's conceptual history of crisis specifically notes alternating legal–political, theological, historical, economic, and medical connotations of the term.

In classical Greek usage, crisis indicated a turning point calling for political decisions to restore justice and order, thereby bringing "subjective" judgments to bear on "objective" conditions. In the Judeo-Christian tradition, crisis additionally acquires eschatological connotations evoking "apocalyptic expectations" of the Last Judgment or "a promise of salvation" (Koselleck 2006: 358–360). Since the second half of the 18th century, the political meaning of crisis is amplified to "external or military situations" (e.g., crises of the balance of power or imperial order) whose resolution posed stark alternatives of fundamental change (survival vs. demise, or revolution) of the political order or "a simple change of government" (reform) (Koselleck 2006: 368–369, 391–392). In the philosophy of history, crisis becomes an "epochal concept" and "a structural signature of modernity;" "a final reckoning of universal significance [...] incorporating the theological idea of the Last Judgment" as well as a call "for the execution of tendencies revealed through critique" (Koselleck

2006: 371–375, 385). In historically dominant medical and in modern economic terms, crisis is seen as a recurrent phenomenon encapsulating diagnosis and treatment, or an inevitable development that "can be overcome through proper prognosis and planning" (Koselleck 2006: 377; see also 370, 389–397).

From a macroscopic perspective, the conceptual history of crisis may appear as a series of dualisms posed and intensified (albeit not necessarily in mutually exclusive ways) by the concept: "subjective" decision and/vs. attention to "objective" conditions, judgment and/vs. salvation, revolution vs. reform, life vs. death, exceptional measures vs. enduring critique, crisis resolution vs. crisis management. Similar bifurcations also characterize contemporary treatments of crisis.

An example is Milton Friedman's "crisis hypothesis" which Naomi Klein (2008: 166) identifies as the wellspring of the global victory of the neoliberal "shock doctrine" since the early 1970s. According to Friedman (with ironic Bolshevik echoes), "[o]nly cris[e]s" can "produce real change" (quoted by Klein 2008: 166) by creating the space "for emergency measures, a state of exception during which the rules of democracy [can] be suspended" and economic decisions made by experts (Klein 2008: 186). Given the opportunities they present, crises however also call for "intellectual disaster preparedness" (in academia, think tanks, the media) or even active efforts to provoke crises (for instance, through the IMF's structural adjustment programs) (Klein 2008: 167; see also 190–193, 307–315). Writing in a rather different normative key, Milstein (2015: 146) submits that crises present situations in which "the objective force of history" presses upon the participants "a decision on their own fate." Rather than seeing crises as leading into "democracy-free zones" (Klein 2008: 167) of exceptionalism and expertocracy however, Milstein interprets them as calls for collective reflection, civic participation, and collective responsibility for the destiny of the relevant "crisis community" (Milstein 2015: 143, 146–147, 151–152, 155), which "hint[s] at a 'democratic' structure" of reciprocal recognition and "emancipatory" potentials (Milstein 2015: 153, 154; see also 156).

Dualisms such as exceptionalism/decisionism and expertocracy along with those of judgment and salvation, universal fate and particular criticisms/contingencies, life and death, etc. not only establish "crisis" as a "structural signature of modernity" (Koselleck), but also resemble and inform what Dean, following intellectual paths charted by Foucault, Schmitt, and Agamben, calls "the signature of power." In its "key form," the latter refers to "a relationship between sovereignty and reign, on the one hand, and economic management and government, or governance, on the other" (Dean 2013: 14; see also 216, 221). Similarly to the historical semantics of crisis, the signature of power then is less a dualism that separates than a duality that relates its "Schmittian" transcendent-sovereign and its "Foucauldian" immanent-governmental poles. Following Agamben's (2011) archeology of the "governmental machine of the West" (xii), Dean locates the unity of this duality in an economic theology, "'in which the Kingdom [i.e. *Regno* or Reign] of providence legitimates and founds the Government of fate, and the latter guarantees the order that the former had established and renders it operative'" (Agamben 2011: 129 quoted by Dean 2013: 187). The upshot of the signature of power is that Foucauldian studies of governmentality need to be articulated or supplemented with "the operation of sovereign power and authority" (Dean 2013: 195).

While Foucault (2007: 107) in principle agrees that governmentality far from evacuating the problem of sovereignty makes it "more acute than ever," in practice he tends to consign sovereign concerns with spectacle and territory to a pre-governmental past. Dean seeks to recover the "spectacular," territorial and legal dimensions of sovereign power by reference to Agamben's account of Roman-Christian practices and rituals of "glorification" (splendor, publicity, acclamation) and Schmitt's geopolitical mythology of world order, or *nomos*. Indeed, the two are connected insofar as the "glorification" of sovereignty not merely adorns, but effectively founds and justifies contemporary political and world order (Dean 2013: 129, 133–136, 209–210, 222, 226–227; see also Agamben 2011: 230 and Dean 2004). The signature of power therefore illuminates that:

> *the now globally imagined economy in crisis* is both the exception to sovereignty and law, and thus the rationale for governmental action and individual conduct and self-formation, and at the same time the collectively willed providential order constantly glorified in sporting events and advertising, by celebrity and financial reporting, and by *crisis intervention* and catastrophe management.
>
> (Dean 2013: 217, my emphases)

The following analysis shows how crisis semantics instantiate a particular version of the signature of power in BRICS' approach to global governance.[11] Rather than referring to the conjunctural condition of the global financial crisis (2008–2009) alone, the discursive mobilization of crisis around and by BRICS has occasioned both biopolitical and ordoliberal governmentalities on the one hand, and calls for the respect for sovereignty, international law, and multipolarity on the other. Apart from academic literature on BRICS (here treated as part of BRICS discourse), the illustration of BRICS' "crisis-ridden" signature of power focuses on BRICS summit meetings and the declarations and initiatives that have issued from them. Much like summit meetings of other international groupings such as the EU, the G-7, G-20, or the UN General Assembly, the very staging of BRICS summits through designated websites, logos, and summit-city "branding" exemplifies the "glorification" materializing BRICS' signature of power.

Heeding Dean's (2013: 14, 196, 211, 221) caveat against treating the signature of power as a general, transhistorically valid theory, the notion is used merely heuristically to illustrate some specificities of BRICS' intertwining of governmental-economic and sovereign-multipolar modalities of power. However, even the heuristic use of the signature of power with respect to

BRICS will be complicated by pointing to its inherently "deconstructive" quality. The latter emerges from the fact that typical instrumentalities of statecraft figure prominently in the rationalization or implementation of governmental-economic (including neoliberal) programs, and that conversely nonsovereign forms of dissemination (e.g., by think tanks) contribute to the "glorification" of BRICS as stalwart of sovereignty and harbinger of multi-polarity. Overall, BRICS' deconstructive signature of power expresses a dis-tinctive post-neoliberal global governmentality.

### Riding the crisis of neoliberalism: Towards (state) governmentality and a (nonstate) sovereign-multipolar nomos

#### Crisis, governmentality, and multipolarity in BRICS discourse

*Pace* Glosny's (2010: 110) claim that "BRIC cooperation is not a product of the current global economic and financial crisis," crisis narratives (centered on but not limited to the latter) envelop virtually every account of BRICS' economic and geopolitical formation. Sum (2013) traces the construction of BRIC(S) as a governmental technology of crisis management and recovery by international investment banks, economists, international organizations, think tanks, business media, and policymakers. As such, BRIC(S) involved discursive and material dimensions[12] (mediated by both affect and calcula-tion) and moved through three distinct (though overlapping) phases extol-ling BRIC(S) as a crisis-transcending site of investment, consumption, and lending.

"Crisis" also looms large in treatments of BRICS not framed in terms of governmentality. Stuenkel (2015) demonstrates that BRICS' "global project" (Stuenkel 2015, x) not only activates governmental technologies centered on practices of investing, consuming, and borrowing/lending, but also a "signa-ture" dual political rationality of the reform of global financial governance and multipolar world order. Corresponding to this duality, BRICS mobilizes an array of programs of institutional change and biopolitical regulation targeting global health, food security, and development (not least through the compilation of relevant statistics) on the one hand (see also Jaeger 2014: 215–216), and conventional politicodiplomatic techniques of multilateral cooper-ation including BRICS leaders' summits (with the associated pageantry of "family photos," media briefings, summit declarations, action plans, etc.), a host of more practically oriented ministerial and "sherpa" meetings, and transgovernmental bureaucratic and technical/expert channels on the other.[13]

Stuenkel outlines a cascade of the financial crisis into a legitimacy crisis of the international financial order and eventually a "sense of crisis [...] of global order in general" resulting in "the birth of BRICS as a political group" with their first summit in 2009 (Stuenkel 2015: 9, 30; see also 14–15, 31, 33–34, 63). Institutionally, BRICS' founding rationale of crisis recovery has become most tangible in its Contingency Reserve Arrangement (CRA) "to tackle any possible financial crisis in the emerging economies." The CRA displays BRICS' post-neoliberal signature of power with quasisovereign "precautionary" emergency provision of liquidity to developing countries "facing currency crises" ("as an additional line of defense" to IMF support) on the one hand, and more governmental welfarist–actuarial concerns with strengthening "the global financial safety net" on the other (Stuenkel 2015: 113–116; see also BRICS 2015: #16; 2018: #68).

The constitutive rather than merely conjunctural role of crisis for BRICS is also highlighted by Xing and Christensen who identify a dual crisis of neoliberal "market fundamentalism" and "the hegemony of the existing world order" at the root of BRICS' rise. They further disaggregate this dual crisis into "cris[e]s of functionality" (of existing multilateral institutions), "scope" (in the range of global governance challenges), "legitimacy" (of liberal policies to deliver "a secure and just world order") and "authority" (due to the shifting balance of power from the West to emerging powers) (Xing 2014: 8–11; Christensen and Xing 2016: 5–8, 16; similarly, see also Cooper and Alexandroff 2010: 1, 14). Schematically, the crises of functionality, scope, and efficiency loosely point towards the governmental-economic, and those of legitimacy and authority towards BRICS' multipolar pole of power.

Apart from explicitly crisis-centered accounts, virtually all global governance literature/discourse on BRICS is suffused by an air of crisis, even when only mentioned in passing. Laïdi (2012: 618–619), for instance, articulates a widely shared sense that "the economic and financial crisis in 2008–2009 affirmed the prominent role played by emerging countries in the international system more than ever before." Hongyu and Xing (2014: 114) see "[t]he global economic crises since 2008" and "global crises" of "overpopulation, ethnic conflict, environmental degradation, resource scarcity, and the collapse of failed states" as indicating "the need for alternative global governance" by BRICS and the G-20. Van Noort (2017a: 124) implicitly substantiates the generative character of crisis for an alternative global governance project by identifying "global recovery" as one of BRICS' "strategic narratives." Nayyar (2016: 578) evokes a more material than discursive sense of crisis-generativity in marking 1980 as the approximate "turning point" towards current BRICS economic-growth trajectories, which implicitly points to the oil and economic crises of the 1970s and the debt crisis of the 1980s as catalysts for BRICS' economic take-off.

Some commentators have recently suggested that BRICS themselves may be in crisis economically and politically (or even become the incubator for the next global economic crisis) (Pant 2013: 97; Kiely 2016: ch. 4; Toloraya and Chukov 2016: 72, 75; Elsenhans and Babones 2017: 1). Rather than necessarily representing an impediment however, BRICS' putative crisis may induce further governance efforts.[14] Far from constituting an interpretative imposition by analysts, the diagnosis of the BRICS-generative character of crisis also animates BRICS' signature of power in both its governmental–biopolitical-economic and sovereign-multipolar dimensions in their official declarations.

"Crisis" has been a leitmotif in BRICS' communications from the group's first stirrings. Both the Joint Communiqué of the first BRIC Foreign Ministers' Meeting in 2008 and the "Joint Statement on Global Food Security" issued during the first BRIC summit in Yekaterinburg in 2009 prominently reference the concurrent global food, and economic and financial crises of 2007–2008 (BRIC 2008, #4; BRIC 2009a). Much as Foucault (2007, ch. 2) relates the problem of grain scarcity to the emergence of physiocratic governmentality in 18th-century France, the global food crisis can be seen as an instigation of BRICS' global governance project. The initial statements regarding the food crisis were followed up by Declarations of BRIC(S) Agriculture Ministers, BRICS' Action Plan for Agricultural Cooperation, and the creation of the BRICS Agriculture Information Exchange System and Agricultural Research Platform. Along with consultations on foreign policy, finance, trade, health, and national statistics, agriculture has continued to be among the most tangible and active fields of BRICS intergovernmental and transgovernmental cooperation.[15] And along with BRICS' interest in global health, agricultural, and food-security cooperation perhaps most directly testify to a biopolitical orientation towards safeguarding (biological) life and the wellbeing of populations (see Foucault 2003: 243–244; 2007: 104–108), dubbed BRICS' "strategic partnership for the welfare of our peoples" (BRICS 2017: #5).[16]

Even more than the food crisis, the global financial crisis constituted BRICS' original political *raison d'être* in both its governmental-economic and sovereign-multipolar dimensions. References to the financial crisis open the first two BRIC summit declarations to establish the G-20 (rather than the G-7/8) as the primary forum for global economic governance (BRIC 2009b, ##1–2; 2010, #3). In the 2010 declaration, the financial and economic crisis simply becomes "the crisis," which is directly linked to "the need for corresponding transformations in global governance" and "support for a multipolar, equitable and democratic world order" (BRIC 2010, ##1–3). Apart from "world economic recovery" driven by growth in emerging and developing economies, BRIC see "a reformed and more stable financial architecture that will make the global economy less prone and more resilient to future crises" as the main remedy for the predicament (BRIC 2010, ##6–13).

Comprising institutional reforms of the Bretton Woods institutions aiming at improved "regulation and supervision" of financial markets (BRIC 2010, #13) and BRICS' recently created New Development Bank and Contingency Reserve Arrangement as supplementary financial institutions (see Stuenkel 2015, ch. 6), the crisis remedy unwittingly internationalizes an ordoliberal governmental script (sometimes called the "post-Washington Consensus"). The latter stipulates that imperfectly self-regulating markets, and competition more generally, require an appropriate institutional "framework" (BRICS 2015, #11) to secure their functioning. Similarly to the ordoliberalism deployed in West Germany's postwar recovery in which the economy's institutional "framework" or "economic constitution" helped reactivate political sovereignty (Foucault 2008: 120–121, 138–140, 163–164), BRICS' proposal of a new "constitution" for the world economy simultaneously activates the potential for multipolar world order (by shifting the balance of voting power in the international financial institutions and the G-20 in favor of emerging economies, BRIC 2010: ##9, 11). As suggested by Dean's notion of the signature of power, BRICS' governmentality thus supports multipolarity as much as, conversely, the project of multipolar order "frames" the conditions of BRICS' global governance programs. The crisis-induced ordoliberal–governmental and multipolar themes have been recurrent features in all BRIC(S) summit declarations.

The 2014 Fortaleza Declaration concluding the first cycle of BRICS summits officially inscribes "the global crisis" into BRICS' political genealogy (BRICS 2014, #10) and offers the most comprehensive explicit treatment (diagnosis and remedy) of crisis as BRICS' signature political rationality, while also displaying certain "deconstructive" features (as explained below). Typifying the dramatization of crisis discourse, the summit ostensibly marks "a crucial juncture" with "challenges of [...] recovery from the global financial crises, sustainable development, [...] climate change, [...] persistent political instability and conflict in various global hotspots" all occurring within "international governance structures [...] show[ing] increasingly evident signs of losing legitimacy and effectiveness." Against this background BRICS are presented as "an important force for incremental [...] reform" of international financial institutions and "the main engines" for global economic recovery (BRICS 2014: ## 5–7, 9). The declaration rehearses the governmental–ordoliberal theme in terms of "inclusive macroeconomic and social policies" based on "[s]trong macroeconomic frameworks," "orderly competition" and statistically supported policy, and the multipolar theme (in attenuated form) in terms of "multilateral and plurilateral initiatives" and a "shared [...] commitment to [...] multilateralism" (BRICS 2014: ## 1–2, 4, 21).

After the Fortaleza "crisis manifesto" explicit references to crisis (apart from those to local crises in the Middle East and Africa; BRICS 2015: ##36, 39, 45, 47, 49; 2018: ##43–44) largely disappeared from BRICS' summit declarations. However, crisis continues to define BRICS' burgeoning global governmentality. Expressed in terms of "systematic strengthening of economic partnership for the recovery of the global economy" (BRICS 2015: #12; see also #11, 2016: #24 and Van Noort 2017a: 124) and enhancements of national and global "resilience" to counter persisting "risks" (BRICS 2016: #24; 2017: ## 7–8, 10, 30; 2018: ##54–55), crisis has effectively been institutionalized as BRICS' political rationality. Concurrently with the narrative of permanent crisis BRICS have added national and transnational deviance (crime, corruption, drugs, piracy), population policy, migration, expanded efforts in global health, gender equality, and reproductive rights to their biopolitical portfolio (BRICS 2014: ##57–58; 2015: ##28, 29–31, 34, 58–61; 2016: ## 53, 71–75, 99, 102; 2017: ## 20, 64–65; 2018: ## 32, 78–79, 90–91, 100), in part under the characteristically liberal/neoliberal–governmental umbrella of public–private partnerships (including "civil society") (BRICS 2014: #49; 2015: ##70, 74; 2017: ##10, 12; 2018: #27; see Foucault 2008: 349–357).

Overall, BRICS may appear to confront crisis with a predominantly governmental temper of international ordoliberal reform and biopolitical activism rather than a sovereign-multipolar one of "decisionist" or "revolutionary" reordering of the international system. Compared to the prominent explicit endorsements of multipolarity in early summit declarations (BRICS 2009, #12; 2010, #2; 2011, #7; 2012, #3) BRICS' sovereign-multipolar flank may appear muted, multipolarity now being sublimated as multilateralism. However, a closer look at BRICS' governmental-multipolar configuration reveals a different picture. On the one hand, BRICS' ostensible ordo-/neo-liberalism (especially governance through institutional frameworks for markets and through resilience[17]) is punctuated by narratives and practices of developmental-state capitalism. On the other hand, sovereign-multipolar discourse now manifests itself in a different, "glorified" guise.

### *BRICS governmentality and multipolarity "deconstructed"*

With respect to their governmental-economic dimension it is conventional wisdom that BRICS countries (despite individual differences and variations) have long followed – before and during the period of intensified neoliberalism from the 1980s to the financial crisis – models of "state-capitalist" economic development with industrial policies promoting national champions or state ownership, significant public investments (especially in energy and infrastructure) and state-sponsored export strategies (see Kiely 2015, ch. 3; Elsenhans and Babones 2017, chs. 1–2). Corresponding (pre- and) postneoliberal notes also surface in BRICS summit endorsements of promotion of industrial development through state-owned companies (BRICS 2013, #18; 2014, #23); technology development and innovation in mining, resource-extraction, metal industries, pharmaceuticals, (petro-)chemicals, and the ICT sector; and investment in transportation infrastructures, logistics, and renewable energy (BRICS 2015: ## 23, 52; BRICS 2016: ##36–37, 46; 2017: #13; 2018: ## 56, 66, 74–75; see also van Noort 2017a: 124–125).[18] BRICS' New Development Bank (NDB) is mandated to facilitate such efforts on a multilateral basis and in cooperation with other development institutions including the World Bank and the Asian Infrastructure Investment Bank (BRICS 2017, # 31). All this demonstrates that BRICS' neoliberal governmental pole of power is shot through with, or effectively "deconstructed," by a substantial dose of the kind of statism anathema to the "state-phobic" architects of neoliberalism. However, as seen with the adaptation of the German ordoliberal model in France, this kind of governmental ambiguity has a precedent in the history of neoliberal governmentality.

While initially often touted as its most significant attribute (see Papa 2014; Jaeger 2014: 214–215), BRICS' sovereign-multipolar axis of power seems to have lost some of its former sheen. However, the attenuation of sovereignty discourse and demands for multipolar order in BRICS summit declarations since 2013[19] does not mean that BRICS' sovereign-multipolar aspirations have faded. Rather as insinuated by scholars highlighting BRICS' cultural-symbolic dimension (Fourcade 2013), "social imaginary" (Mielniczuk 2013), soft power (Chatin and Gallarotti 2016), or multicivilizational character (Toloraya and Chukov 2016: 71; Van Noort 2018: 8), BRICS' advertisement of a new multipolar *nomos* has been sublimated into "glorification"; specifically in (the secularized form of) ceremonial symbols and attempts to stimulate the popular acclamation of BRICS. Van Noort (2017b) depicts BRICS' glorification of multipolar world order in terms of the "visual narration" of BRICS through their summit and NDB logos as well as BRICS Film Festivals since 2016.[20] The "iconic" logos, she argues, communicate the complementarity, connectivity, and temporal continuity within the BRICS group vis-à-vis their oft-alleged incoherence, brand the summit host nations and cities, and, in the words of India's foreign minister (quoted by Van Noort 2017b), express "the Brics [sic] spirit." The latter also features as "our valuable asset and an inexhaustible source of strength for BRICS cooperation" in the 2017 Xiamen Declaration (BRICS 2017, #3).

BRICS' "liturgical" glorification is also apparent in their increasing emphasis on "people-to-people" contacts among BRICS countries "to garner more popular support for BRICS cooperation [...] thus making BRICS partnership closer to our people's hearts" (BRICS 2017, #6; see also 2012, #48; 2015, #56).[21] The most recent summit declarations identify "people-to-people exchanges" as "the third pillar of BRICS cooperation" (alongside "global economic governance" and "international peace and security") geared to "foster a meaningful resonance of the BRICS partnership amongst its peoples" (BRICS 2017: #60; see also 2018: 5). The "people-to-people" pillar encompasses miscellaneous initiatives including cultural cooperation through "BRICS Alliance[s] of Libraries, [...] Museums, [...] and [...] [Children's and Youth] Theaters," a prospective BRICS Cultural Council, BRICS Culture and Film Festivals and joint film productions; educational cooperation through the BRICS University League and BRICS Network University; sports cooperation through BRICS Games and Football Tournaments; the promotion of tourism; parliamentary exchanges; and transnational "Fora" of BRICS Media, Friendship Cities and Local Governments, Youth, Young Diplomats, Young Scientists, Political Parties, Think Tanks and Civil Society Organizations (BRICS 2017: ##61–63, 66; see also Annex I, pp. 35–36; BRICS 2014: #59; 2015: ##56, 63–64, 70, 73–74; 2016: ##78–79, 100 and Action Plan, ##81–87; 2018: ##86, 92–100).

Following Agamben's excavation of the significance of glory/glorification through "acclamations, ceremonies, liturgies, and insignia" (Agamben 2011: 188) in the Western political-theological imaginary, BRICS' post-Western mobilization of "profane acclamations" should not be considered epiphenomenal. "Glorious" rallying of popular support not only adorns, "but found[s] and justif[ies]" (Agamben 2011: 230; see also 207–208) political and economic power in the reciprocal operation of "transcendent" sovereignty/ order and "immanent" governmentality/economy. "[T]he BRICS spirit" invoked in the Xiamen Declaration is thus said to embody sovereign "equality," "mutual respect" and (effectively multipolar) "solidarity" with "emerging" and developing countries as well as "governmentally" contributing to "an open world economy," "common development," and "benefit[ing] the world at large" (BRICS 2017, #3). People-to-people initiatives traverse BRICS' governmental-multipolar duality: on the one hand, innocuous cooperative activities among libraries and museums are designated as "Alliances" (evoking a geopolitics of culture), while, on the other, biopolitical–governmental cooperation in health, development and population issues appears – seemingly incongruously – alongside cultural, educational, and other transsocietal activities within the people-to-people pillar (see BRICS 2017: ##60–66 and Annex I, pp. 35–36; 2018: ##87–88, 90–91), as though "[a]ll economy must become glory, and all glory become economy" (Agamben 2011: 210).

BRICS summit declarations associate multipolar order and respect for sovereignty with "democracy" at the level of the international system (BRIC 2009: #12; 2010: #2; BRICS 2011: #7; 2016: ##6–7; 2018: ##6–7, 16; see also Laïdi 2012: 617; Mielniczuk 2013: 1081). While the practice of acclamations may appear to belong to an authoritarian political tradition (especially when encouraged by China or Russia), Agamben suggests that glorification does not disappear in contemporary democracy, but shifts to the arena of public opinion, "founded upon [...] the efficacy of acclamation, multiplied and disseminated by the media" (Agamben 2011: 255–256). Assuming this observation may apply to BRICS' aspiration to democracy in the international system, the "Action Plan of Promoting BRICS Media Cooperation" adopted by 27 BRICS media organizations in 2017 holds considerable interest.

According to the Action Plan, media exchanges among BRICS countries constitute "an important basis for [...] mutual learning among civilisations" and will "boost people-to-people ties" and "amplify a sense of BRICS identity" by "consolidat[ing]" and "accurately guid[ing] public opinion." The BRICS media organizations commit to "rebalanc[ing] international public opinion" by promoting "a fairer and more rational global governance system," and by highlighting BRICS' contributions to world economic growth and development, social progress, and "an open global economy" (BRICS Media Forum 2017). BRICS media cooperation then places glory in the form of (international) public opinion at the center of the nexus between "democratic" multipolar world order (here expressed in terms of a "fairer and more just" balance of international public opinion) and BRICS' contributions to global economic governance constituting the group's distinctive signature of power.

If BRICS' governmental-economic power axis is "deconstructed" by its state-capitalist elements, its sovereign-multipolar counterpart exhibits a similar tendency. Laïdi captures one sense of this when arguing that BRICS' attachment to state sovereignty as essential to a multipolar world signifies both strength and weakness, providing a unifying cause while simultaneously limiting their solidarity. Since "national sovereignty" narrowly conceived "cannot be the source of a collective political project," BRICS paradoxically "share a sovereigntist approach to avoid sharing sovereignty" making "[t]heir place in the international system" one of "radical ambivalence" (Laïdi 2012: 614–615, 623). Our account of BRICS' sovereign-multipolar power axis and its glorification by people-to-people contacts and international public opinion suggests a second inherently deconstructive aspect. Namely, rather than solely pertaining to state institutions, BRICS' symbology of sovereignty and multipolar order invokes the support of miscellaneous nonstate ("civil society") organizations mobilized in connection with people-to-people contacts and media cooperation (think tanks, municipalities, cultural, media, and sports organizations, etc.). To these "deconstructive" forces, we may add multipolar propagandists "freelancing" for BRICS, such as the controversial Russian right-wing philosopher Alexander Dugin and others who disseminate their acclamations through political movements, media outlets, think tanks/academic centers, academic journals, and websites.[22]

To be sure, Dugin's Theory of the Multipolar World (TMW)[23] and his Eurasian movement do not provide readymade political rationalities for BRICS' global project, since they promote a wide range of political objectives and alliances beyond BRICS. However, in addition to occasional direct references to BRICS (and related "internal crises of globalisation"[24]) Dugin explicitly endorses coordination of "the common multipolar paradigm" among the leaders of "the multipolar club" and preparation for "information wars […] for influence upon public opinion," while simultaneously (and deconstructively) calling for strengthening ethnocivilizational nonstate actors over obsolescent nation-states (Dugin 2014). Along with Brazilian philosopher and performer Flavia Virginia, Dugin has also cofounded a Russian-Brazilian Center for Multipolarity Studies.[25] Discourses and practices like these simultaneously glorify and deconstruct, and thereby introduce fundamental ambiguity into BRICS' official proclamations of a state-centric multipolar order.

### Conclusion: Crisis, "statist" governmentality, and "glorified" multipolarity

Vis-à-vis portrayals in terms of familiar dynamics of global capitalism or geopolitics, I have argued that BRICS' birth from a generalized early 21st century sense of crisis has imbued it with a distinctive postneoliberal global governance approach characterized by the interplay of governmental-economic and sovereign-multipolar modes of conduct. By characteristically heightening the stakes, crisis discourse has not only infused BRICS' emergence with an air of epochal change (however, plausible or implausible) but also predisposed its governmentality towards oscillation between "reformatory" modes of ordoliberal-cum-biopolitical economic crisis management and more "exceptional" demands for a fundamental shift in world order.

However, both poles of BRICS' signature of power are afflicted by "deconstructive" ambiguities putting in doubt a categorization of BRICS as a stable governmental-sovereign constellation (or a developmental-multipolar collective identity; see Mielniczuk 2013). Not necessarily signifying that BRICS' "global project" is destined to fail, BRICS' ambiguities in 21st century global politics at least complicate existing interpretations. BRICS' signature of power is neither simply a reproduction of class and power dynamics of global capitalism nor a mere rekindling of hegemony or the international balance of power by different players, though the notion comports with the "commonsensical" observation that BRICS have both a political and economic governance project (De Coning et al. 2015: ch. 1). BRICS' signature of power not only entails the concrete identification of the ordoliberal rationalities, biopolitical materialities, and practices and symbologies of sovereignty and world order constituting these, but – through its deconstructive inflection – also brings into relief a distinctively postneoliberal conjunction of "statist" governmentality with popularly "glorified" multipolarity.

BRICS' discursive mobilization of "crisis" illustrates and amplifies Jordheim and Wigen's (2018) argument about a shifting temporal "ordering of the international" in which "crisis" replaces "progress" as the key concept. BRICS' lexicon coagulates many crises into the "collective singular" (Koselleck quoted by Jordheim and Wigen 2018: 423, 429, 431–433) of a global crisis. This aggregation allows "crisis" to structure contemporary global experience and political conduct much as "progress" did in the past two centuries. Whereas the Eurocentric notion of "progress" implied international ordering in terms of hierarchically arranged cultural difference (say, between "primitive" and "civilized" peoples, or the "first" world and the "third") (Jordheim and Wigen 2018: 427), the potentially more global or pluricentric "crisis" may entail more sovereign-egalitarian or even "democratic" international relations, as suggested (however incongruously) in BRICS' governmental-multipolar discourse. Confirming Agamben's and Dean's conjecture that the signature of power is sutured by "glorification" or acclamation, BRICS discourse has recently turned to mobilizing international public opinion as a response to the putative crisis of global order (or BRICS' own crisis).

In the context of BRICS' signature of power, international public opinion evokes both Wilsonian echoes as a foundation of international governance and Hobbesian ones of the sovereign's governing of opinions to maintain order. However, the inherent volatility of public opinion as acclamation in a context of perceived crisis may also open pathways towards a potentially emancipatory or democratic scenario (see Milstein 2015). As argued by Bond (with reference to capitalist contradiction rather than discursive deconstruction), BRICS' apparent inability to address "the world's [...] economic and ecological crises" indicates the need and potential for a "BRICS-from-below strategy" – or, if you will, a crisis counter-governmentality – heeding "poor and working people's needs" (Bond 2016: 611, 615, 624; see Bond and Garcia 2015: chs. 24–25). Thus, while BRICS' postneoliberal construction of a political globality of agonistic cooperation may be preferable to its "psycho-pathological," alternately schizoid and narcissistic, US counterpart, BRICS' governmental-multipolar signature of power may in itself – and perhaps ought to – be(come) liable to more profound sub- and transglobal political challenges and demands for a life beyond governmental economy and sovereign law from those expected to glorify it by acclamation.

## Notes

1 BRIC (Brazil, Russia, India, China) held their first summit meeting in 2009. South Africa joined the group in 2011 changing the acronym to BRICS.

2 The distinction between these two lines of interpretation is of course schematic, since most accounts of BRICS usually touch on both. However, they are rarely systematically connected (see Stephen 2014 though) but instead prioritize either BRICS' economic-developmental or sovereign-multipolar parentage. Where both lines come into view, unifying categories of "identity and interests" (Mielniczuk 2013), "international political economy" (Xing 2014) or "strategic narratives" (Van Noort 2017a) tend to gloss over their interplay and BRICS' distinctive approach to global governance.

3 While not foreclosing governmentality as an analytical category for variable forms and levels of the conduct of self and others, my use of the concept thus mostly straddles the line between Walters' (2012: 11–13) liberal and state-genealogical senses of the term referred to in the introductory chapter.

4 BRICS' global governance approach may thereby illustrate a broader movement towards synchronizations of "international" temporalities in terms of crisis (Jordheim and Wigen 2018).

5 However, for a similar interpolation of geopolitical and biopolitical logics of security, see Dillon and Lobo-Guerrero (2008).

6 Sovereignty arguably constitutes the "defensive" and multipolarity the "reconstructive" side of BRICS' geopolitical project.

7 For an exception, see Kiersey (2009).

8 Somewhat dialectically, other economic crises, "the major crises of the seventeenth century: [...] the Thirty Years War, [...] the great peasant and urban uprisings; [...] the financial crisis, as well as the crisis of means of subsistence" initially also blocked the further development of the art of government pioneered by police science in the sixteenth century" (Foucault 2007: 101).

9 Foucault fleetingly notes that the state-phobia marking the crisis of liberalism parallels the "crisis of governmentality" in the second half of the 18th century in which "criticism of despotism, tyranny, and arbitrariness" matured into liberalism in the first place (Foucault 2008: 76). While acknowledging links between crises of capitalism and crises of liberalism, he rejects reducing the latter to the former (Foucault 2008: 70, 176).

10 Ordoliberalism received considerable inspiration from a trilogy of books by Wilhelm Röpke – Foucault (2008: 104) calls it "a kind of bible" of German neoliberalism – the first one of which was titled *The Societal Crisis of the Present* (*Die Gesellschaftskrisis der Gegenwart*, 1942).

11 The focus here is on BRICS as a group rather than individual BRICS countries. Of course, different BRICS governments may conceive "crisis," "sovereignty,"

multipolarity," etc. differently and emphasize different aspects of BRICS' common agenda.

12  For instance, narratives of BRIC(S) as "dream" or "hope," and BRIC funds, reports, "growth maps," videos and webtours, respectively.

13  The Action Plan of BRICS' Johannesburg summit lists 23 interministerial and more than 50 meetings of bureaucrats or experts in 2018 (BRICS 2018: Annex 1).

14  Based on BRICS' economic and population statistics, Elsenhans and Babones (2017) provide a kind of governmentality manual to this effect.

15  See www.brics.utoronto.ca/docs/index.html (accessed 25 September 2018) and Stuenkel (2015: 175–184).

16  For BRICS' specifically biopolitical concerns with equilibrium, milieus, and circulations (Foucault 2003: 249; 2007: 18, 20–23, 29) see Jaeger (2014: 215–216).

17  Whether resilience is inherently neoliberal is contested (see Bourbeau 2018).

18  See also BRICS' interministerial declarations on industrial and trade policy: www.brics.utoronto.ca/docs/index.html, accessed 25 September 2018.

19  Exceptions are BRICS (2016: ##6–7; 2018, ##15–16).

20  As such, BRICS' modes of glorification resemble and mimic the strategies of visual self-legitimation of other informal multilateral "clubs" such as the G-7/8 and G-20 (see Gronau 2015: 51–58).

21  Agamben (2011: 174) notes the etymological derivation of liturgy from *laos*, the "people."

22  See www.geopolitica.ru/en/person/alexander-dugin, accessed 25 September 2018.

23  TMW is a curious amalgam of Schmittian geopolitics, Heideggerian philosophy, "Gramscianism of the right," Huntington's "clash of civilizations," post-Eurocentric IR and apocalyptic mysticism befitting the perception of an age of crisis. For samples of Dugin's writings see www.geopolitica.ru/en or http://katehon.com/about-us, accessed 25 September 2018.

24  See www.theory-talks.org/2014/12/theory-talk-66.html, accessed 25 September 2018.

25  See www.geopolitica.ru/en/person/alexander-dugin and www.portalcem.com/, accessed 25 September 2018.

## References

Abdenour, Adriana E, Paulo Esteves and Carlos FPS Gama (2014) 'BRICS and Global Governance Reform: A Two-Pronged Approach', *Papers of the Fifth BRICS Academic Forum: Partnership for Development, Integration and Industrialisation*, pp. 52–59, www.academia.edu/7709035/BRICS_and_Global_Governance_Reform_A_Two-Pronged_Approach, accessed 15 June 2018.

Agamben, Giorgio (2011) *The Kingdom and the Glory: For a Theological Genealogy of Economy and Government* (Stanford: Stanford University Press).

Armijo, Leslie Elliott and Cynthia Roberts (2014) 'The Emerging Powers and Global Governance: Why the BRICS Matter' in Robert Looney (ed.) *Handbook of Emerging Economies* (New York: Routledge), www.leslieelliottarmijo.org/wp-content/uploads/2011/02/ArmRobts-13-July-20-BRICS.pdf, accessed 25 September 2018.

Biebricher, Thomas (2013) 'Critical Theories of the State: Governmentality and the Strategic-Relational Approach', *Constellations*, 20:3, 388–405.

Bond, Patrick (2016) 'BRICS Banking and the Debate Over Sub-Imperialism', *Third World Quarterly*, 37:4, 611-629.

Bond, Patrick and Ana Garcia (eds) (2015) *BRICS: An Anti-Capitalist Critique* (London: Pluto Press).

Bourbeau, Philippe (2018) 'A Genealogy of Resilience', *International Political Sociology*, 12:1, 19-35.

BRIC (2008) BRICs Foreign Ministers' Meeting – Joint Communiqué, Yekaterinburg, 16 May 2008, www.brics.utoronto.ca/docs/080516-foreign.html, accessed 5 July 2018.

BRIC (2009a) BRIC's Joint Statement on Global Food Security, Yekaterinburg, 16 June 2009, www.brics.utoronto.ca/docs/090616-food-security.html, accessed 5 July 2018.

BRIC (2009b) Joint Statement of the BRIC Countries' Leaders, Yekaterinburg, 16 June 2009, www.brics.utoronto.ca/docs/090616-leaders.html, accessed 5 July 2018.

BRIC (2010) Second BRIC Summit of Heads of State and Government, Brasilia, 15 April 2010, www.brics.utoronto.ca/docs/100415-leaders.html, accessed 5 July 2018.

BRICS (2011) Sanya Declaration, Sanya, 14 April 2011, www.brics.utoronto.ca/docs/110414-leaders.html, accessed 5 July 2018.

BRICS (2012) Fourth BRICS Summit: Delhi Declaration, New Delhi, 29 March 2012, www.brics.utoronto.ca/docs/120329-delhi-declaration.html, accessed 5 July 2018.

BRICS (2013) BRICS and Africa: Partnership for Development, Integration and Industrialisation, eThekwini Declaration, Durban, 27 March 2013, www.brics.utoronto.ca/docs/130327-statement.html, accessed 5 July 2018.

BRICS (2014) The Sixth BRICS Summit: Fortaleza Declaration, Fortaleza, 15 July 2014, www.brics.utoronto.ca/docs/140715-leaders.html, accessed 5 July 2018.

BRICS (2015) VII BRICS Summit: Ufa Declaration, Ufa, 9 July 2015, www.brics.utoronto.ca/docs/150709-ufa-declaration_en.html, accessed 5 July 2018.

BRICS (2016) Eighth BRICS Summit: Goa Declaration, Goa, 16 October 2016, www.brics.utoronto.ca/docs/161016-goa.html, accessed 5 July 2018.

BRICS (2017) BRICS Leaders Xiamen Declaration, 4 September 2017, www.brics.utoronto.ca/docs/index.html, accessed 5 July 2018.

BRICS (2018) Tenth BRICS Summit Johannesburg Declaration, Johannesburg, 25–27 July 2018, www.brics.utoronto.ca/docs/index.html, accessed 1 August 2018.

BRICS Media Forum (2017) Action Plan of Promoting BRICS Media Cooperation, Beijing, 8 June 2017, www.xinhuanet.com/english/2017-06/08/c_136350356.htm, accessed 5 July 2018.

Castañeda, Jorge (2010) 'Not Ready for Prime Time', *Foreign Affairs* 89:5, 109–122.

Chatin, Mathilde and Giulio M Gallarotti (2016) 'The BRICS and Soft Power: An Introduction', *Journal of Political Power* 9:3, 335–352.

Christensen, Steen F and Li Xing (2016) 'The Emerging Powers and the Emerging World Order: Back to the Future?' in Christensen and Xing (eds) *Emerging Powers, Emerging Markets, Emerging Societies: Global Responses* (New York: Palgrave Macmillan), 3–29.

Cooper, Andrew F and Alan S Alexandroff (2010) 'Introduction' in Alexandroff and Cooper (eds) *Rising States, Rising Institutions* (Washington DC: Brookings), 1–14.

Dean, Mitchell (2004) 'Nomos and The Politics of World Order' in Wendy Larner and William Walters (eds) *Global Governmentality: Governing International Spaces* (New York: Routledge), 40–58.

Dean, Mitchell (2010 [1999]) *Governmentality: Power and Rule in Modern Society*, second edition (London: Sage).

Dean, Mitchell (2013) *The Signature of Power: Sovereignty, Governmentality and Biopolitics* (London: Sage).

De Coning, Cedric, Thomas Mandrup and Liselotte Odgaard (eds) (2015) *The BRICS and Coexistence: An Alternative Vision of World Order* (New York: Routledge).

Dillon, Michael and Luis Lobo-Guerrero (2008) 'Biopolitics of Security in the 21st Century: An Introduction,' *Review of International Studies* 34:2, 265-292.

Dugin, Alexander (2014) 'The Multipolar World and the Postmodern', *Journal of Eurasian Affairs* 2:1, www.eurasianaffairs.net/the-multipolar-world-and-the-postmodern/, accessed 17 July 2018.

Elsenhans, Hartmut and Salvatore Babones (2017) *BRICS or Bust? Escaping the Middle-Income Trap* (Stanford: Stanford University Press).

Foucault, Michel (1990) *The History Of Sexuality, Vol. I: An Introduction* (New York: Vintage Books).

Foucault, Michel (2003) *"Society Must Be Defended:" Lectures at the Collège de France 1975-1976* (New York: Picador).

Foucault, Michel (2007) *Security, Territory, Population: Lectures at the Collège de France 1977-1978* (New York: Palgrave Macmillan).

Foucault, Michel (2008) *The Birth of Biopolitics: Lectures at the Collège de France 1978-1979* (New York: Palgrave Macmillan).

Fourcade, Marion (2013) 'The Material and Symbolic Construction of the BRICs: Reflections Inspired by the RIPE Special Issue', *Review of International Political Economy*, 20:2, 256–267.

Glosny, Michael (2010) 'China and the BRICs: A Real (But Limited) Partnership in a Unipolar World', *Polity*, 42:1, 100–129.

Gronau, Jennifer (2015) 'Die Welt im Rücken: die Selbstlegitimation der G8 und der G20 in Zeiten multilateraler Konkurrenz', *Zeitschrift für Internationale Beziehungen* 22:2, 34–67.

Hongyu, Lin and Li Xing (2014) 'G20 and C2: Sino-US Relations as an Institutional Cooperation Game' in Xing (ed.) *The BRICS and Beyond: The International Political Economy of the Emergence of a New World Order* (Burlington, VT: Ashgate), 111–128.

Jaeger, Hans-Martin (2014) 'Neither Cosmopolitanism Nor Multipolarity: The Political Beyond Global Governmentality', in Japhy Wilson and Erik Swyngedouw (eds) *The Post-Political and Its Discontents: Spaces of Depoliticisation, Spectres of Radical Politics* (Edinburgh: Edinburgh University Press), 208–228.

Jessop, Bob (2011) 'Constituting Another Foucault Effect: Foucault on States and Statecraft', in Ulrich Bröckling, Susanne Krasmann and Thomas Lemke (eds) *Governmentality: Current Issues and Future Challenges* (New York: Routledge), 56–73.

Jordheim, Helge and Einar Wigen (2018) 'Conceptual Synchronisation: From *Progress* to *Crisis*', *Millennium: Journal of International Studies*, 46:3, 421–439.

Kiely, Ray (2015) *The BRICs, US 'Decline' and Global Transformations* (London: Palgrave Macmillan).

Kiely, Ray (2016) *The Rise and Fall of Emerging Powers: Globalisation, US Power and the Global North-South Divide* (London: Palgrave Macmillan).

Kiersey, Nicholas J. (2009) 'Neoliberal Political Economy and the Subjectivity of Crisis: Why Governmentality Is Not Hollow', *Global Society*, 23:4, 363–386.

Klein, Naomi (2008) *The Shock Doctrine: The Rise of Disaster Capitalism* (Toronto: Vintage Canada).

Koselleck, Reinhart (2006) 'Crisis', *Journal of the History of Ideas* 67:2, 357–400.

Laïdi, Zaki (2012) 'BRICS: Sovereignty Power and Weakness', *International Politics* 49:5, 614–632.

Lemke, Thomas (2007) 'An Indigestible Meal? Foucault, Governmentality and State Theory', *Distinktion: Scandinavian Journal of Social Theory*, 8:2, 43–64.

Lipschutz, Ronnie D. (2002) 'The Clash of Governmentalities: The Fall of the UN Republic and America's Reach for Empire', *Contemporary Security Policy* 23:3, 214–231.

Mielniczuk, Fabiano (2013) 'BRICS in the Contemporary World: Changing Identities, Converging Interests', *Third World Quarterly*, 34:6, 1075–1090.

Milstein, Brian (2015) 'Thinking Politically About Crisis: A Pragmatist Perspective', *European Journal of Political Theory*, 14:2, 141–160.

Nayyar, Deepak (2016) 'BRICS, Developing Countries and Global Governance', *Third World Quarterly*, 37:4, 575–591.

Pant, Harsh V (2013) 'The BRICS Fallacy', *Washington Quarterly*, 36:3, 91–105.

Papa, Mihaela (2014) 'BRICS' Pursuit of Multipolarity: Response In the United States', *Fudan Journal of Social and Human Sciences*, 7:3, 363–380.

Patrick, Stewart (2010) 'Irresponsible Stakeholders? The Difficulty of Integrating Rising Powers', *Foreign Affairs* 89:6, 44–53.

Roberts, Cynthia (2010) 'Polity Forum: Challengers or Stakeholders? BRICs and the Liberal World Order – Introduction', *Polity*, 42:1, 1–13.

Robinson, William I (2015) 'The Transnational State and the BRICS: A Global Capitalism Perspective', *Third World Quarterly*, 36:1, 1–21.

Stephen, Matthew D (2014) 'Rising Powers, Global Capitalism and Liberal Global Governance: A Historical-Materialist Account of the BRICs Challenge', *European Journal of International Relations*, 20:4, 912–938.

Stuenkel, Oliver (2015) *The BRICS and the Future of Global Order* (Lanham, MD: Lexington Books).

Sum, Ngai-Ling (2013) 'A Cultural Political Economy of Crisis Recovery: (Trans-) National Imaginaries of "BRIC" and Subaltern Groups in China', *Economy and Society*, 42:4, 543–570.

Taylor, Ian (2016) 'BRICS and Capitalist Hegemony: Passive Revolution in Theory and Practice', in Steen F Christensen and Xi Ling (eds) *Emerging Powers, Emerging Markets, Emerging Societies: Global Responses* (New York: Palgrave Macmillan), 55–84.

Thakur, Ramesh (2012) 'Cementing BRICS as a Coalition of the Global South' in BRICS Research Group (ed) *BRICS New Delhi Summit 2012: Stability, Security and Prosperity* (London: Newsdesk Media), 84–85, www.brics.utoronto.ca/newsdesk/index.html, accessed 15 June 2018.

Toloraya, Georgy and Roman Chukov (2016) 'BRICS to Be Considered?', *International Organisations Research Journal* 11:2, 70–81.

Van Noort, Carolijn (2017a) 'Study of Strategic Narratives: The Case of BRICS', *Politics and Governance* 5:3, 121–129.

Van Noort, Carolijn (2017b) 'Strategic Narratives of the BRICS: A Visual Analysis', e-international relations, www.e-ir.info/2017/11/09/strategic-narratives-of-the-brics-a-visual-analysis/, accessed 12 July 2018.

Van Noort, Carolijn (2018) 'Brics Issue Narrative on Culture: Strategic or Trivial?', *International Journal of Cultural Policy*, published online 5 April 2018, www.tandfonline.com/doi/full/10.1080/10286632.2018.1459589.

Vasilache, Andreas (ed.) (2014) *Gouvernementalität, Staat und Weltgesellschaft* (Wiesbaden: Springer).

Walters, William (2012) *Governmentality: Critical Encounters* (New York: Routledge).

Xing, Li (2014) 'Introduction: Understanding the Hegemony and the Dialectics of the Emerging World Order', in Xing (ed.) *The BRICS and Beyond: The International Political Economy of the Emergence of a New World Order* (Burlington, VT: Ashgate), 1-23.

Xing, Li and Óscar García Agustín (2014) 'Constructing and Conceptualising "Interdependent Hegemony" in an Era of the Rise of the BRICS and Beyond' in Li Xing (ed) *The BRICS and Beyond: The International Political Economy of the Emergence of a New World Order* (Burlington, VT: Ashgate), 53–74.

# 10 Governmentality of the Arctic as an international region

*Mathias Albert and Andreas Vasilache*

## Introduction[1]

From the late 1990s onwards, the Arctic had a major comeback in terms of global public attention, discursively integrating the Arctic into the representational scope of world politics and globality. Not only did it epitomize the consequences of global climate change. It also – again – served as a point of reference from which grand thought schemes with global impact could be projected. Thus, for example, the prospect of ice-free sea lanes along the Northern Sea Route and through the Northwest Passage gave rise to a wealth of predictions about a major shift in the global shipment of goods.

The present contribution argues that the prospects for the Arctic are strongly intertwined with dominant perceptions and depictions of it as an international region, subject to emerging practices of governmentality.[2] Practices of "governmentality" here, as will be further outlined below, are understood as rationalities, technologies, and mechanisms that (co-)constitute, change, and govern social entities by shaping institutions, actors, subjectivities, normative orders, and cognitive maps in a comprehensive fashion. We argue that an assessment of the future of the Arctic needs to take patterns of Arctic governmentality into account, that is, patterns which constitute and regulate the Arctic as a social and political space.

In the following, we present what is primarily a conceptual argument for the added value of a governmentality perspective on the Arctic. Having said this, we will apply governmentality also as a theoretical and analytical lens to current Arctic affairs and policies.[3] The contribution will proceed in three main steps. First, we will briefly survey the current situation in, and the discussions about, the Arctic. Second, we will introduce some conceptual aspects of governmentality, of the regionalization focus applied, as well as of the role of perceptions and representations for governmentality. Third, and drawing on the concepts developed in the previous part, we will argue that the construction and representation of the Arctic takes place through a number of intertwined discourses and related practices and that these, taken together, constitute the governmentality of a unique international region.

## The current situation in the Arctic

There is no "neutral" or "objective" current state of affairs with regard to the Arctic. Quite to the contrary, over the last decade, it has almost become a showcase of how quickly wholesale discursive constructions of a region can change.[4] The common denominator regarding change in the Arctic pertains to the decrease in the extent of year-on-year sea ice in the Arctic Ocean as well as the decrease in the mass of inland ice on Greenland. The region has witnessed an exponential increase in global attention since the early/mid-2000s and this is probably because nowhere else has global warming become so immediately visible. While the local impact of global climate change on flora and fauna, as well as on the local communities living on the shorelines of the Arctic Ocean has already been profound and has received increased attention, the major focus regarding the global impact of developments induced by global climate change in the Arctic has been on economic and resulting geopolitical interests.

Economic interests in the Arctic relate to the possibility of accessing vast crude oil and mineral offshore resources that up to now have been beyond the scope of exploration because of the challenges posed by the ice cover and the harsh climatic conditions. In addition, the melting of the sea ice has fostered interests in new Arctic shipping routes. The prospects in this respect have underpinned a long and intensive discussion about the future of the Arctic in the face of both environmental and economic globalization. Emboldened by a range of highly symbolic moves, most notably the planting of a Russian flag on the seabed under the North Pole in 2007, this prospect of the economic use of the Arctic has supported a vast debate of a coming "Cold War" there, a new "scramble for the Arctic," etc. and has been framed in terms of the prospects for cooperation or conflict in the Arctic region (cf. Brosnan et al. 2011; Stephen and Knecht 2017; Young 2011).

The discursive hype notwithstanding,[5] however, the Arctic has never been a region prone to manifest territorial conflict. Quite to the contrary, inter-state territorial disputes remain very limited. They pertain, most notably, to the exact location of the boundary between the US and Canada in the Beaufort Sea, to the dispute between Canada and Denmark with regard to the tiny Hans Island in the Kennedy Channel of Nares Strait, the question of whether the Northwest Passage constitutes an international shipping lane or a domestic shipping route within Canadian waters, and unresolved issues in relation to Svalbard's Exclusive Economic Zone (EEZ). The Arctic Ocean remains subject to the UN Convention on the Law of the Sea (UNCLOS), and although there are vast differences between riparian states regarding claims as to the extension of their continental shelves (and associated rights of economic exploitation), thus far all states involved have sought to abide by UNCLOS rules and have submitted their scientific data and claims for a necessary decision on the issue to the Commission on the Limits of the Continental Shelf (CLCS). In addition, the Arctic Council has proved to be a fairly effective and efficient body for discussing all matters pertaining to the

Arctic (save issues of security), exerting a strong pull for a range of states who have sought observer status.

What we take as a starting point for the discussion of current governmental developments in the region are representations, depictions, and imaginaries of the Arctic. Neither is the Arctic a region that can be characterized by supposedly "neutral" facts, nor is it amenable to arbitrary social constructions "at will," so to speak. As with other spatial formations that are subject to some form of political authority, the Arctic region can be conceptualized as a specific and evolving conglomerate of a relation between power and knowledge that is expressed through and reproduced by a range of discursive strategies. It is against this background that we believe that the concept of governmentality can help to shed light on the specific constellation of the Arctic power/knowledge nexus that constitutes and shapes the Arctic as an international region.

## Governmentality and regionalism

At first glance, it might seem counterintuitive using the Foucauldian concept of governmentality when discussing the Arctic region. Foucault's interest was in the practices and strategies of governmentality that were associated with the emergence of the modern state, and in the specific formulations of disciplining power connected to it (Foucault 2004a, 2004b). For a long time, governmentality studies did not pay much attention to trans- or international relations, but adhered to Foucault's focus on the governmentalization of and within modern, and, in most cases, Western societies (cf. Burchell et al. 1991; Dean 1999). While we can already find some first reflections on international governmentality in Dean's approach to governmental theory and politics in 1999, the early governmentality discourse concentrated on politics within (mostly liberal) states and societies. Using governmentality in relation to the Arctic, therefore, seems at first glance to be at best a borderline case of governmentality studies, in the sense that past and present attempts to bind the inhabited parts of the Arctic into the framework of modern statehood could be traced. In this respect, one could argue that these attempts nowadays particularly work through a discourse on, and a normative and legal practice of, "indigeneity" (Lindroth 2011), that ties autonomy to the framing of a sovereign territorial state. However, while not negating the assertion of territorial statehood, however limited,[6] and, in particular, not denying the ongoing relevance of state interests and state sovereignty patterns, as well as juridical and institutional policies in areas of the "High North", we will take a different approach and look at the Arctic mainly as a subject for, and an object of, inter- and transnational governmentality. Given the abundance of governmentality approaches we will, however, abstain from giving yet another exegetical overview on the theory of governmentality, but will only briefly sketch, contextualize, and justify our perspective. Our more detailed reading of governmentality will then be deployed step by step in the course of the analytical part of this article. We deliberately concentrate on governmentality, and do not focus on notions and concepts of traditional state sovereignty or governance.[7]

For Foucault, the governmental type of power is systematically distinct from – or rather even opposed to – what he calls sovereign power and describes as state-centric, juridical, institution-based, and repressive – and which he believes to be an anachronistic power mode that is not prevalent in modern politics any more. Although Foucault pointed out that sovereign power techniques might be instrumental for governmentality and put forward the idea that the transition from sovereign to disciplinary, and then to governmental power should be understood as a genealogical passage and not as a sequential replacement of one power type by another, for Foucault this does not put in doubt the systematic and conceptual distinctions between these different forms of power and the corresponding rationalities of politics (Foucault 1997: 32–34, 2001, 2004a: 17–26, 134–165, 2004b: 427, 435ff.; cf. Vasilache 2019). However, while our present look at the Arctic follows Foucault's conceptual sketch of governmentality, we do not intend to imply that sovereign or disciplinary rationalities and frames of power (the latter rather on the microlevel of power exertion than on the regional macrolevel) have ceased to exist[8] or are irrelevant in the Arctic space. Quite on the contrary, it is obvious that some major Arctic actors, Russia, for instance, rely strongly on sovereign approaches and policies towards the Arctic.

A considerable range of adaptations of the governmentality lens exists in International Relations (IR) that emphasizes various aspects of Foucault's late work and addresses a variety of transborder topics. As Zanotti (2013: 289) argues, there are basically two different streams in governmental IR, a more heuristic and a more descriptive one. While we agree to this assessment, our reference to the governmentality discourse in IR is not focused on systematic differences, but rather on a reading that emphasizes the overlapping foci of interest of governmentality approaches, resulting not least from the interrelatedness between the different conceptual facets of and within Foucault's approach. Taking into consideration the relevance of the dispositifs of security for the governmental art of governing (Foucault 2001), governmentality-oriented approaches to IR have been adopted, first and foremost, in security-related research in a broad sense. This research addresses the governmental framing of inter- and transnational security rationalities and politics as well as governmental securitization dynamics (Aradau and Van Munster 2007; Bigo 2008; De Larrinaga and Doucet 2008; Evans 2010; Vasilache 2014). Related to approaches that focus on security, a considerable number of adaptations of governmentality theory in IR draw in particular on Foucault's concept of biopolitics in order to discern and analyze biopolitical implications of and within international politics (Aradau and Blanke 2010; De Larrinaga and Doucet 2008; Dillon 2007, 2010; Duffield 2007). In addition, there is considerable interest in the colonization and shaping of the international by rationalities and techniques of liberal political economy (Duffield 2007; Jabri

2006; Kiersey 2011). Along with research that addresses a variety of empirical issues, the governmentality angle in IR also includes broader, conceptual approaches that discuss tendencies of "global governmentality" (Grondin 2010; Larner and Walters 2004), the governmental rationalities of globalization (Lipschutz and Rowe 2005) or "*The International* as governmentality" (Neumann and Sending 2007, original emphasis).

Critics of using Foucault's theories broadly with regard to IR[9] argue that governmentality "refers to the conduct of conduct, especially the technologies that govern individuals," and that it "captures the way governments and other actors draw on knowledge to make policies that regulate and create subjectivities" (Bevir 2010: 423). Therefore, governmentality theory is seen as being applicable to the governing of individuals, mainly in Western states, rather than to IR or even to global politics (Joseph 2010; Selby 2007). Related to this criticism, Chandler (2010: 135) argues that governmentality in IR depends on taking for granted the existence of a global liberal order and therefore tends to turn "methodology into a dogmatic a priori approach." While we cannot invest further in this debate, it seems that the criticism of taking governmentality to the global level does not oppose, but much rather suggests, applying a regional governmentality perspective. In conceptual terms, a regional focus does not depend on presupposing a boundless and denationalized liberal global order. In addition, a regional approach allows for taking into account a range of actors on various scales (states, populations, individuals, inter- and transnational organizations, etc.), without methodologically prioritizing – as in methodological nationalism – or excluding any particular type of actor.

Because of the systematic openness in this regard it seems that, first, a regional view can be expected to be relevant for governmentality studies because it adopts the middle ground and fills the systematic gap between the state-confined and the boundless/global views in governmentality approaches. Taking a regional perspective allows observing and describing both subregional dynamics and impacts of the global level, as well as the discursive and representational integration of the regional level into the realm of globality. However, looking at regions from a governmentality perspective is, second, justified also in thematic terms. While regional patterns and dynamics both play a significant role in international politics and have received a lot of scholarly attention since the 1990s (for an overview, see Söderbaum 2015), the governmentality view has not often turned towards regionalism (with a few exceptions, such as Larner and Walters 2002; Walters 2004) or to particular world regions. The increased relevance of regionalism as a focus and regions as areas of political and economic regulation, as well as their liberal framing, not only suggests going beyond mainstream governance approaches to regionalism (cf. Stokke and Hønneland 2007) but, in particular, supports the governmentality focus on regions. In addition, the few regional applications of the governmentality lens usually address the EU (Walters and Haahr 2005) or, in a few cases, the Middle East (Busse and Stetter 2014) or the Association of Southeast Asian Nations (ASEAN) (Freistein 2014). Unlike these political regions, the Arctic has not yet been subject to institutionalized political regionalization attempts. It is a geographical space that is uninhabited in large parts. Only a minor part of the Arctic is covered by territorial states and it is basically subject to maritime law. These characteristics constitute a systematic distinction between the Arctic and political regionalization processes worldwide. Third, taking a closer look at the Arctic region, therefore, seems relevant as it might provide insights into the dynamics of a genuinely international regional space. Fourth, this specific characteristic of the Arctic entails the necessity as well as the possibility of widening the view beyond the conduct of states, institutionalized governance, or international organizations and of taking into account discursive representations of the region. Therefore, we will broaden the empirical perspective and trace facets of governmentality in the Arctic with a focus on representations, depictions, conceptualizations, and perceptions, as well as on related practices.

To put an emphasis on ideas, discourses, and practices is, however, not only appropriate because of the particular situation of the Arctic region (i.e., on the empirical level), but also in theoretical terms. Such a focus results from the conceptual feature of governmentality as being both a rationality and regime of governing, as well as a perspective for analysis (see, in particular, Dean 2007; Neumann and Sending 2010). The inextricable interrelation between governmental rationality and practices corresponds to the core role of discourses in Foucauldian thinking in general (Foucault 1975, 1976, 1980, 1984) and, in particular, to the importance that Foucault assigns to the study of discourses, perceptions, depictions, and representations for the understanding of politics and governmentality (Foucault 1991b). By drawing on both Foucault's writings[10] as well as on governmentality studies in IR, we will use governmentality as a heuristic framework and seek to take into account the interrelatedness of the core conceptual aspects of governmentality analysis and politics. In doing so, we will outline and discuss how the Arctic is affected by governmental security rationalities, by specific logics of political economy and order-building, and by circuits of liberal economic flows, as well as how it is subjected to biopolitical rationalizations and imaginaries.

## Facets of Arctic governmentality

Approaching the Arctic as a region of governmentality requires acknowledging a wealth of discourses that both represent and "make" the region. Here, we follow both Foucault as well as the vast majority of Foucauldian readings, and treat discourses in the widest possible sense, encompassing mentalities, practices, semantics, and representations. On an empirical level, the discursive making of the Arctic is probably best expressed by the fact that definitions of the regional boundaries vary widely. While obviously a function of the criteria applied (e.g., the location of the polar circle, the tree line, the 10°C July isotherm, etc.), it is equally obvious that the application of one criterion or another in most cases follows discursive purposes and related interests. While it is not possible here to enumerate all discourses that feed into the representation and production of the Arctic as a region of governmentality, a number of the most important ones can easily be identified. These include representations of the Arctic as: an open and still-wild space, a site of conquest and struggle; an economic zone, rich in natural resources; a living space for (indigenous) people(s); a site for cooperation and possible conflict between nation-states; and a regulative space. While a detailed analysis of these discourses is far beyond the scope of the present contribution, we observe their existence as a starting point and argue that it is the shape and rationalities of these discourses and imaginaries of the Arctic (Steinberg et al. 2015), their changes, and their modifications that characterize the Arctic region as an international region and as a space in the process of governmentalization.

### Shaping a region and making a regional space governable

The discourse on the conquest and exploration of the Arctic as frontier and as an unknown, wild, and challenging space is the oldest one, as it is intimately linked to the early days of polar exploration from the 18th century onwards. For a long time, this discourse was the dominant representation of the Arctic (as well as of Antarctica). While this dominance has long been weakened, it still provides a powerful way of depicting the region. In a direct continuation of historical narratives of exploration, this representation can be found, for instance, in attempts to actualize past heroism and tragedy for present purposes (e.g., then Canadian Prime Minister Harper at the bow of one of the vessels that miraculously then found one of the Franklin expedition ships just a few days later). It is expressed more broadly and pervasively, however, in depictions of people, expeditions, ships, etc. that seem to challenge the cold and the wilderness (in the case of people often posing for commemorative snapshots with a rather triumphant expression), in rituals of national conquest (the by now infamous flag-planting on the seabed under the North Pole by a Russian submarine), and in metaphors of extremity (most notably the "Far North").

This broader discourse feeds on the "authenticity" of the struggle and effort expressed in the more traditional one on conquest and exploration.[11] However, in addition to these heroic discourses and practices that reflect traditional sovereign projections of land appropriation rather than governmental imaginaries, we see recent discursive representations that go along with, but also overwrite and question the idea of an open and hostile space conquered by brave individual explorers representing their states. Taken together, these more current approaches to the Arctic contribute to a (re)definition and constitution of it as a region and a governable space. This takes place along five interrelated discursive, representational, and political moves.

First, there is a growing and expanding interest of international institutions and organizations in the Arctic. While international governmentality is not limited to activities of international institutions and organizations, Merlingen (2003) has demonstrated their impact on, and importance for, transboundary governmental steering. In respect of the Arctic, we see increasing attention from institutions, in the Foucauldian sense of problematization (Foucault 1983), that can be traced in both the growing number of international organizations dealing with the Arctic, as well as in the increasing relevance of Arctic issues to international organizations. Arctic-related topics have gained relevance beyond the institutional framework of UNCLOS and the Arctic Council, and are addressed in numerous institutional contexts, differentiated along specific thematic concerns (e.g., the new Arctic Economic Council). The Arctic has become a topic in a wide range of fora on economic and environmental issues, on tourist development, on issues of agriculture, and on indigenous and human rights, etc. In addition, the rising interest in the Arctic from institutions is mirrored in the increasing visibility and actual political relevance of the Arctic Council itself. This rise in visibility and relevance of the Arctic within international institutions has been accompanied by riparian states reformulating their Arctic policies and strategies, but also by countries far away from the Arctic, such as China and India, developing an interest in the region – and, for example, seeking and gaining observer status in the Arctic Council. Taken together, we witness an inclusion of the Arctic into the global political system and into the horizon of globality.

Second, related to the increasing relevance of the Arctic to institutions that we have witnessed during the last few years, there has also been a substantial increase in the number and dedication of actors dealing with the Arctic. This includes international institutions and nonriparian states that were formerly barely involved (and sometimes, not even interested) in Arctic policies and politics. However, the increasing number of actors involved in Arctic affairs goes far beyond states and institutions, and includes both a broad variety of different nongovernmental organizations (NGOs), as well as individual actors. Ranging from private companies with obvious economic interests, transnational trade, and industry associations, through environmental and climate protection actors, biodiversity actors, indigenous representatives, and indigenous rights activists, to a multidisciplinary variety of scholars and experts, a broad spectrum of actors have captured the Arctic discursively. They address manifold topics from their respective specialized perspectives and with different political, economic, ecological, cultural, or academic interests and goals (see Jensen and Hønneland 2015 for a recent overview). The expansion of actor diversity and the activities of these actors in Arctic discourses go along with Arctic topics attracting more media attention. Broadcasters and media organizations contribute to actor variety by both diffusing the expanding and specialized Arctic discourses to a broad public and – as actors in their own right – by participating in Arctic agenda-setting. This multiplicity of actors dealing with Arctic affairs, their specialization, and polyphony, the inclusion of Arctic inhabitants as subjects and objects of governmental (self-)observation and (self-)enhancement, as well as the lack of a clear legal political hierarchy in Arctic politics, are characteristic features of governmentality as "[t]he ensemble formed by the institutions, procedures, analyses and reflections, the calculations and tactics that allow the exercise of this very specific albeit complex form of power" (Foucault 1991a: 102; see also 2004a: 416). While governmentality might historically be linked inextricably with the emergence of the modern state and, thus, with governmental practices of state institutions, governmentality in the context of the emergence of the Arctic as an international region draws on governmental practices of both state institutions as well as nonstate actors.

Third, the growing number and thematic range of Arctic actors is accompanied by a multiplication of knowledge on the Arctic. While still a marginal and specialized subject compared to mainline subjects in most scientific disciplines, the marginality of the Arctic seems to have been gradually reduced by the growing realization that it is not only a region of natural phenomena, but embedded in global networks and "flows of people, money, ideas and influence" (Dodds and Nuttall 2016: 37).

This systematic knowledge production on the Arctic is not only both a precondition and technique of governmentality (Foucault 1991a: 96, 102; 2004a: 114, 118–121, 162–163, 346), but also, fourth, contributes to the *normalization* of the Arctic – i.e., to its *deexceptionalization* and epistemic taming through rationalization and intelligible permeation – which is another core facet of governmentality (see Foucault 2004a: 90–100).

Fifth, taken together, the aspects mentioned not only show that several characteristic traits of governmental rationality are being projected onto the Arctic, but add to the definition and constitution of the Arctic as a region. The broad and diversified framework of actors and of knowledge production covering the Arctic, as well as its normalization, contributes to reframing an open and wild area as a concrete and defined space. This is also reflected by a remarkable change in spatial perspectives on the Arctic. While former heroic narratives concentrated either on single geographical spots (North Pole) or particular routes (Northwest Passage), such Pole or Far North representations have been superseded by spatial representations of the Arctic that conceive it as an encompassing region or even as a placeholder for a global "New North" (Smith 2012). The interest in specific spots within an open, undeveloped area has been overwritten by a comprehensive view that depicts the Arctic as a concrete space and as a particular "historical-natural milieu" (Foucault 2004a: 42, our translation, see also 40–44). Corresponding to governmental rationalities, the discursive construction of the Arctic as a region is based on an assemblage of actors, knowledge, and representations aimed at defining, understanding, assessing, and ordering the respective space. It can be seen as an example of "how imaginative geographies reflect (and allow) folding of [...] discourses as well as biopolitical strategies" (Prasad and Prasad 2012: 358).

The particular relevance of discourses and representations for the constitution of the Arctic as a region is underpinned by the fact that questions of territorial and legal belonging of the Arctic to particular states do not constitute the core of Arctic debates. Because of its missing national foundation, the development of the Arctic differs strongly from other regionalization initiatives around the world. Unlike regional projects such as the EU, ASEAN, Mercosur, etc. Arctic regionalism and its governmental framing do not and cannot originate primarily from nation-states establishing a regional institution, whose demarcations are then clearly defined by the territorial areas of the member states. Since the Arctic lacks a clear national-territorial basis that characterizes other political regions, it is an international regional space that is held together neither by member states alone nor mainly by law, but much more by the mentioned assemblage of discourses, imaginaries, and the entirety of political and societal actors and initiatives addressing the Arctic and its populations. Because there is no primacy of the national and the juridical in Arctic affairs, we see a rather subordinated and instrumental function of the law – which corresponds to governmental rationalities in that "the 'rule of law' [works] as rule 'through' law" (Rajkovic 2010: 29; see Foucault 2004a: 150).

This, again, does not mean to underestimate the relevance of institutional and, thus, juridical aspects of Arctic politics – for example, regarding questions of indigenous rights. And, while it needs to be emphasized that governmentality works mostly "indirectly" by shaping the frames in which others make sense of their actions, this does not deny the relevance of more "direct" paths of action – as, for instance, traditional government practices and more sovereign, sometimes repressive techniques – parallel to, alongside, and within politics of governmentality (see Dillon 2004: 76). To use but one example, it has been argued that, in relation to Arctic region-building, some actions taken by the governments involved, most notably the Ilulissat Declaration, were state- and government-centric and deliberately framed to exclude others (see Moe et al. 2011).[12]

### Knowledge production, normalization, and security

As hinted at already, there is a substantial increase in, and specialization with regard to, knowledge production on the Arctic, as well as a particularly close relation between scholarly observation and policy advice.[13] According to governmentality theory – but already in accordance with Foucault's earlier concept of the inseparability of the power/knowledge nexus (Foucault 1980) – knowledge production is a necessary requirement for the governmentalization of spaces (Foucault 1991a: 96, 102; 2004a: 114, 118–121, 162–163, 346) and, thus, an important activity field and technique of governmental power. Diverse and specialized expertise does not only open up the possibility for concrete governmental intervention in respective thematic areas. Rather, the expertise-based, systematic detection of risks and aberrations requires the elaboration of scholarly political problem-solving strategies and intervention through preventive measures (Aradau and Van Munster 2007: 91, 102–106; Foucault 2004a: 53, 57; 2004b: 101; Rose 1993).

Likewise, the multidisciplinary scope of Arctic knowledge production and its depth can be read as a contribution to the governmentalization of the

Arctic through its normalization. However, it is a type of normalization that, on the one hand, refers to the governmental, i.e., knowledge-based meaning of the term (Bigo 2008: 99–104; De Larrinaga and Doucet 2008: 520; Foucault 2004a: 90–100) while, on the other hand, it includes the colloquial usage of the term in the sense of a trivialization of the Arctic as a mundane, rather unspectacular space. Having said this, we see a normalization of the Arctic space through thematic enlargement and knowledge differentiation along-side disciplinary expertise. This normalization move consists of the discursive transformation of an area of unexpected extremity to a space of predictable order – with predictability being a core target of the governmental security dispositif. Following Foucault, security is an encompassing ordering principle that pervades the politics of governmentality (Foucault 2001, 2004a: 19, 39–44, 53, 162; 2004b: 101–102) and pervades all aspects of life, aiming at an arrangement and an order of things that minimizes the risk of undesirable or unexpected incidences, as well as of aleatory events. By doing so, it reduces uncertainty (Foucault 2004a: 52ff., 57). In order to enable the deployment of a governmental regulation of space, its circulation patterns and biopolitical focus, the governmental security dispositif – understood as a general impera-tive and ordering principle of governmental steering – works through pre-ventive risk detection, which is realized through socioengineering techniques of observation and surveillance, as well as cost–benefit calculations and risk analyzes. Reshaping the Arctic from the unexpected to the calculable, there-fore, also implies moving away from the logic of threats to a rationality of expertise-based risk assessment as well as resilience rationalities (Aradau and Van Munster 2007; Castel 1991; Dean 1999: 177; Foucault 2004a: 57; 2004b: 101). This is reflected in current discursive representations and projections of the Arctic. Although representations in relation to "trad-itional" security issues still abound, the Arctic is increasingly seen as a social and inhabited area that needs to be comprehensively managed (e.g., Anderson 2009), in this respect also endowing it with a history that is retold as not being "marginal" (see Grant 2016). In line with the governmental ideal of establishing and maintaining favorable conditions for the normal course of life and its supposed natural regularities (Foucault 2004a: 53, 78ff., 346, 501–505), the Arctic experiences governmental securitizing moves (see Palosaari and Tynkkynen 2015) that transform it from a place of (possible) death to a place of life, in which future developments become controllable through the knowledge-based prevention of undesirable and/or unforeseeable incidents and sudden breaks in the normal course of events.[14]

The governmental triangle of systematic knowledge production, normal-ization, and securitization is also mirrored in the fact that heroic polar explor-ation has been replaced by scientific missions. In structural equivalence to Foucault's remark that the universal philosopher has been replaced by the specific technical expert (Foucault 1980: 126–129), we see the polar adven-turer being replaced by the scientist specializing in Arctic studies. Indeed, there are major systematic differences between these two types of Arctic travelers.

While the first aimed at putting his (almost never: her) feet on a geographical spot that was not seen as being in reach for normal humans and – if lucky – coming back immediately after successfully getting there, the second comes here to stay – i.e., to spend a longer period of time in a research station or in the environment of Arctic towns with a high density of research organization representatives. Former heroic polar expeditions were about braving the elements and overcoming life-threatening dangers. In contrast to the heroic era, the prototype of contemporary polar explorers is not the group of – more or less crazy – hotshots, but the interdisciplinary team of experts, who apply for a sabbatical to do field research. This corresponds to the almost complete absence of the image of the Arctic as "terra nullius" in such contexts, which serves as a flexible point of reference in other, more traditional "heroic" discourses (see Steinberg et al. 2015: 31ff.). Furthermore, even the depiction of recent more or less "heroic" (or, according to perspective, completely nonsensical) performances of the human body in an Arctic environment, such as running a marathon to the North Pole, differs from the logics of traditional explorations. Such an event is detached from the extraordinary characteristics and the uniqueness of an existential, potentially life-threatening challenge, but rather symbolically as well as metaphorically includes the Arctic space within the regular realm of sportive events – with sports being an activity that particularly fits with the governmental ideal of the biopolitical subject voluntarily enhancing his or her fitness in the sense of a continuous "souci de soi" (Foucault 1984).

### Unleashing economic potential and circulation

Governmentality is both based on, and enables, structures and processes of liberal political economy. Understood as a broad political rationality that frames the entire social order (Foucault 1991a: 92; 2004a: 142–145, 159), the concept of liberal political economy, on the one hand, goes beyond the economy as a single policy field. On the other hand, however, the economy as a subject matter provides a prototypical area of activity and the guiding rationalities of governmentality (Foucault 2004a: 144ff.). Liberal economic patterns and policies offer a blueprint for the wider political economy of governmentality. The discourse on the Arctic as an economic zone is the one that most directly draws on the observation of the regional effects of climate change, most notably the reduction of year-on-year ice in the Arctic Ocean and the receding of inland ice in Greenland. It focuses on the expectation of the (not necessarily always confirmed) presence of vast resources of sought-after raw materials in the region. This is related first and foremost to oil and gas (Mikkelsen and Langhelle 2008) as well as to minerals to be exploited on or below the seabed. Such expectations explain the high interests and stakes invested in the delimitation of the continental shelves of riparian states – which demonstrates that territorial questions, although not central to Arctic debates, are of course neither absent nor irrelevant. Another thematic field of the economic discourse focuses on the usefulness of shipping routes that might become available as a result of the receding year-on-year ice, most notably the Northwest Passage and the Northern Sea Route (along the north shore of Russia). It is these that have often been infused with projections for a new global role for the Arctic as possible alternatives to the Panama and Suez Canal routes.

In considering recent discourses on the Arctic, we not only discern the particular relevance of economic expectations, but also a governmental framing of these economic aspirations in that they are, first, targeted at unleashing the, until now, fallow economic potential of the Arctic – as well as human capacities and individual energies in general – by, second, enabling circulation flows. Current economic discourses and representations not only describe the development of the Arctic in terms of a purposeful establishment or an accurately planned construction of a regional economy. Rather, they are also characterized by the governmental rationality of freeing already existing potentials, unleashing available, but latent forces, which until now were obstructed and – both metaphorically and literally – frozen in perpetual ice (see e.g., Eurasia Group 2014). In contrast to a foundational or creational logic that is linked to sovereign rationalities (Foucault 1991a: 95, 102), the governmental approach strives to enable economic deployment according to the (supposed) momentum and inner regularities of economic dynamics. Therefore, economic development is not seen primarily in terms of structures and institutions, but rather projected in patterns of movement, circulation, and free trade.

Within governmental rationalities, enabling and maintaining circulation play a crucial role beyond simple economic necessities or technical/logistical requirements. Rather, it can be understood as a nonmaterial pattern that contributes to constituting, ordering, and securing a governable space (Aradau and Blanke 2010). As Dillon puts it, "distribution is the spatial figuration that characterizes traditional geopolitical rationalities and technologies of security, circulation is the spatial configuration that characterizes the biopolitics of security" (Dillon 2007: 11; see also Bigo 2008: 107). However, circulation is important not only in terms of biopolitical security, but also as a crucial ordering principle for the deployment of liberal political economy and its regulation (Foucault 2004a: 36ff., 40, 100).

Looking at economic aspirations towards Arctic space, we can actually detect three different, but closely interrelated projections of circulation. First, the exploitation of Arctic raw materials appears as a promise to include Arctic goods into global trade flows (see Glomsrød and Aslaksen 2008). However, this target is connected to a much broader aspiration. It appears, second, also as a hope for maintaining, furthering, and securing global economic circulation through the (speculative) increase in natural gas and crude oil supply from Arctic deposits (Eurasia Group 2014), creating a new global hot spot for gas and oil production in addition to the Gulf region, Russia, and Venezuela. Third, new shipping routes are supposed to expand the global map of liberal circulation (Humpert 2014). Thus, governmental circulation projections onto the Arctic are encompassing, since they address the regional as well as the global level. Thereby, circulation is framed and envisaged in both a systematic and a material fashion. The Arctic is represented as a region that might not only benefit regionally from its inclusion into global circulation, but that could also contribute to enabling and ensuring global circulation – thus intensifying and furthering the globality of the world.

### Biopolitics

Over the past two to three decades, the status and livelihoods of people that actually live in the Arctic have, after a long history of neglect and displacement, played an increasing (although varied) role within the individual riparian states. The rights of indigenous peoples have become a more prominent issue in national as well as in international–regional contexts as a result of the increasing prominence of the global normative framework for indigenous rights. Some indigenous peoples now play an important role in the construction of the Arctic as a region, as witnessed most notably in their representation in the Arctic Council. While it is probably an exaggeration to talk about a nascent collective identity of different groups and peoples as a somehow common Arctic people, both the relations between indigenous peoples in the Arctic and their participation in (the formation of) regional institutions have increased over the years (see Shadian 2006; Tennberg 2010).

Beyond and in addition to a rights-oriented approach, inhabitants of the Arctic have become addressees of an encompassing biopolitical concern. This biopolitical interest does not so much focus on legal structures and rights, but more on provisions that regulate a sociobiological ecosystem, in which "power comes to take species existence as its referent object" (Dillon 2010: 64) in order to make life live and flourish (De Larrinaga and Doucet 2008: 520; Dillon 2010; Foucault 2004a: 78ff., 108ff., 158, 346, 501–505). Thereby, biopolitics are connected to and framed along governmental security rationalities since they "revolve around the properties of biological being" (Dillon 2010: 65). In contrast to a sovereign, rather traditional understanding of security, governmental security does not follow a restricting, limiting logic, but aims to enable and safeguard the full deployment of the potentials of a biopolitical ecosystem and its various social milieus. In this context, humans are not conceptualized primarily as citizens, legal objects/subjects, or rights-holders, but constituted as populations that are differentiated along statistical distribution and social milieus and are being addressed by specific subjectivation processes and (self-)improvement policies and measures (Bigo 2008: 103–106; Busse 2015; Foucault 2004a: 70–72, 95, 98, 156ff.).

Taking a look at the more prominent role of Arctic inhabitants in recent Arctic discourses and politics, as well as at the way in which people living in the Arctic are represented discursively, we can indeed identify the deployment of biopolitical rationalities and their corresponding security logics, which are based on, and reflected in, an all-encompassing interest in the life and life conditions of Arctic populations.[15] Fueled by the melting of Arctic ice, aspirations to integrate Arctic populations into regional and global economic circulation patterns through the development of an agricultural and/or tourist sector go along with a thorough analysis of the living patterns of Arctic inhabitants. Thereby, addressing Arctic indigenous peoples includes, but also transcends the circulation aspect. There are both broad as well as specialized observations of the political, social, economic, legal, and cultural life situation of Arctic populations, of their indigenous traditions, their health, education, life chances and risks, economic potential, language and communication patterns, gender and generational relations, preferences, cultural thinking patterns, personal goals, and so on. This focus on Arctic populations and the interest in, basically, all aspects of their life, as well as in their statistical behavior, reflects the rise of biopolitical rationalities in the Arctic and is crucial from a governmental perspective.

Systematic knowledge on the population and its milieus is necessary for the continuous governmental assessment of possible chances and risks. It provides the basis for specific interventions and measures aimed at the socioeconomic management and the (re)allocation of chances and risks. In order to develop and safeguard the release of potentials thus far unrealized, governmental politics aim at regulative settings that encourage particular (majoritarian) milieus and their behavioral patterns while discouraging other (marginal, minoritarian) milieus, ways of life, and behavioral preferences – which have to be detected and subjected to normalization and abnormalization procedures (Bigo 2008: 103–106). The governmental logic of enabling and safeguarding the growth and flourishing of life (in the broadest sense) requires knowledge also on undesired and risky milieus lurking to interrupt the governmental course of things. Thus, the population is addressed according to its statistical distribution and its milieus undergo differentiated biopolitical assessment and are targets of specified intervention and (self-)regulation incentives and measures.[16]

At the same time, the biopolitical perspective on the Arctic, in empirical terms, goes beyond the immediate focus on populations. In order to allow for the development and growth of the biopolitical "habitat" according to its inherent dynamics and regularities, the scope of governmental regulation comprises both the populations themselves and the whole ecosystem, in which populations and their milieus are embedded (Foucault 2004a: 70–72, 95, 98, 156ff.). This corresponds to the perspective on the Arctic that is interested in the entire ecosystem with its climate conditions, its prospective alterations through climate change, its overall environmental configuration, its biological diversity, infrastructure, resources, and raw materials as well as in the possible ratio between industrialization and sustainable protection in the region, and related topics (see Nordic Council of Ministers 2014: 13).

Although being aware that the majority of scholars undertaking governmentality studies follow Foucault (2004a: 150) in subordinating the law to governmental rationalities,[17] we see that legal aspects – and in par-ticular claims to autonomous rights – play an important role with regard to Arctic populations. Nonetheless, and without neglecting the importance of the law, we can, however, also detect a governmental, biopolitical constitution of Arctic populations, which focuses rather on life contexts than on rights, rather on biopolitical managerial strategies than on legal procedures, "with rights used tactically in this process" (Lindroth 2014: 341; see also Foucault 2004a: 70). Also, the genuinely inter- and transnational setting of the Arctic seems to promote a regulative and governmental rather than a legalist approach to its populations.

## Concluding thoughts

While clearly being linked to the image of the wild and still-to-be-explored territory, and also to images of the region as one of new economic oppor-tunities, discourses on the Arctic also tie in with issues of climate change, of cooperation and conflict, of Arctic governance, of international law, of the situation and rights of indigenous people, as well as of great-power pol-itics. Taken together, these aspects indeed characterize a region whose making comprises a range of features that distinguish it from institution-centered regionalization exercises in other parts of the world.

We have argued that the Arctic can be usefully analyzed as a region of unfolding governmentality, and that its regional peculiarity is reflected in the variety and plurality of representations, discourses, perceptions, and imaginaries. Governmentality, both as an analytical concept and as a pol-itical way of governing, relies on an inextricable entanglement between its parts. Having said this, we can indeed observe that all the main characteristic aspects of governmentality are being projected onto the Arctic region and that these governmental techniques, approaches, and rationalities are closely interlinked. The political, economic, societal, and scholarly multiplication of knowledge production on the Arctic, together with its thematic inclu-siveness, formalization, and disciplinary diversification constitutes a power–knowledge–nexus that is a core requirement of governmental rationalities and politics. This contributes to both addressing and thereby establishing the Arctic as a defined regional space, while at the same time, it furthers the governmental normalization of the Arctic as a regular governable space. Governmental expertise-based regulation and normalization demands the continuous assessment of regularities, normal distributions, and possible risks for the well-ordered course of things. It is therefore inseparably tied to the security dispositif of governmentality that draws through all aspects of life aiming at reducing uncertainty through preventive arrangements that minimize the risk of undesirable and unexpected incidences. Furthermore, both the embeddedness of economic prospects in securitization logics and the particular relevance of economic aspirations in Arctic discourses correspond to the guiding role of economic thinking in governmentality. Apart from this,

Arctic economic projections display a liberating political economy aimed at unleashing existent, but fallow economic potentials that need to be freed in order to develop according to their inner dynamics and regularities. In addition, the release of untapped economic potentials is configured as patterns of circulation, which are a spatial order characteristic of governmentality. Finally, we have seen that Arctic discourses are pervaded by an encompassing biopolitical concern. The biopolitical imperatives of unleashing human potentials as well as of overall life enhancement and securitization are reflected in the broad and systematic interest in virtually every possible aspect of Arctic populations, their socioeconomic milieus, their living, educational, social, health, cultural, and behavioral patterns, as well as in aspirations of deploying and realizing Arctic population capacities. The governmentalization of the Arctic, in sum, contributes to both curbing exceptionalist representations of the Arctic and integrating the Arctic into the horizon of world politics and globality.

We think that showing how governmental logics and imaginaries are being projected onto the region has a useful role to fulfil, complementary to other approaches, in portraying the Arctic both as a sociopolitical space in its entirety, as well as an international region sui generis in the process of discursive constitution. The discourses and practices of governmentality permeating the Arctic contribute to its spatial, figurative, and political reframing and aim at making it a governable region that can be addressed by, and be accessible for, ordering rationalities and measures. Thus, we see this heuristic for understanding the Arctic region also as an argument for encouraging governmentality studies to apply its conceptual vocabulary to regions, as phenomena within the ideational and imaginary realm of globality, while being located "above" the nation-state, but "below" the global level. As we have highlighted before, the Arctic is an important region worthwhile studying in this respect, but it is not "exceptional." It differs from other regions in degree, and also somewhat in kind as an "international" region, but not in its "regionness," so to speak, if that regionness is taken to primarily pertain to the place of regions in a global context (see Albert 2021). It is in this sense that the Arctic as an international region can be seen as a building bloc of, and for, globality. "Governmentalization" would, in this sense, be nothing else but the structural consolidation of that building bloc.

## Notes

1  This is a revised and shorter version of an article that appeared in *Cooperation and Conflict*, Vol. 53, No. 1. We thank Jan Busse for comments on the present version.
2  For an earlier view on the emergence of the Arctic as an "international region," yet focused primarily on the international comparative region-building discourse, see Keskitalo (2007). See Tennberg (2000) for an earlier account of governmentality in relation to the Arctic, focused on issues concerning Arctic environmental

cooperation. For a Foucault-inspired discourse analysis of Norway's role in Arctic politics, see Jensen (2016); see also Salter (2019).

3 Regarding the three different conceptualizations of governmentality outlined in the introductory chapter of this volume, we mainly refer to the first and the third conceptualization, i.e., governmentality as a heuristic tool and governmentality as a historical formation of a particular regime of power.

4 The literature on the individual aspects of, and developments in, the Arctic is by now extensive. For a recent overview, see Jensen and Hønneland (2015).

5 For an analysis of this discursive hype from the angle of the theory of social differentiation, see Albert (2015).

6 See Adler-Nissen and Gad (2014); for a case study on Greenland, see Gad (2014).

7 Consequently, the adjectival use of "governmental" in this article refers to "governmentality," not to "governance" or to the institution of "government."

8 In fact, the simultaneity of governmentality and sovereign governing modes might add to and reinforce each other in a reciprocal manner (Vasilache 2014, 2019).

9 For a discussion of the critique of governmentality in IR, see also the introductory chapter of this volume.

10 While not excluding earlier writings, we concentrate mainly on the lectures at the Collège de France (Foucault, 2004a, 2004b) as well as on related texts on governmentality (Foucault, 1991a, 1991b, 2001).

11 See Dittmer et al (2011), whose article has some overlap with the present one, but takes the approach of critical geopolitics. For a recent critical geopolitics perspective on the Polar Regions, see Wehrmann (2018).

12 For a similar argument in relation to why, after long attempts leading nowhere, the boundary dispute between Norway and Russia was surprisingly resolved in 2010, see again Moe et al. (2011).

13 An exemplar of this is the Arctic Human Development Report II by the Nordic Council of Ministers (2014).

14 See Jørgensen and Sörlin (2013) for an account of the technology/environment nexus in the Arctic.

15 The Arctic Human Development Report II (Nordic Council of Ministers 2014) is an exemplar of this and the following.

16 See, for example, the behavioral biopolitical perspective on health enhancement in the Arctic in the International Journal of Circumpolar Health (IJCH).

17 On the role of the law in the concept of governmentality, see Biebricher (2014).

## References

Adler-Nissen, Rebecca and Gad, Ulrik P (2014) 'Postimperial sovereignty games in Norden', *Cooperation and Conflict*, 49:1, 119–129.

Albert, Mathias (2015) 'The polar regions in the system of world politics: Social differentiation and securitization', Geographische Zeitschrift, 103:4, 217–230.

Albert, Mathias (2021) 'Regions in the system of world politics' in Paul J Kohlenberg and Nadine Godehardt (eds) *The Multidimensionality of Regions in World Politics* (London: Routledge), 59–74.

Anderson, Alun (2009) *Life, Death and Politics in the New Arctic* (London: Virgin Books).

Aradau, Claudia and Blanke, Tobias (2010) 'Governing circulation: A critique of the biopolitics of security' in Miguel de Larrinaga and Marc G Doucet (eds) *Security and Global Governmentality* (London: Routledge), 44–58.

Aradau, Claudia and Van Munster, Rens (2007) 'Governing terrorism through risk: taking precautions, (un)knowing the future', *European Journal of International Relations,* 13:1, 89–115.

Bevir, Mark (2010) 'Rethinking governmentality: Towards genealogies of governance', *European Journal of Social Theory,* 13:4, 423–441.

Biebricher, Thomas (2014) 'Souveränität und Recht in der Staatsanalytik Foucaults' in Andreas Vasilache (ed) *Gouvernementalität, Staat und Weltgesellschaft* (Wiesbaden: Springer VS), 21–41.

Bigo, Didier (2008) 'Security: A field left fallow' in Michael Dillon and Andrew W Neal (eds) *Foucault on Politics, Security and War* (Basingstoke: Palgrave Macmillan), 93–114.

Brosnan, Ian G, Leschine, Thomas M and Miles, Edward L (2011) 'Cooperation or conflict in a changing Arctic?', *Ocean Development & International Law,* 42:1–2, 173–210.

Burchell, Graham, Gordon, Colin and Miller, Peter (eds) (1991) *The Foucault Effect* (Chicago: University of Chicago Press).

Busse, Jan (2015) 'The Biopolitics of Statistics and Census in Palestine', *International Political Sociology,* 9:1, 70–89.

Busse, Jan and Stetter, Stephan (2014) 'Gouvernementalität im Nahen Osten: Machtpraktiken in Israel und Palästina aus weltgesellschaftstheoretischer Perspektive' in Andreas Vasilache (ed) *Gouvernementalität, Staat und Weltgesellschaft* (Wiesbaden: SpringerVS), 197–224.

Castel, Robert (1991) 'From dangerousness to risk' in Graham Burchell, Colin Gordon and Peter Miller (eds) *The Foucault Effect* (Chicago: University of Chicago Press), 281–298.

Chandler, David (2010) 'Globalising Foucault: Turning critique into apologia', *Global Society,* 24:2, 135–142.

De Larrinaga, Miguel and Doucet, Marc G (2008) 'Sovereign power and the biopolitics of human security', *Security Dialogue,* 39:5, 517–537.

Dean, Mitchell (1999) *Governmentality* (London: SAGE).

Dean, Mitchell (2007) *Governing Societies* (Maidenhead: Open University Press).

Dillon, Michael (2004) 'The security of governance' in Wendy Larner and William Walters (ed) *Global Governmentality: Governing International Spaces* (Abingdon: Routledge), 76–94.

Dillon, Michael (2007) 'Governing terror: The state of emergency of biopolitical emergence', *International Political Sociology,* 1:1, 7–28.

Dillon, Michael (2010) 'Biopolitics of security' in Peter J Burgess (ed) *The Routledge Handbook of New Security Studies* (Abingdon: Routledge), 61–71.

Dittmer, Jason, Moisio, Sami, Ingrama, Alan and Dodds, Klaus (2011) 'Have you heard the one about the disappearing ice? Recasting Arctic geopolitics', *Political Geography,* 30:4, 202–214.

Dodds, Klaus and Nuttall, Mark (2016) *The Scramble for the Poles* (Oxford: Polity).

Duffield, Mark (2007) *Development, Security and Unending War: Governing the World of Peoples* (Cambridge: Polity).

Eurasia Group (2014) *Opportunities and Challenges for Arctic Oil and Gas Development* (Washington, DC: Wilson Center).

Evans, Brad (2010) 'Foucault's legacy: Security, war and violence in the 21st century', *Security Dialogue*, 41:4, 413–433.

Foucault, Michel (1975) *Surveiller et punir* (Paris: Gallimard).

Foucault, Michel (1976) *La volonté de savoir* (Paris: Gallimard).

Foucault, Michel (1980) *Power/Knowledge: Selected Interviews and other Writings 1972-1977* (New York: Pantheon Books).

Foucault, Michel (1983) *Discourse and Truth: The Problematisation of Parrhesia'* English lecture transcript, www.foucault.info/parrhesia/, accessed 06 September 2018.

Foucault, Michel (1984) *Le souci de soi* (Paris: Gallimard).

Foucault, Michel (1991a) 'Governmentality' in Graham Burchell, Colin Gordon and Peter Miller (eds) *The Foucault Effect* (Chicago: University of Chicago Press), 87–104.

Foucault, Michel (1991b) 'Politics and the study of discourse' in Graham Burchell, Colin Gordon and Peter Miller (eds) *The Foucault Effect* (Chicago: University of Chicago Press), 53–72.

Foucault, Michel (1997) *Il faut défendre la société: Cours au Collège de France 1976* (Paris: Gallimard).

Foucault, Michel (2001) 'Désormais, la sécurité est au-dessus des lois' in Daniel Defert and François Ewald (eds) *Dits et écrits II 1976-1988* (Paris: Gallimard), 366–368.

Foucault, Michel (2004a) *Geschichte der Gouvernementalität I: Sicherheit, Territorium, Bevölkerung* (Frankfurt am Main: Suhrkamp).

Foucault, Michel (2004b) *Geschichte der Gouvernementalität II: Die Geburt der Biopolitik* (Frankfurt am Main: Suhrkamp).

Freistein, Katja (2014) 'Gouvernementalität und Regionales Regieren: Konkurrierende Ordnungsvorstellungen' in der ASEAN' in Andreas Vasilache (ed) *Gouvernementalität, Staat und Weltgesellschaft* (Wiesbaden: SpringerVS), 225–258.

Gad, Ulrik P (2014) 'Greenland: A post-Danish sovereign nation state in the making', *Cooperation and Conflict*, 49:1, 98–118.

Glomsrød, Solveig and Aslaksen, Iulie (eds) (2008) *The Economy of the North 2008* (Oslo: Statistics Norway).

Grant, Shelagh D (2016) 'Arctic governance and the relevance of history' in Dawn Alexandrea Berry, Nigel Bowles and Halbert Jones (eds) *Governing the North American Arctic: Sovereignty, Security, and Institutions.* (Basingstoke: Palgrave Macmillan), 29–50.

Grondin, David (2010) 'The new frontiers of the national security state: The U.S. global governmentality of contingency' in Miguel de Larrinaga and Marc G. Doucet (eds) *Security and Global Governmentality* (London: Routledge), 79–95.

Humpert, Malte (2014) *The Future of Arctic Shipping: A New Silk Route to China?* (Washington, DC: The Arctic Institute).

Jabri, Vivienne (2006) 'War, security and the liberal state', *Security Dialogue*, 37:1, 47–64.

Jensen, Christian L (2016) *International Relations in the Arctic. Norway and the Struggle for Power in the New North* (London: I.B. Tauris).

Jensen, Christian L and Hønneland, Geir (eds.) (2015) *Handbook of the Politics of the Arctic* (Cheltenham: Edward Elgar).

Jørgensen, Dolly and Sörlin, Sverker (eds) (2013) *Northscapes: History, Technology, and the Making of Northern Environments* (Vancouver: University of British Columbia Press).

Joseph, Jonathan (2010) 'The limits of governmentality: Social theory and the international', *European Journal of International Relations,* 16:2, 223–246.

Keskitalo, Carina (2007) 'International region-building: Development of the Arctic as an international region', *Cooperation and Conflict,* 42:2, 187–205.

Kiersey, Nicholas J (2011) 'Neoliberal political economy and the subjectivity of crises: Why governmentality is not hollow' in Nicholas J Kiersey and Doug Stokes (eds) *Foucault and International Relations* (Abingdon: Routledge), 1–24.

Knecht, Sebastian and Stephen, Kathrin (eds) (2017) *Governing Arctic Change: Global Perspectives* (London: Palgrave).

Larner, Wendy and Walters, William (2002) 'The political rationality of 'new regionalism': toward a genealogy of the region', *Theory and Society,* 31:1, 391–431.

Larner, Wendy and Walters, William (eds) (2004) *Global Governmentality* (London: Routledge).

Lindroth, Marjo (2011) 'Paradoxes of power: indigenous peoples in the Permanent Forum', *Cooperation and Conflict,* 46:4, 543–562.

Lindroth, Marjo (2014) 'Indigenous rights as tactics of neoliberal governance: Practices of expertise in the United Nations', *Social & Legal Studies,* 23:3, 341–360.

Lipschutz, Ronnie D and Row, James K (2005) *Globalization, Governmentality and Global Politics* (Abingdon: Routledge).

Merlingen, Michael (2003) 'Governmentality: Towards a Foucauldian framework for the study of IGOs', *Cooperation and Conflict,* 38:4, 361–384.

Mikkelsen, Aslaug and Langhelle, Oluf (eds) (2008) *Arctic Oil and Gas: Sustainability at Risk?* (Abingdon: Routledge).

Moe, Arild, Fjærtoft, Daniel and Øverland, Indra (2011) 'Space and timing: Why was the Barents Sea delimitation dispute resolved in 2010?', *Polar Geography,* 34:3, 145–162.

Neumann, Iver B. and Sending, Ole J (2007) "The international' as governmentality', *Millennium,* 35:3, 677–701.

Neumann, Iver B. and Sending, Ole J (2010) *Governing the Global Polity: Practice, Mentality, Rationality* (Ann Arbor: University of Michigan Press).

Nordic Council of Ministers (2014) *Arctic Human Development Report II* (Copenhagen: Nordic Council of Ministers).

Palosaari, Teemu and Tynkkynen, Nina (2015) 'Arctic securitization and climate change' in Jensen, Christian L and Hønneland Geir (eds.) (2015) *Handbook of the Politics of the Arctic* (Cheltenham: Edward Elgar), 87–104.

Prasad, Amit and Prasad, Srirupa (2012) 'Imaginative geography, neoliberal globalization, and colonial distinctions', *Cultural Geographies,* 19:3, 349–364.

Rajkovic, Nikolas M (2010) "Global law' and governmentality: reconceptualizing the 'rule of law' as rule 'through' law', *European Journal of International Relations,* 18:1, 29–52.

Rose, Nikolas (1993) 'Government, authority and expertise in advanced liberalism', *Economy and Society,* 22:3, 283–299.

Salter, Mark (2019) 'Arctic Security, territory, population: Canadian sovereignty and the international', *International Political Sociology* 13:4, 358–374.

Selby, Jan (2007) 'Engaging Foucault: Discourse, liberal governance and the limits of Foucauldian IR', *International Relations,* 21:3, 324–345.

Shadian, Jessica (2006) 'Remaking Arctic governance: the construction of an Arctic Inuit polity', *Polar Record* 42:2, 249–259.

Smith, Laurence C (2012) *The New North: The World in 2050* (London: Profile Books).

Söderbaum, Frederik (2015) *Rethinking Regionalism* (Basingstoke: Palgrave Macmillan).

Steinberg, Philip E., Tasch, Jeremy and Gerhardt, Hannes (2015) *Contesting the Arctic: Politics and Imaginaries in the Circumpolar North* (London: I.B. Tauris).

Stokke, Olav Schram and Hønneland, Geir (2007) *International Cooperation and Arctic Governance: Regime Effectiveness and Northern Region Building* (Abingdon: Routledge).

Tennberg, Monica (2000) *Arctic Environmental Cooperation: A Study in Governmentality* (Aldershot: Ashgate).

Tennberg, Monica (2010) 'Indigenous peoples as international political actors: A summary', *Polar Record*, 46:3, 264–270.

Vasilache, Andreas (2014) 'Great power governmentality? Coincidence and parallelism in the new strategic guidance for the US Department of Defense', *Security Dialogue*, 45:6, 585–600.

Vasilache, Andreas (2019) 'Security in the sovereignty-governmentality continuum', *Cambridge Review of International Affairs*, 32:6, 681–711.

Walters, William (2004) 'The political rationality of European integration' in Wendy Larner and William Walters (eds) *Global Governmentality: Governing International Spaces* (Abingdon: Routledge), 155–173.

Walters, William and Haahr, Jens Hendrik (2005) *Governing Europe: Discourse, Governmentality and European Integration* (Abingdon: Routledge).

Wehrmann, Dorothea (2018) *Critical Geopolitics of the Polar Regions: An Inter-American Perspective* (Abingdon: Routledge).

Young, Oran R (2011) 'The future of the Arctic: Cauldron of conflict or zone of peace?', *International Affairs*, 87:1, 185–193.

Zanotti, Laura (2013) 'Governmentality, ontology, methodology: re-thinking political agency in the global world', *Alternatives*, 38:4, 288–304.

# 11 Conclusion

## How we should, and how we should not, widen the scope of governmentality studies[1]

*Iver B. Neumann and Ole Jacob Sending*

## Introduction

This volume demonstrates that the concept of global governmentality is analytically useful in order to understand emergent policies as well as emergent modes of governing. It also brings us a step closer to understanding the nature of the overall conditions of globality under which we now live. This is no small feat for an edited volume. The book's introduction gives a clear conceptual analysis of the term governmentality and a full précis of the uses to which the concept has been put in the study of world politics. The following chapters expand those uses and discuss further vistas. In this conclusion, we discuss the strengths and limits of the chapters in the volume. In so doing, we give our reasons why we think Foucauldian governmentality analyses are incommensurable with foundational approaches, Marxism included, and also why the much-discussed issue of the pros and cons of scaling-up governmentality analyses constitute a non-problem for scholars of governmentality.

In the introduction to this volume, Busse and Hamilton (p. 17) write that:

> It is [...] the common extension of governmentality *upwards* to the global realm that this volume takes issue with. Globality is not merely an extension of the state. Globality thus cannot be equated with the international level. Rather, it is constitutive, entangled, and deserving of an analysis unto itself. The conduct of global conduct is comprised of rationalities and subjectivities of a genuine character. As a result, one needs to overcome the methodological nationalism that is inherent both in IR theorizing and most governmentality research in IR.

We agree. Our third concern in this conclusion is how governmentality analysis stands in relation to other approaches, and particularly to processual sociology analyses as spearheaded by Norbert Elias. We do this to highlight how a broader research agenda may develop and help scholarship on governmentality move towards a broader engagement with International Relations scholarship. Elements of such a broader engagement are on display in this volume, but we think it important to stress what can be gained by living down a tendency to ignore insights from colleagues who rely on different vocabularies in addressing similar phenomena. We want to criticize a tendency which is perhaps most pronounced in much scholarship in International Political Sociology (IPS), namely a tendency to focus on the ins and outs of a particular concept and its uses within the discipline, to the detriment of focusing on how that concept, and the tradition from which it grows may be brought into dialogue with other concepts and traditions so that we may produce better analyses of the world.

## Governmentality versus foundationalism

Foucault acquired his fame for the works on what he came to call discipline, that is, a mode of power where resistance could be effective in the short run, but not in the long one. Discipline was to be understood as a mode of power that came in addition to what Foucault saw as an everpresent mode of power in society and called sovereignty. Where sovereignty had the form of an open game, that is, a game that it was not clear at the outset who would win, discipline had the form of a closed game, that is, one that was rigged so that the challenger had to lose in the long run. Discipline was on particularly prominent display in total institutions, such as asylums and prisons, but Foucault also suggested that modern society was, not a prison, but *like* a prison, in the sense that the seemingly evergrowing demands on the subject were such that the possibility for resistance to be effective in the long run was forever shrinking (Ransom 1997). Amongst the more interesting of the critiques waged against the early Foucault, was one that will sound very familiar at this point in time, given the prominent place of identity politics, namely that Foucault's analyses occluded agency. Foucault famously decentered the individual, saw it as a subject no more persistent than a figure drawn in sand. Equally famously, he underlined the need to cut the King's head off, that is, to decenter the state. Critics rightly pointed out that such decentering, while refreshing in opening new avenues of analysis, could also hamper political resistance, by not allowing any site for the agency that resistance needs in order to be successful.

The late Foucault's answer to this critique was to develop a third mode of power, to stand beside sovereignty and discipline, namely governmentality. This book has done a great job of demonstrating how this indirect form of power works in International Relations, to mention but one example through the site that is BRICS (see Jaeger's chapter above), and it has discussed the limits of that view. However, we spot a problem. Some of the more Marxist-inspired readings on display here seem eager to return to structural analyses where everything turns on how futile resistance is within a capitalist society. As pointed out already in the introduction to this volume, that is exactly the position that Foucault wanted to leave when he developed the concept of governmentality in the first place. More fundamentally, the entire point of Foucault's break with structuralism turned on this point. Structuralism, one will recall, defined the analyst's job in two steps. First, to study *manifest* – that is, observable – structures, say of gendered division of labor, or of cooking; and secondly, to compare these manifest structures with a view to identifying a society's underlying and unobservable *latent* structure. What Foucault and others that came to be called poststructuralists did in the late 1960s to earn that moniker was in principle very simple. They asked how we should think about society and of the analyst's job if we first postulated that there was no such thing as a latent structure, if all we had to work with was manifest structures. This is the challenge of any Foucauldian undertaking, governmentality studies amongst them. If one simply insists that "capitalism" is a latent structure that underlies today's societies, then one does not need a governmentality perspective to understand either that society at large, or the individual room for maneuver that that particular society actually contains. In the terms used by Foucault, it does not make sense to study governmentality if one believes that only the power mode of discipline exists, and that discipline may only disappear if a postulated "latent structure" that guarantees it is changed. To be blunt, Jonathan Joseph is surely right when he argues in his chapter above that an analysis of governmentality to remain Foucauldian cannot be carried out from a structuralist, a Marxist or a critical realist perspective, for that would mean insisting on the very kind of ontological foundation from which Foucault tried to disentangle his empirical analyses in the first place.

## Scaling-up

A governmentality approach is certainly analytical, and it's certainly critical. The degree in which any one use of the term will yield critical analyses does of course vary. We note, and agree, with Mitchell Dean and Oscar L. Larsson's charge above that our way of using the concept, including how we approach it in this conclusion, comes with a liberal bias. Whether it is a corollary of this that we come to "reproduce a liberal imaginary of the current international domain, rather than one that allows us a critical or analytical distance," as they put it, will be in the eye of the beholder. As already noted, in the introduction to this volume, Busse and Hamilton write that this volume takes issue with the scaling of governmentality upwards to the global level. And indeed, the volume is doing a very nice job of demonstrating how conditions of globality – our conceptualization of social space around the planet as being of a piece – has its own political logic that must be understood in its own terms, from its own presuppositions. Busse and Hamilton are also right in pointing out that methodological nationalism – or rather statism – is a danger. Given that the international or "internationality" – understood as relations between states and between groups that are primarily conceptualized as residing in different states – was until fairly recently the dominant frame for our analyses, it is hardly surprising that remnants of yesterday's habits are still coloring much analysis. In some degree, it should, for relations between states are still definitely worthy of much analytical attention. Having said that, conceptualizing globality is the new challenge, and so it should by definition take precedence as an analytical concern of the avant-garde.

It also seems clear that, if globality has its own logic, then we cannot get at that logic by simply transposing the logic of the international to the realm of globality. That would be presupposing isomorphism – similarity of form – between the two, and such a presupposition would be as unwarranted as presupposing that the international may be analyzed in terms of the domestic. This so-called domestic analogy lingered as a widespread, and yet erroneous, starting point for analyses of the international as late as in the first half of the 20th century. If there is one thing that the discipline of International Relations has accomplished, it is to do in the analogy between the domestic and the international. It takes time to change analytical frames and do away with remnants of the old, but it is not impossible.

What is not clear to us, however, is that the IR literature on global governmentality is guilty of making the mistake of analyzing globality in terms of the international. Is it the case that there is a "common extension of governmentality upwards to the global realm" in the literature, as Busse and Hamilton (p. 17) suggest, or is this simply a misplaced charge? We would argue the latter. Let us begin by looking at how Foucault himself saw the matter. Foucault touched directly on the issue of the international in the published text that kicked-off the entire governmentality undertaking. In commenting on Frederick the Great's book *Anti-Machiavel* Foucault writes:

> He [Frederick] says, for instance, let us compare Holland with Russia: Russia may have the largest territory of any European state, but it is mostly made up of swamps, forests, and deserts, and is inhabited by miserable groups of people totally destitute of activity and industry; if one takes Holland, on the other hand, with its tiny territory, again mostly marshland, we find that it nevertheless possesses such a population, such wealth, such commercial activity, and such a fleet as to make it an important European state, something that Russia is only beginning to become. To govern, then, means to govern things.
>
> (Foucault [1978] 2000: 209–210)

Frederick the Great is clearly what we would now call a methodological nationalist, for he takes states as given and bounded entities, and then compares them as such. Foucault, on the other hand, is not a methodological individualist. A key concern in hatching the concept of governmentality in the first place was to capture a phenomenon that was exactly *not* bounded by states, but that cropped up all over Europe from the 16th century onwards, namely that one could and should govern rather than rule. Rather than trusting the sword to cut down subjects that made problems, as would an old-fashioned ruler, the point was to govern citizens in such a way that they would be more productive. To repeat, Foucault started his analysis from the observation that governmentality was not limited to one state, but existed throughout Europe. In other words, his point of departure was exactly not methodological nationalist, but Europe-wide. While the specificity of the relations between polities, or states, was not Foucault's core focus, we think it is defensible and also necessary to scale-up in one way or the other in order to try to theorize about globality, globalization, or the international.[2] Halvard Leira's chapter in this book does a good job of identifying elements of such an analytic in Foucault's own works, which are there for us to adjust and expand upon.

Moreover, any effort to theorize phenomena that we call global or international must necessarily involve some form of scaling-up. In this volume, such scaling is implicitly done whenever the concept of "entanglement" is used. With the exception of Zanotti's chapter, which has an extensive discussion of the presuppositions of this concept in quantum theory that leans on Karen Barad's work (esp. Barad 2007), it is used as a claim of what we could call maximalist co-constitution, where "spooky action at a distance" (Einstein's term) is going on. But absent a specification of what entanglement means, and empirical illustrations to this effect, invoking entanglement seems to imply some form of scaling-up or generalizing from the micro to the macro, where local relations can be extrapolated to the global. Our point here is not that there is anything problematic with entanglements as such, but that a claim about entanglements should also be justified and explained. This raises the issue of scaling more generally.[3] We think scaling is embedded in the very concepts used to denote an object or phenomenon (e.g., "state"), where a particular concept – such as representation or performance – is invoked to link disparate elements together to form an image of the state. Or it takes the form of implicit generalizations from the study of some small-scale practice or process that can be empirically observed (such as assembling a war-fighting machinery, providing development assistance, measuring, and assessing state "performance" on economic indicators, etc.) to a larger scale phenomenon of relations between states, or a pervasive governmental logic. To repeat, the scaling-up itself is not a problem. What is problematic is to do so without due concern for what is assumed or implied in the analytical concept used. In the case of governmentality, we think it is perfectly fine to engage in scaling-up, as long as one specifies the types or relations or objects being studied, and for what purpose.

Indeed, analytical developments in IR and elsewhere in the social sciences make scaling-up easier now than before. When Foucault wrote his oeuvre more than 40 years ago, we had no specific concept beyond the negative one of decentering with which to denote the kind of focus that he applied. We do today. It is what Mustafa Emirbayer (1997; for an IR application, see Jackson 2011) has baptized relationalism. Foucault presupposes that relations between political entities – in this case, flows of ways of conceptualizing what it is to rule and govern – are a more fruitful point of departure for analysis than the existence of units – in this case, states. We would side with Foucault and Emirbayer here, as we have done in our previous work on global govern-ance. The starting point is relations between units. Governmentality existed as European-wide phenomenon in the 16th century. Today, it exists as a phe-nomenon on the global level. We therefore believe it is misplaced to argue, as do Busse, Hamilton and a number of others, that Foucault's, and for that matter, our, application of the concept of governmentality to globality is a case of "scaling-up" a concept that was hatched for analysis of states or the international to the level of the global.[4] The reason is that the concept of governmentality was not hatched to analyze the levels of the domestic or the international in the first place. It was, on the contrary, hatched as a concept to capture relational logics in a European-wide setting, where there were not yet any clear-cut states in evidence.

If this argument puts paid to Busse's and Hamilton's charge, however, it does not in and of itself ward against Jonathan Joseph's charge (2012, and again in this volume) that it is Euro-centric to transpose the concept of governmentality, which Foucault explicitly hatched for use in a European setting, to the global level. If Euro-centrism is "the notion that the West prop-erly deserves to occupy the centre stage of progressive world history, both past and present" (Hobson 2004: 2), then it is by definition Euro-centric to use a concept hatched for use in a European setting in other settings without regard to whether they fit that particular setting. We would argue, however, that such regard is usually being paid when the concept of global governmentality is being used. It is to be expected that governmentality will be one of those relational logics that will spread, under conditions of "internationality" and globality both. Of course, governmentality will be in evidence in different degrees in different places, and there will be different kinds of and degrees of hybridization with other modes of government. A relationist would expect nothing else. The point is that, under conditions of globality, governmentality should be expected to crop up in an increasing number of specific places, in an increasing degree. Indeed, what would be the point of talking about globality if it were not to capture processes such as the spread of governmentality analytically?

## Compatible approaches

Let us now try to step out of Foucauldian concepts and onto the stage of social critique at large, to see if we may locate additional weaknesses with the kind of governmental analyses on display elsewhere in this volume. Foucault's foil when developing his power analyses was nothing less than modernity and its thinkers at large, and particularly the very French idea of "civiliza-tion." Where modern thinkers had underlined the advantages of building a strong state and highlighted the progress made, Foucault, again famously, insisted on discussing the disadvantages incurred and questioning progress as such. To Foucault, each society inscribed violence in its own way, and the key analytical challenge was not to celebrate how the use of direct violence diminished, but to document the exact practices used to produce more or less docile subjects. In this, he heartily succeeded. However, if the social sciences are about documenting how society is possible in the first place and how societies survive over time, then we cannot do away with generalization altogether. Some kind of balance has to be struck between documenting different ways of constructing and maintaining society on the one hand, and generalizing about the human condition on the other. Foucault himself certainly tried to do that in his own works on governmentality, but to repeat, within a wider field, that is to say within the social sciences at large, he comes down firmly on the side of stressing the disadvantages of being disciplined and of having one's conduct conducted. So, let's have a look at the more positively inclined opposition.

The key French Enlightenment thinker, Voltaire, highlighted that Louis XIV "succeeded in making of a hitherto turbulent nation a peaceful people dangerous only to its enemies [...] manners were softened" (cited in Elias 2000: 42). The key institutionalizer of French social sciences, Durkheim, saw the state not only as a softener of manners, but as the very precondition for individualization to take place. By opening a space that transcended the family and the guilds, and by transcending these institutions, the state did not only grow stronger itself, but also made it possible for the individual to be strengthened vis-à-vis state and society both. "It is the State," Durkheim (1992: 64) wrote:

> that has rescued the child from patriarchical domination and from family tyranny; it is the State that has freed the citizen from feudal groups and later from communal groups; it is the State that has liberated the craftsman and his master from guild tyranny

However, this necessarily had to happen at a price, for the simple reason that:

> Every society is despotic, at least if nothing from without supervenes to restrain its despotism. Still, I would not say that there is anything artificial in this despotism; it is natural because it is necessary, and also because, in certain conditions, societies cannot endure without it. [...] From the moment the individual has been raised in this way by the collectivity, he will naturally desire what it desires and accept without difficulty the state of subjection to which he finds himself reduced.
>
> (Durkheim 1992: 61)

The last sentence of the latter quote from Durkheim should ring a bell for a reader who is just finishing a book on governmentality, for Durkheim and Foucault are at one in highlighting how societies produce individuals/subjects. To repeat a point, where they differ is in highlighting the advantages (Durkheim) or disadvantages (Foucault) of this process.

The social scientist who has brought Voltaire's and Durkheim's perspective on the civilizing role of the state the furthest, remains Norbert Elias. In his magnum opus, originally published in German as two separate volumes in 1939, he began, with Durkheim and Sociology in general, from the postulate that the emergence of the individual psyche ("psychogenesis") is shaped by the emergence of society ("sociogenesis"; Elias 2000). Elias then went on to demonstrate in some detail how the behavior of the "secular upper classes in the West" (the subtitle of his first volume) changed in a less violent direction during the first centuries of the second millennium. In the second volume, Elias detailed how state formation in what was becoming France during the same period took the shape of forceful acquisition by evergrowing polities of their neighboring polities. The basic thrust of the analysis is that there is a correlation between the two, a "civilizing process" (the title of the entire volume), whereby stronger social control of the use of force by the state (a Weberian theme) leads to and correlates with a growth in self-control of the use of violence and unpredictable behavior by individuals (a Durkheimian theme). The following quote may serve as a nutshell précis:

> if in this or that region the power of a central authority grows, if over a larger or smaller area the people are forced to live in peace with each other, the moulding of affects and the standards of the drive-economy are very gradually changed as well.
>
> (Elias quoted in Linklater 2016: 195)

Building on the two volumes that were subsequently merged under the title *The Civilization Process*, Elias spent the rest of his career on further empirical studies of how the "civilization process" played out in specific courts, states, and fields. To pick but two apposite examples in this context, he discussed the change away from putting criminals to death towards incarcerating them as an example of civilizational progress (Spierenburg 2004), and the increased popularity of sports as a channeling of violent energies previously spent in duels and on the battlefield in a less lethal direction (Long 2006). When we include the work of his numerous followers, which include prominent IR scholar Andrew Linklater (esp. 2016), it all adds up to an entire school of what is often named "configurational" or "processual" sociology.[5]

Linklater's (2016) empirical analyses of changing "harm conventions" in what he calls Western states systems (the Hellenistic states system, the suzerain Roman system, Latin Christendom, the renaissance city-state system, and the European states system) stresses how these conventions have, mutatis mutandi, not only grown in strength, but have also been more radically internalized by individuals. Writing roughly about the same period which first served as a stepping stone for Foucault's governmentality analyses, Linklater (2016: 110 fn1) notes how:

In the case of British ducal families in the fourteenth and fifteenth centuries, around forty-six per cent of male children that reached the age of fifteen suffered a violent death. Three hundred years later, and as a consequence of "the domestication of the European nobility," the death rate fell to around four per cent.

Having suborned most free peasants throughout Europe during the high middle ages, surviving nobles were ever more aware of their increasing interdependence in and out of Europe's courts, and "relied on experts in Roman law emerged in response to the incentives to pacify or 'civilize' intra-court relations" (Linklater 2016: 111). The new order also imposed restraints on the nobles:

> Those whose lives were woven together in court society developed a collective awareness of the need for self-restraint in relations with the members of the other dominant strata. Throughout the transition to the realization that they were partners as well as adversaries, the two groups tended to "oscillate between the desire to win major advantages over their social opponents and their fear of ruining the whole social apparatus"
> (Elias quoted in Linklater 2016: 197)

As will be readily seen, Elias's and Foucault's projects have considerable overlap, not only where subject matter and choice of empirics are concerned, but also in execution. There seems to be no question of direct Eliasan influence; at least Elias is nowhere mentioned in Foucault's oeuvre.[6] The added value for a Foucauldian of considering Elias's perspective lies elsewhere. First, in Foucault's own terms, power is productive. It follows that governmentality is productive. It is, therefore, not satisfactory only to consider the disadvantages incurred by an increase in governmentality. We also have to specify the advantages that Foucault hints at when he underlines how governmentality produces an "addition to life." Foucault seems to have in mind the production of goods and services; Elias complements this by documenting how order and efficiency are also increasing as violence and the use of force are decreasing. Foucault's moral point, that violence is simply inscribed differently, and that there is a change in which subjects and groups of subjects bear the brunt of violence, does not change the substantial point that looking at the positive, and not only the negative, aspects of a social change makes for a richer analysis of the phenomenon under scrutiny.

If the first added value of complementing a governmentality perspective on social change with an Eliasian one is substantial, a second point is epistemological. It has been noted many times that Foucault is great on individuation, but bad on individuals. Even when he writes short monographs about a Pierre Rivière or a Herculine Barbin, his focus is on how society creates them, not on their agency. Governmentality certainly was a good way for Foucault of getting agency back into his analyses of power, but it did not go that far in working in specific agents. Elias, on the other hand, gives running examples of changed individual behavior, so gets closer to his subjects, and thereby also the subject common to himself and Foucault of how changing society changes individuals.

A third and final advantage for governmentality studies of also bringing in an Eliasian perspective is that processual and configurational thrust of Elias's work opens up new avenues of research that link governmentality studies to broader debates in IR and elsewhere in the social sciences. Stephan Stetter's contribution to this volume demonstrates the utility of such an approach by drawing on works by the Stanford school, Luhmann and Bourdieu to argue that this thing we call "international politics" has evolved as an integral subsystem or field of the global. While such expansions of the theoretical toolbox may, at least initially, produce some inconsistencies, they have the virtue of engaging with broader debates in IR scholarship about the boundaries, functioning, and transformation of distinct spheres of political activity. We would argue that the discipline of IR, and particularly the overlapping field of IPS, have reached a point of fragmentation. Fighting tribes structure their analyses around specific concepts – practice, assemblage, new materialism, emotions, critical race studies, governmentality. There is a seemingly evergrowing focus on turning inward, towards disciplinary in-fighting, instead of aiming for the kind of cross-fertilizing dialogue that we need to produce more inclusive and incisive analyses of the world.

## Conclusion

To sum up, we have argued that governmentality scholars should leave aside two concerns and focus on a third. We should stop discussing the relationship between governmentality and approaches which presuppose that the social is kept together by some underlying latent structures, such as structuralism, Marxism and Critical Realism, for governmentality rests on the incommensurable ontological wager that the world is forever in flux. We should stop worrying that governmentality involves an unwarranted scaling-up of domestic analysis to the international and global levels. It does not, for governmentality was always, from the very first text that Foucault published on the matter, not exclusively an attempt at studying a specific set of social relations, but social relations in general. Those were the negatives. On the positive side, we should not be tribal about the concept of governmentality or the Foucauldian tradition, but take what we can use from that tradition and, while observing the risks of mixing traditions that may rest on different epistemological and ontological presuppositions, mix it with other concepts and traditions that can help us get on with the job of analyzing power relations. The main challenge should not be to win some disciplinary in-fight within IPS, IR, or the social sciences in general, but to analyze the social at large. This volume demonstrates that governmentality studies are highly suited to the study of power relations under today's conditions of globality. Let us make it even more so.

## Notes

1  We should like to thank Jan Busse for comments to an earlier draft of this chapter.
2  The concept of scale, and the issue of how they interact (the cliché would be the global in the local, the glocal), is being criticized by ANT and new materialism scholars. While we think it a valid and worthy thing to do to place a "flat ontology" wager on analyses and disregard scale for certain analytical purposes, such a wager works to the detriment of power analyses, which are predicated on a working analysis of hierarchy and so scale in order to work. Given that governmentality is a form of power, it follows that one cannot place a flat ontology wager and engage in governmentality studies at the same time.
3  For a discussion of debates on this previous to the present volume, see Hamilton and Neumann (2017).
4  Again, we are not against such scaling-up, we simply think that governmentality analysis is not a case thereof.
5  Note that, to Eliasians, a civilizing process is not necessarily a positive thing only. We are not moving on the level of stories people themselves tell about how very civilized they are here, but on the analytical level. The civilizing process, then, "does not refer to some normative vision of 'civilized' existence but to shifts in the standards of self-restraint that people have imposed on themselves and on each other in the course of responding to the new potentials for organizing harm that occurred as cultural development replace biological evolution as the principal influence on the history of the species" (Linklater 2016: 9). Linklater also highlights how the concept of civilization has from the very beginning been used to legitimate what we would today consider cruelty, as when those in the Roman world "who had challenged the political order were often punished by being thrown to the beasts; as enemies of 'civilization', they forfeited the right to be protected from predatory animals" (Linklater 2016: 97).
6  This is not necessarily surprising, for although Foucault wrote his "little dissertation" on a psychoanalytic whose works were only available in German at the time, he only discovered the Frankfurt School late in life, so must be considered exceptionally Gallo-centric.

## References

Barad, Karen (2007) *Meeting the Universe Halfway: Quantum Physics and the Entanglement of Matter and Meaning* (Durham: Duke University Press).

Durkheim, Émile ([1913] 1992) *Professional Ethics and Civic Morals* (London: Routledge).

Elias, Norbert ([1939] 2000) *The Civilization Process: Sociogenetic and Psychogenetic Investigations* (Oxford: Blackwell).

Emirbayer, Mustafa (1997) 'Manifesto for a Relational Sociology', *American Journal of Sociology* 103:2, 281–317.

Foucault, Michel ([1978] 2000) 'Governmentality' in James D Faubion (ed) *Power: Essential Works of Foucault 1954-1984* (Harmondsworth: Penguin), 201–22.

Hamilton, Scott T and Iver B Neumann (2017) 'Governnmentality' in Michael Outhwaite and Stephen Turner (eds) *The SAGE Handbook of Political Sociology, vol. 1* (London: Sage), 293–311.

Hobson, John (2004) *The Eastern Origins of Western Civilization* (Cambridge: Cambridge University Press).

Jackson, Patrick T. ([2011] 2016) *The Conduct of Inquiry in International Relations: Philosophy of Science and Its Implications for the Study of World Politics* (London: Routledge).

Joseph, Jonathan (2012) *The Social in the Global* (Cambridge: Cambridge University Press).

Linklater, Andrew (2016) *Violence and Civilization in the Western States-Systems* (Cambridge: Cambridge University Press).

Long, David (2006) 'Quidditch, Imperialism, and the Sport-War Intertext' in Daniel H. Nexon and Iver B Neumann (eds) *Harry Potter and International Relations* (Lanham, MD: Rowman & Littlefield), 127–156.

Ransom, John S (1997) *Foucault's Discipline: The Politics of Subjectivity* (Durham, NC: Duke University Press).

Spierenburg, Petrus Cornelis (2004) 'Punishment, Power, and History: Foucault and Elias' *Social Science History* 28:4, 607–636.

# Index

Printed in the United States
by Baker & Taylor Publisher Services